"A business model is like the rudder of a ship. Though hidden from view it is the point of highest leverage for quickly shifting course to avoid turbulence and find the most direct route to new opportunities. The authors of this thoughtful book understand business models and how to make them a source of sustainable competitive advantage."
—Michael C. Ruettgers, Executive Chairman, EMC

"*The Ultimate Competitive Advantage* is filled with examples and ideas on how to continually improve existing business models and to innovate to create even better models; contains many helpful hints for business managers."
—Robert S. Kaplan, Marvin Bower Professor of Leadership Development, Harvard Business School, co-author of *The Balanced Scorecard, The Strategy-Focused Organization*, and *Cost & Effect*

"This book could be re-titled, *From Start-Up to Number One*. Looking every day at how you can reinvent your company should be your top priority. *The Ultimate Competitive Advantage* has all the questions and advice you need to succeed."
—C. Richard Reese, Chairman and CEO, Iron Mountain

"Mitchell and Coles challenge outworn practices and stodgy assumptions. They offer a brilliant Baedeker to those open to new ideas for creating vibrant and successful organizations."
—Deborah Wadsworth, President, Public Agenda

"*The Ultimate Competitive Advantage* is for anyone looking for a new and powerful paradigm for creating success out of the chaos in today's dynamic business climate. Whether you are a nonprofit organization or a for-profit company, you will receive examples and advice to help you add valuable benefits at no additional cost, utilize sensible pricing strategy to gain and retain customers, and slash costs that add no value for, or even worse, harm customers and employees. Whether you are a sole proprietor working at home or run a huge multinational, this book is directed to your most pressing concerns and important opportunities. It offers best practices with a heart, a smile, and a pat on the back. You'll like it."
—Richard C. Whiteley, Whiteley Group, author of the bestselling book *Customer-Driven Growth*

"Get ready for a guided, hands-on approach to analyzing the key components of your business plan from top to bottom. The authors have delivered a learning opportunity that focuses on asking the right questions to help executives keep their sights on the right targets. The opportunity for improving a business plan is always there, and this book provides the methodology for creating and discovering new perspectives and strategies to increase stakeholder loyalty and satisfaction."
—George Zimmer, CEO, Men's Wearhouse

"Mitchell's and Coles' book, *The Ultimate Competitive Advantage*, provides business leaders with real-life examples and the tools necessary to develop a winning business model in a globally competitive environment. They challenge the status quo and provide insightful new ways for business leaders to think."
—Don R. Graber, Chairman, President, and CEO, Huffy

"True innovation is about continuously evolving your organization to meet every changing market condition. *The Ultimate Competitive Advantage* provides thought provoking questions and insightful advice that will keep your business ahead of the pack."

—Stephen M. Shapiro, Founder, The 24/7 Innovation Group,
author of *24/7 Innovation*

"Packed with sound advice on what to do (and what to avoid) when thinking about your business model, *The Ultimate Competitive Advantage* will be an asset to anyone who's searching for new ways to achieve growth and profitability."

—Emanuel Rosen, author, *The Anatomy of Buzz*

"From humble beginnings, great success can develop when based on the right values. *The Ultimate Competitive Advantage* shows you how to see and perform business basics in new and more exciting ways. For example, view your best product improvement as just the beginning of what's possible. Instead of reducing costs, get the world's best advice for free to make what you offer better at a lower price. Rather than do more with less, learn how to do more of what counts."

—Irwin D. Simon, Chairman, President and CEO,
The Hain Celestial Group

"Every company wants the 'Ultimate Competitive Advantage.' In this book, Don Mitchell and Carol Coles show how strategic innovation can separate your company from the pack, deliver stronger results, and drive shareholder value."

—John F. O'Brien, President and CEO, Allmerica Financial Corporation

"In business, 'trying to make ends meet when they keep moving the ends' is a great analogy for the need to continually change and reinvent the business model. In today's operating environment, trends and cycles are shorter, increasing the need to reload faster and more frequently. Mitchell's and Coles' *The Ultimate Competitive Advantage* provides real examples of what's worked and what hasn't."

—Larry G. Kirk, CEO, Hancock Fabrics

"This book should encourage every management group to dedicate themselves to exploiting their company's unique attributes. Executives now have a roadmap to follow in building value for their investors, employees and society."

—William F. Mahoney, Executive Editor, *Shareholder Value Magazine*

"*The Ultimate Competitive Advantage* offers executives the tools they need for competing successfully amid today's changing business landscape."

—Harold M. Messmer, Jr., Chairman and CEO, Robert Half International

"History is littered with companies that failed to adjust their business models to changing conditions. *The Ultimate Competitive Advantage* offers the reader a useful toolset for adapting one's business model for the ever changing environment. A useful read for any business leader."

—David T. Farina, Principal and Head of Technology Research at
William Blair & Company

THE ULTIMATE COMPETITIVE ADVANTAGE

Secrets of Continually Developing a More Profitable Business Model

Donald Mitchell and Carol Coles

BERRETT-KOEHLER PUBLISHERS, INC.
San Francisco

AUG 3 1 2004   292958

Berrett-Koehler Publishers, Inc.
235 Montgomery Street, Suite 650
San Francisco, CA 94104-2916
Tel: (415) 288-0260   Fax: (415) 362-2512   www.bkconnection.com

ORDERING INFORMATION
Quantity sales. Special discounts are available on quantity purchases by corporations, associations, and others. For details, contact the "Special Sales Department" at the Berrett-Koehler address above.
Individual sales. Berrett-Koehler publications are available through most bookstores. They can also be ordered direct from Berrett-Koehler: Tel: (800) 929-2929; Fax: (802) 864-7626; www.bkconnection.com
Orders for college textbook/course adoption use. Please contact Berrett-Koehler: Tel: (800) 929-2929; Fax: (802) 864-7626.
Orders by U.S. trade bookstores and wholesalers. Please contact Publishers Group West, 1700 Fourth Street, Berkeley, CA 94710. Tel: (510) 528-1414; Fax: (510) 528-3444.

Berrett-Koehler and the BK logo are registered trademarks of Berrett-Koehler Publishers, Inc.

Printed in the United States of America

Berrett-Koehler books are printed on long-lasting acid-free paper. When it is available, we choose paper that has been manufactured by environmentally responsible processes. These may include using trees grown in sustainable forests, incorporating recycled paper, minimizing chlorine in bleaching, or recycling the energy produced at the paper mill.

Library of Congress Cataloging-in-Publication Data

Mitchell, Donald, 1946–
    The ultimate competitive advantage : secrets of continually developing a more profitable business model / Donald Mitchell, Carol Coles.
        p. cm.
    Includes bibliographical references and index.
    ISBN 1-57675-167-8 (alk. paper)
    1. Competition. 2. Strategic planning. 3. Industrial management. I. Coles, Carol. II. Title.
HD41.M57 2003
658.4'012—dc21
                                                                2002190856

First Edition
08 07 06 05 04 03   10 9 8 7 6 5 4 3 2 1

Copyedited by Bernice Pettinato, Beehive Production Services. Composition and production services by Westchester Book Group.

To all those who taught us to look for a better way.

CONTENTS

FOREWORD

Every decade or so, businesses have to master an essential new task in order to prosper. Today, business model innovation is that task, and you need to become good at it before your competitors do. *The Ultimate Competitive Advantage* is the template you need to master this critical challenge.

Few businesses ever develop a business model innovation by accident. Instead, better business models are the result of establishing a useful focus through an ongoing process for constantly improving how you serve customers and their stakeholders while satisfying your own stakeholders. Most companies stick to their old business models, and hope that their competitors will too. Increasingly, that hope is misplaced as competition from new entrants and established companies gets tougher. You can expect to face new, more effective business models that will make your current ones obsolete.

Because their companies have lacked the necessary focus on and processes for continuing business model innovation, few CEOs today have successful experience in locating and implementing opportunities for such innovation. Until this book, the inexperienced leader in business model innovation had no place to turn for guidance. At the same time, the successful business model innovator had few resources to find out what methods have worked well for others that have not yet been tried in the innovator's own company.

These deficiencies are remedied by *The Ultimate Competitive Advantage*. A leader can learn how to establish a continually improving process for successful business model innovation by reading this book.

For today's reader, it's a little like being at the start of the Oklahoma land rush. A lot of progress in staking out new competitive territory is about to happen because of this book. You need to get busy. In fact, if you read and apply the lessons of only one business book in the next few years, I encourage you to consider this one.

At Paychex, we are dedicated to helping small businesses become more successful by improving their effectiveness in providing for and communicating with their employees. For that reason, I was pleased to see that this book has a heavy emphasis on how a small business can develop the vision and management necessary to grow from its current size into global leadership. Many chapters feature case histories of repeated, successful business model innovations by small companies, a number of which are now global leaders. Many of these case histories and the lessons in this book pay particular attention to involving employees more effectively in business model innovation. That's a focus I heartily endorse based on our experiences at Paychex.

At the same time, *The Ultimate Competitive Advantage* has plenty of practical advice for the big companies. There are even lessons for how big companies can get some of the advantages that smaller companies normally enjoy, while benefiting more from their larger size.

Continuing business model innovation has been a priority at Paychex. I'm delighted that our story is shared with you in the book's Introduction and Chapter 1. I hope that establishing a business model innovation process turns out to be as helpful for you as it has been for us.

B. Thomas Golisano
Chairman, President, and CEO Paychex, Inc.

FOREWORD

The Ultimate Competitive Advantage provides a valuable roadmap for leaders to maximize the potential of their organizations through continuous learning and innovation that pays off. Like any good roadmap, the book lets you look at your choice of route from start to finish, beginning with founding a company on through achieving profitable market leadership.

Many leaders associate innovation with their company laboratories or new product units. While those forms of innovation are important, the book points you toward an equally significant requirement—continually improving your fundamental business model in order to provide, profitably, more benefits for customers and other stakeholders. As a leader, you have to set the right tone and direction for continual improvement to happen. If it doesn't, your organization may falter when circumstances change or competitors lead with their own business model adjustments.

Have you ever been given bad directions to a destination? If you've been told you only have to lower the costs of your present operations, then you've had that experience. It didn't help buggy whip makers, and it won't help you today.

The business innovation stories in this book are based on the successful recent experiences of top-performing companies of all sizes and types. Company leaders found that business model innovation allowed them to be more successful than simply getting better at the old model. That finding corresponds with my own experience at Education Management. You'll read more about that in Chapter 6.

The book is filled with high-performing examples that you can use in your business. That's one way to learn. However, most people learn best by doing. The authors have made the doing easier for you with thought-provoking questions and tasks at the end of each chapter. Responding to those questions and assignments will prompt your thinking.

Organizations do better when they concentrate on refining their effectiveness through continuous learning. This book helps you establish a continual process of business model improvement, something few companies have today.

Robert B. Knutson
Chairman and CEO of
Education Management Corporation

PREFACE

You must become an ignorant man again
And see the sun again with an ignorant eye
And see it clearly in the idea of it.
—Wallace Stevens ("Notes Toward a Supreme
Fiction," 1947)

This is the book we've always wanted to read . . . but could never find. *The Ultimate Competitive Advantage* answers the question: What one thing can most improve a company's growth and profitability? Our investigations and experience show that the answer is having the best process in your industry for continuing business model innovation.

So if you want to perform at your best, lead the pack to win the competitive race and then move on to greater accomplishments, this is the book for you.

Centuries pass from the time an important idea is first expressed to its widespread implementation. For example, universal literacy and education were advocated after the printing press was invented. Their broadscale application did not begin in many countries until the latter half of the nineteenth century. Even today, these basics are not observed in all countries.[1] Businesses didn't begin to study how to systematically improve until the twentieth century. Today, most ways to improve are ignored in more businesses than they are used. That's because a business can focus on only a few things. You need simpler, more effective ways to improve.[2]

The most fundamental concept of progress is that of continual learning. Yet business has been slow to pick up on that concept, and applies it sporadically and only to parts of what a company does. Most organizations focus on learning how to do better what they did poorly yesterday, activities that usually aren't very important for tomorrow. For example, endless studies will go into fine-tuning a mass production line, when the company really needs to learn how to make better, customized products inexpensively. That's like stooping to pick up a penny while a hundred dollar bill wafts by unnoticed. Instead, you need to work on what will help you and your stakeholders (including but not limited to customers, end users, employees, partners, suppliers, distributors, lenders, shareholders, the communities in which you operate and the parts of society that you impact) the most. These tasks are continually performing business model innovation (which we define and describe in the introduction to Part One), finding better ways to prepare for unexpected future events and enhancing your highest potential performances that supply the most valued benefits. Most companies totally ignore at least one of these three areas. Many ignore all three. It's no wonder that so many companies briefly prosper before withering. In this book, we've detailed a management process for superbly pursuing all three essential tasks that combines the best practices of today's best performing companies.

WHAT WE EXAMINED

There have been many studies of "strategic best practices," but none quite like or as significant to you as what you are about to read here. We sought to find the simplest, most effective management methods that the most successful companies have used since 1992 to continually outperform competitors. We hoped to find these methods by tracking and studying top-performing companies while they thought of and made the changes that created these competitive achievements. That kind of real-time measurement and study of creating competitive advantages across many different industries has never been done before.

Instead, prior strategic studies have attempted to look backward to earlier periods for the causes of today's success and then tried after the fact to describe all of the elements of creating that best performance. In such backward looks, cause and effect can easily be confused in the process since many changes are only coincidentally associated with each other. Afterwards, memories fade and those who tell their stories may be more interested in enhancing their roles than in accurately describing what worked and what didn't.

Those prior strategic studies also unintentionally missed two critical points. First, management effectiveness in outperforming competitors reached a higher level in the 1990s than had been seen before through a new, rapidly expanding management practice: continuing business model innovation. As a result, studying what people did prior to the 1990s is of limited usefulness in understanding the current gold standard in creating and improving on lasting competitive advantages. Second, the management process behind simultaneously improving performance across many company activities was often kept secret during the 1990s by those who practiced continuing business model innovation. Only if you looked in the right places while this innovation was going on could you find how this practice was flourishing.

As a result of these unintended limitations of prior published strategic studies, much of what you have learned about creating competitive advantages is of less value now compared to what you are about to read concerning the state-of-the-art and potential of continual business model innovation.

In the course of this examination of continual business model innovation, you will become aware of implications concerning events that you may not have thought of before, even though you have seen these events happening all around you. Open your mind to reinterpreting what you have seen and heard about. In helping you do so, we rely heavily on the companies and their leaders to tell you how they saw the causes of their success . . . as they created that success. We then allowed the test of time to validate or refute those statements, so that we report to you here what the leaders said would work that did, in fact, work.

Who We Examined First

In 1992, we began annually identifying and studying 100 CEOs and their companies based on three criteria: (1) the companies had been publicly held for several years and were above a minimum market capitalization size; (2) their stock prices grew the fastest during the previous three years within the group that met the first criterion; and (3) the same CEO was in place throughout the three years. Our study period begins in 1989 and continues through the present. From 1992 on, we looked at, spoke with, queried and visited a new group each year that met our criteria, with the minimum size adjusted to reflect changes in stock price levels. We didn't know what we would find, but suspected that something important would pop up.

Most CEOs and their companies were on the list briefly, but a handful frequently repeated. We paid more attention to those perennial winners, and interviewed many of them every year. Beginning in 1995, we began to notice that they had made large changes to improve their business models. Then we noticed that they did it again. And again. And again.[3] We began visiting these companies, such as Dell Computer, EMC, Paychex and Tellabs, for in-depth investigations and expanded our knowledge further. We interviewed others about how their efforts had contributed to their extraordinary success, and continually studied the actions and performance of all the most frequent repeaters.

Although the perennially successful CEOs kept practicing business model innovation, each did so differently. When we arrived to ask them about continuing business model innovation, however, they knew what we were talking about because that's what they and their companies were consciously doing.

We asked these CEOs who else had come to talk to them about continuing business model innovation. No one had raised the subject until we arrived. Yet, they were visited routinely by most of the best-selling business book authors as part of their studies of what made these companies successful.

We asked these CEOs who else was good at business model innovation outside of their industry. They usually could provide no examples. When we mentioned cases we had examined, they were always curious to learn more. From these conversations, we learned that these innovations were the result of intense interest in and study of customer and stakeholder needs, rather than emulating best strategic practices elsewhere.

How We Found Additional Examples

We began to look at the earlier history of business model innovation, and we saw that improved business models usually came from start-ups and new entrants. We became curious about the frequency with which companies enjoyed ongoing success in improving their business models. To understand this frequency, we read profiles of all public companies described in the *Value Line Investment Survey* from 1989 during the fall of 2000. We noted companies that seemed to have completed at least two successful business model innovations during those years, without regard to their stock-market performance. As a result of either lower stock-price growth or changes in CEOs, many of them did not make our CEO 100 lists during the prior years. We contacted the companies we identified in *Value Line* by e-mail to request interviews with their CEO and some of the other senior executives.[4] From these contacts, we were able to arrange CEO interviews at over forty companies during late 2000 and the first half of 2001. We performed literature searches on another few dozen companies that confirmed they had been frequent business model innovators, but these companies declined to be interviewed. From this investigation, we became convinced that at least seventy public companies had performed at least two successful business model innovations in the same business between 1989 and 2000.

We then began a year-long analysis. We took what we learned and summarized it in simple form so that more companies could understand how to choose and successfully follow this path. To test our thinking, we discussed our work in progress with many of the CEOs and their staffs as well as top strategic thinkers in other companies. Many valuable corrections and improvements to our findings and explanations were made as a result. You can read about who some of these people are in the Acknowledgments.

Next, we sought out individual, small company, and nonprofit organization examples to portray in the book that beautifully capture the themes that emerged from analyzing our study group of public companies that have been continuing business model innovators. As you will see, many of these examples are drawn from our personal experiences with the subjects or our long-term interest in their work. This approach allowed us the perspective of many years in drawing key lessons from these examples. You will find most of these examples at the beginning of a chapter.

Finally, we kept in touch with all of the individuals and companies so that the information we provide in the book is as up-to-date as possible.

OUR PURPOSE

Our purpose in writing this book is to redirect your perception of what must be done to lead and operate a successful business or organization. We believe that you and your colleagues have the knowledge and skills to achieve vastly more. You have observed how to accomplish everything you need to do for continuing business model innovation in some other area of your life, but have not yet applied those observations to the most important areas of your business. You, your organization and your stakeholders simply need to apply your knowledge and those skills in new ways and more often. New questions raised in this book will help shift your focus into more productive directions.

The message of *The Ultimate Competitive Advantage* is to develop and implement a superior management process that continually improves an organization's business model—its ways of serving customers and outperforming competitors—as well as fairly and appropriately rewarding all stakeholders. This book is designed to help you plan, start and invest in new businesses; turn start-ups into seasoned operations; turn around problem businesses; move from a weak position to industry leadership; and build from industry leadership into expanding the scope, growth and profitability of the industry. Most of the companies described in this book were start-ups under the current CEO within the past twenty-five years. Students and young people developing business careers can learn important leadership and management principles and responsibilities from the many examples we present here. Readers will benefit by employing the strategic management process described in the book. Specific questions about your business at the end of each chapter and examples are designed to stimulate useful thinking and help inspire progress.

RELATED READING

The Ultimate Competitive Advantage is the third volume in Mitchell and Company's library of business books designed to improve organizational performance. Like the prior two books, *The 2,000 Percent Solution* (AMACOM, 1999)[5] and *The Irresistible Growth Enterprise* (Stylus, 2000),[6] this volume can be understood and employed independently of the others. At the same time, the skills and perspectives developed in each volume are also designed to be complementary to and mutually supportive of one another. Reading the three books expands the usefulness of each volume in the series.

If you have not read any of the books in this series, we suggest that you begin with *The Ultimate Competitive Advantage* because it addresses organizational issues in the broadest way. With the benefit of this book's perspective, *The Irresistible Growth Enterprise* is a good choice for your next book in the series. Part Two of that book will help you apply many key ideas in this book. Finish with *The 2,000 Percent Solution*, which teaches world-class problem solving. You can use the skills developed in that book to create more and better business model innovations.

Throughout the book, we note other books that can help you apply specific lessons from *The Ultimate Competitive Advantage*. Some of these are in the text and others are found in the Notes section.

Finally, we would be delighted to answer any questions you have. Please contact us at mitchell@mitchellandco.com.

Donald Mitchell
Carol Coles
Wellesley, Massachusetts
January 2003

INTRODUCTION

BUILD MARKET LEADERSHIP
AND PROSPERITY

Change the environment; do not try to change man.
—R. Buckminster Fuller

This is the book you didn't know you need. Until now, you haven't seen the critical opportunities and threats we raise and address here. In this book, we introduce you to a new life-changing question, answer that question and show you how to make best use of the answer.

The question was originally posed to us as we were driving from our hotel to Dell Computer's headquarters in Round Rock, Texas, for two days of site visits and discussions. In the back seat was Mr. Robert R. McEwen, CEO of Goldcorp, a gold-mining company based in Toronto. He was one of several executives who would be participating in this meeting of Twenty Times Progress, an organization devoted to improving company effectiveness, being held at Dell's facilities.

Mr. McEwen leaned forward to speak to us in the front seat and asked a question that we had never heard before:

Do you think that a CEO would be better off working on improving the company's business model or the efficiency of the way the company operates now?

After we responded that the most successful companies we had studied were, like Dell Computer, constantly improving their business models, Mr. McEwen said that he agreed. He had decided to focus his company in that way. Just the week before, he had launched an experiment—the Goldcorp Challenge—to find more gold in its main mine. This online contest for geologists would cost several hundred thousand dollars, taken from the exploratory drilling budget. He felt he had little to lose, and possibly something to gain. If this experiment didn't work, he would try some other way to find more gold less expensively.

The experiment paid off beyond his wildest dreams. Within two years, his company found more gold in that mine than it had in the prior fifty, and greatly reduced the cost and effort involved. Because of this success, fewer miners will risk accidents there to find gold, while being assured of much more work extracting ore. Shareholders and suppliers will do well, too. And that's just the beginning of what Goldcorp can accomplish with its new business model of inexpensively accessing the world's best geological thinking. Best of all, you can adapt key lessons from Goldcorp's success to help your own business.

Mr. McEwen's question and subsequent success in pursuing the answer helped focus our attention on the importance of sharing what we have learned about business model innovation. At the beginning of the Prologue, "Profiles in Business Model Innovation," we tell you more about Mr. McEwen's experiences and future plans for Goldcorp. Throughout the book, we introduce you to path-finding CEOs who can be your models and guides to improved growth and profitability. As you read about their experiences, continually ask yourself how you could apply what they learned to your business.

Definitions

Let's begin by explaining what we mean by certain concepts, with the title as our starting point. *Ultimate* means the greatest, the maximum, the most fundamental, most important, and most desirable circumstance to achieve. *Advantage* means capabilities and performance that are more pleasing and beneficial to customers and other stakeholders than any other available alternative. When you have a *competitive advantage*, your products and services can be provided in ways that deliver more sales, higher profitability and greater cash flow than would occur if a competitor supplied the same customer.

Now let's talk about business models and what we mean by business model innovation. A *business model* is the who, what, when, where, why, and how much a company uses to provide its goods and services and receive value for its efforts. By *business model innovation*, we mean any successful change in any business model element that substantially enhances a company's ongoing performance versus the competition in sales, profits and cash flow. To simplify the text, interpret any reference to "innovation" as meaning "business model innovation."

In the introduction to Part One, you'll find more details on what continuing business model innovation is, and what you should be seeking to accomplish and to avoid in establishing an improved business model. It also includes a simple fictional business that is described in these terms.

LEARN FROM THE NEW INNOVATORS

Virtually unnoticed amid the virulent weeds of limitless greed, corporate charlatans and quick fixes that do more harm than good, the sturdy seeds of a new age of greater and more responsible prosperity are beginning to sprout. Since 1989, company after company has demonstrated remarkable new ways to provide lasting satisfaction and produce wealth by doing as much good for as many people as possible. The values of curiosity, caring, and generosity in sharing benefits greatly facilitated these pursuits. Aided by these values, more and more companies have reinvented their firms every two to four years to improve the benefits received by customers and end users. To succeed, these companies had to learn to focus on business model innovation, inspire and run numerous small-scale experiments and keep overall risk under control as they continually learned how to create large competitive advantages. From the experiences recounted here, you can learn important lessons about what it means to pursue this improved way of doing well by doing good. When enough of us learn how to follow this path in our companies, our ultimate benefit will be a world richer in service to and help for one another.

After you understand *The Ultimate Competitive Advantage*, we hope your heart will be lighter when you leave for work and your hours shorter so that you will have more time to spend with those you love. Here's how we intend to help.

We share lots of stories we hope you'll remember, feel inspired by and enjoy sharing with others. When a problem or opportunity arises, think of these examples and see if they suggest any ideas. We also show you how you can get expert assistance in improving your business model at very little cost through new ways of asking for help.

One of this book's strengths is describing many company reinventions, most of which will be new to you. Most chapters begin with an example from a small business or when a large business was small, specially selected to help the millions of small companies.

You'll find little overlap here with examples from other business books even among the larger firms we describe. That's because this is the first book looking at best practices in continual business model innovation. Until now, these successes have largely swooped in under the radar of academics and consultants alike. Even with the companies you've heard about before, we help you draw new lessons from their examples.

In examining these cases, however, remember that there are no perfect companies, just as there are no perfect people. Examples were selected to help you understand key points about the book's message, not to suggest that these companies should be emulated in other ways. In some instances, the firms have stumbled before or after the time we highlight in the example. We expect that more stumbles and questionable actions will be ahead among the companies we cite here. We hope you will learn to improve on their successes and avoid their errors. As you read about these companies, note your own reservations. That's a valuable way to learn lessons from other companies' experiences. Mistakes can inform us as much or more than success. The elements leading to success can easily escape us in our appreciation for the results, but the causes of failure invariably drill deeply into our minds like high-beam headlights glare into our eyes.

We know that any company is vulnerable to competitors if the company stops frequently improving its business model. When you learn about such setbacks and issues in the future at companies we describe, you can increase your understanding. Armed with this knowledge about changing company status and fortunes, you and your company may be able to accomplish more than the companies have that are described in *The Ultimate Competitive Advantage*. As well as these companies have done, there's still plenty of room for improvement.

Continually Provide More Benefits for Your Customers

Mr. Ray Hughes is a native of the Isle of Man, located in the Irish Sea. There he learned to be an outstanding golf caddie. He served up to two golfers at a time by carrying their bags and providing advice. Based on how much they liked his service, he could hope to get additional jobs from the same golfers. If one pair of golfers wanted to start early and another pair late, he could potentially carry four bags a day. Unfortunately, the winter weather in his native land is bad enough to deter golfers, and work is scarce then. This way of serving golfers on the Isle of Man was his original business model.

(continued)

Mr. Hughes decided to improve his business model. He realized that if he could find a place where there were lots of golfers and good year-round weather, he could earn more money than by being a caddie on the Isle of Man. He decided to move to the Monterey peninsula in California, home of many famous golf courses such as Pebble Beach, Spyglass, Spanish Bay and Cypress Point. The temperature is moderate there year round, and winter weather brings mild rain in which golfers often play. Because of the quality of these courses, golfers fill them from dawn to dusk. As a result, he could work more often. Further, the prices for playing on these courses are very high. Golfers are interested in having a good experience when playing such renowned and difficult courses, and value their caddies more highly than on the Isle of Man. As a result, his income from each golfer also rose. The main drawback was that the cost of living is very high in that area, especially for housing.

The pro shops at these courses often receive requests for caddies, and encourage golfers to make their own arrangements. The pro shops usually refer such requests to caddies who have been praised by other golfers. Because many players told the pro shop they were pleased to have Mr. Hughes as their caddie, he was often recommended.

These introductions became the basis of his next business model innovation. Many of the callers wanted to have more than one caddie. Could he help them? Mr. Hughes is a good judge of golfers and caddies. He inquired about the golfers who would be visiting and matched the golfers with compatible caddies. For example, an inexperienced golfer might be helped by a caddie who had a low-key personality and experience as a teaching pro to help the duffer navigate the course more pleasantly and successfully. As a result of helping other caddies get jobs, they also favored him with referrals in turn. That further increased the number of bags he could carry in a year. Also, those who liked the caddies

Mr. Hughes had assembled for them would often pay him extra for the service, even though he asked for no more pay. The pro shops heard favorable comments about these services as well, and referred larger parties to him.

Mr. Hughes is a very intelligent, inquisitive and interesting man to converse with, and he quickly learned a lot about the golfers who visited these courses. Many of them were attending business conferences at the Pebble Beach resorts. Almost all of the conference sponsors used travel agents and meeting planners to arrange for meeting and sleeping rooms, meals and other resort services. Mr. Hughes asked the golfers and the resorts whether they would be willing to let him play the role of travel agent for these occasions. The resorts and many conference sponsors who had played with him were happy to do so. Naturally, Mr. Hughes still organized the caddies, while adding a major source of income. At this point, he overcame the high cost of living in the area through expanding his role from being a person solely providing a physical service to someone who was also helping make business conferences more successful.

The last time we saw Mr. Hughes, he mentioned that he had added another service. He could now arrange and book business conferences and vacations around the world at top resorts, and, naturally, arrange for golf and wonderful caddies.

As you can see from this example, Mr. Hughes changed every aspect of his initial business model. He continues to work as a golf caddie, but does so in California rather than on the Isle of Man, changing "where" he does his work. He added services by helping arrange meetings, vacations, and caddies, thus changing "what" he does and "who" does it by involving the other caddies and resorts. These new services mean working in the evenings as well as during the day, which changes "when" he works. "Why" changed too. People hire him

(continued)

in order to add value to their meetings, in addition to helping with their putts, club selection and the weight of their bags. His income has gone from being circumscribed by the weather and how many bags he could carry to being limited by his circle of satisfied customers and his ability to learn new ways to serve them, changing "how much" he receives. Notice that his California conference customers pay no more for these services than they did before, even though they benefit more.

SUCCESS SEQUENCE

This book follows the sequence most companies go through to become more adept than their competitors in continually reinventing themselves. Here's what typically happens:

1. They learn how to do one reinvention.
2. They decide to do a second reinvention, and need to expand the scope of what they consider and where they get help.
3. They decide to turn reinvention into a repeating activity, which requires a shift in corporate priorities and attention.
4. Their reinvention success propels them beyond the boundaries of their original marketplaces. They need new targets of opportunity for their subsequent reinventions and must begin searching for them.

Clear Channel Entertains a Better Hearing for Advertisers

Clear Channel Communications was one of the first companies to attract our attention through its remarkable success with continuing business model innovation. It was also unusual in that it used acquisitions to enrich its innovations by changing the businesses it bought. Clear Channel's business model innovations are easy to follow and will help you understand more about our subject.

Let's begin by looking at the magnitude of the company's growth. In 1989 (the first year we studied), the company's stock price traded between $0.45 and $0.70. During 2001, the stock traded between $42.20 and $54.90. Any way you want to measure it, that's enormous growth! Revenues in 1989 were $52.4 million. Revenues in 2001 were $7.9 billion, a more than one-hundred-fifty-fold gain, greatly aided by acquisitions mostly paid for with company shares. In 1989, the company lost $400,000 and in 2001 earned more than $500 million before noncash, goodwill amortization charges.

The company's more than 1,200 radio stations in 2002 serve 11 percent of the radio audience in the United States and make it the industry leader. Clear Channel operates one of the largest radio networks, featuring on-air personalities like Dr. Laura Schlessinger, Jim Rome, Rick Dees and Casey Kasem. The company is also the industry leader in billboards, with over 730,000 in operation. The firm is a leading live entertainment promoter, producing or promoting in excess of 26,000 annual events including music concerts, theatrical shows, and sporting events attended by more than 66 million. Clear Channel is involved with 19 television stations. The company also has an expanding presence in international radio and billboards.

Clear Channel was founded in 1972 by Mr. L. Lowry Mays, who is still the chairman and chief executive officer at this writing. The company started with a single radio station, which Mr. Mays sought to operate better by attracting a bigger audience and selling more advertising. Many other companies were doing the same thing at the time and still are. Clear Channel became very good at this activity and began acquiring other radio stations and similarly improving their operations. By 1984, the com-

(continued)

pany had gone public. Still, this talent for improving station ratings and advertising sales did not provide a lasting competitive advantage over the best operators. However, the next change did, when combined with Clear Channel's high-multiple stock to fund acquisitions.

As licensing limitations on the number of stations that could be owned in a geographical market were loosened in stages by the Federal Communications Commission, Clear Channel began concentrating its ownership in a few places where it could own the maximum number of stations. The broadcasting formats of newly acquired stations were sometimes changed to provide a complementary, ideal audience for local advertisers such as car dealers and department stores, the main sources of revenue for radio stations. To build larger and better audiences for advertisers, a weak rock and roll station might be switched to a country and western format, especially if Clear Channel already had a strong rock and roll station in the market but no country and western station. A news channel might convert to a talk show format to serve market demand and broaden Clear Channel's audience base within the most advertiser-attractive audience. Next, Clear Channel would unstintingly improve the entertainment on the stations to enhance the ratings and audience quality from a local listener's and a local advertiser's point of view. Finally, it provided combined advertising packages involving several of its stations and programs that assembled a higher quality audience for the specific advertiser at a lower cost than could be provided by using any other combination of newspapers, radio and television. Clear Channel could easily offer these advantaged packages due to its combined audience advantages among heavy buyers of specific local products and services.

Other radio station operators either lacked the number of stations or the complementary audience that Clear Channel had in a particular market. Most companies also chose to operate each station to fight for maximum profits and revenues without looking for total market efficiencies for advertisers. As a result, Clear Channel's advantages grew in each local market where it had a full complement of radio stations.

Clear Channel also purchased television stations in some of its radio station markets, expanding the same core concept to provide a broader audience to meld radio and television advertising packages. Other companies used this approach, but usually lacked Clear Channel's strength in local radio audience efficiency. Clear Channel still had the local edge.

The company did this kind of audience development in so many markets that it was eventually able to offer similarly advantaged advertising packages to national advertisers. As the radio industry leader, Clear Channel was the most efficient choice. It had a national advantage because broadcast television and print were much more expensive.

Through acquisitions, Clear Channel next added substantial billboard presences that could be added to the custom advertising packages. This medium provided a further competitive advantage for building inexpensive message frequency for local and national advertisers.

Through other acquisitions, the company expanded the scope of its entertainment and advertising concept internationally by purchasing minority positions in radio stations around the world. In other cases, Clear Channel provided local management and advertising sales representation for international stations.

Most recently, the company acquired talent and sports representation and concert capabilities. As a result, Clear Channel can offer unique talent-based media vehicles for advertisers on the company's media outlets. For example, an advertiser can arrange for a touring music group to appear in its radio, television and billboard ads, make special appearances on its behalf, promote the advertiser at the concert and mention the advertiser during interviews and free ticket give-aways on the company's stations.

(continued)

Providing more appealing entertainment in ways that create better choices for advertisers is the continuing theme of all of these innovations. Clear Channel took this core insight and continually innovated its execution through outstanding programming, advertiser-attractive audience development, advertising sales and acquisitions of additional advertising media into achieving industry leadership in low-cost, cross-media advertising packages.

Any one of thousands of other companies could have done the same, but none did. As entertainment choices proliferate, Clear Channel's opportunities continue to expand.

If you are like us, you didn't expect that kind of constant and substantial improvement in a company's business model. We thought that enormous success occurred only when someone caught hold of a great market with a better product or service, and rode the market's dynamics for a while. Afterward, the executives quietly rode off into the sunset with lots of wealth based on stock options.

The companies we studied differed substantially from that preconception. These CEOs were often like Mr. Mays, having served in their leadership roles since they were young men, when they helped found the company. Most of them were not so young any more, but their entrepreneurial drive was as strong as ever while their business model innovation acumen had grown enormously. The key differentiation from our preconception and what other entrepreneurs do was that the more they improved their business models, the more they focused on continuing business model innovation. Nothing else the company did worked as well for them for improving performance. In the process, they created companies that enjoyed astonishing success for many years compared to competitors, as measured by market share, profitability, employee satisfaction, customer loyalty, recognition and stock-price growth.

In Part One, we focus on three ways to reinvent business models that we found were used most frequently and with a high rate of success. While there are many other choices for reinventing your business, we wanted to point you into the highest potential areas at the start. Part Two focuses on using expanded resources from your first reinvention successes to build a stronger foundation for future reinventions. Without these steps, your business model innovation progress may stall. Part Three looks at how to develop an organizational capability to perform better and more frequent reinventions that deliver more customer and end-user benefits. Part Four explores ways to find larger and higher potential opportunities to reinvent your company through serving new classes of customers and end users.

We hope you will see your own situation more clearly through looking at what others have done. We encourage you to use the questions at the end of each chapter to translate the book's lessons into the context of your business.

While reading the book, keep in mind that you may only need to apply a small portion of what you learn here to outperform your competitors. So if something sounds like it doesn't exactly fit you, focus instead on what does. Remember that no company we profile here is using more than a fraction of these ideas either. In summarizing these secrets from dozens of companies, we're giving you a look at how to move well beyond the best practices of any one company today.

We think a good business model identifies and directs a company to do multiple, appropriate things well in serving customers and other important stakeholders, compared to competitors. Properly done, a company's values, mission, core insights, key competencies, strategy, tactics, processes and reward structure can mutually reinforce one another in pursuit of continual business model innovation. When they do, progress can be remarkable. You'll have a better sense of the potential power behind establishing that congruity after reading parts two through four.

IMPORTANCE OF CONTINUING
BUSINESS MODEL INNOVATION

The Ultimate Competitive Advantage makes a strong claim: There is an ultimate competitive advantage you can gain now by applying what you learn in this book. Do you believe that? Probably not, and with good reason based on your business experience. No individual business advantage usually lasts very long. Everyone quickly tries to copy or outdo what works, or the novelty of the advantage simply wears off. Despite those challenges, recent experience clearly shows that continual business model innovation is the most powerful competitive edge you can have now.

Think of initial skill in business model innovation as being similar to the skill of the world champion chess player. Although the champion will not win every chess game, the champion will win more than anyone else by applying well-developed talent and experience. The only way there will be a substantial setback with such expertise is if the champion bets too much on the results of a single game.

Like a chess match, continuing business model innovation calls for the skill to create new competitive advantages just as rapidly as the opportunities arise. These benefits multiply throughout the match. But unlike chess, each competitive improvement helps lock out competitors and creates ongoing advantages that push the business model innovator ahead in future competitive tussles. It's as though the player with a skill advantage also earns an advantage in the number of playing pieces before the next game based on past wins. In addition, successes bring more involvement by stakeholders and more commitment to the company's improvements. This help is like having a team of chess masters and the top chess computer counsel the chess champion before each move. Further, the business model innovator can change the rules of the game in his or her favor so that his or her pieces are more powerful than the opponent's. These sorts of developing advantages are what we mean when we say that applying skill in business model innovation is the ultimate competitive advantage. Your skill and starting position can advance permanently relative to your competitors.

The opportunity for you is to be like the world champion chess player with an advantage in the number of playing pieces and the rules, while chess masters and the best chess computer advise you. The threat to you is to be that player's opponent.

Paychex Delivers More Benefits and Profitability

Let's look at another star business model innovator and his company, Mr. B. Thomas Golisano, founder, chairman and chief executive officer of Paychex. The company started with three employees in a small office in Rochester, New York, committed to providing payroll services for small employers in Rochester who could not afford to use an outside accountant or a computer-based payroll service like those provided by Automatic Data Processing. Through innovations that are described in Chapter 1, Paychex expanded its sales, stock price and profit margin in a way that serves as a standard for the successful business model innovating company.

By 1983, the company was public. In 1989, revenues were $101.2 million and profits were $9.5 million—or about 9 percent of sales after tax. In 2001, revenues had grown to $869.9 million (while relying very little on acquisitions) and profits zoomed to $254.9 million—or an eye-popping 29 percent of sales after tax. Few companies ever reach such high margins. Not surprisingly, the stock price went from a range of $0.68 to $1.07 in 1989 to a range of $28.30 to $51.00 in 2001. By comparison, industry-standard Automatic Data Processing had an after-tax profit margin on sales of 14 percent in 2001. Some might challenge Paychex's profit margin as excessive, until they appreciate that Paychex's prices are lower than most of its competitors and less than what it costs for most small companies to do the tasks themselves. A special circumstance made Paychex's profit margin expansion possible. The company continually improved its business model to expand sales and reduce costs at the same time by offering many new value-added services to small employers that required its accurate payroll records.

THE FUTURE OF BUSINESS MODEL INNOVATION

We learned from our field work that frequent repetition of business model innovation in the same company was an unintended discovery made simultaneously by dozens of companies in the 1990s. Like Goldcorp, these companies were pleasantly surprised by the effectiveness of their first business model innovation. That success led them to want to repeat. From those repetitions came an increased, continuing focus on business model innovation. Their experiences are the pioneering wave of what we believe will be the most important leadership and management activity of the next ten years.

Globalization will speed this process. By 2013, more than half of all companies in developed countries will face foreign competitors as their most significant challenge.

For example, there have been many business model innovations in car dealerships. We can expect new forms of adding value. For instance, all of a consumer's diverse car and truck needs may be provided for one annual fee (including trucks for moving, a sports car for vacation, as well as a car or SUV for everyday use). Such an offering may come from car rental companies, such as Enterprise. This business model, in turn, may face competition from similar offerings priced through auctions, using e-commerce methods. Such new competitors could supply surplus vehicles in a less costly way through accessing the vehicle rental and leasing companies with the most excess inventory (much as Priceline.com is doing now for rental car companies at major airports).

As a result, the local car dealer in Dallas may be overwhelmed by online competitors from elsewhere. The local dealer may find tough competition from people offering such advanced vehicle service auctions on the Internet, hosted by companies located anywhere in the world. Bangladesh can potentially beat Dallas in such a competition for a Dallas customer, if the Bangladesh company's business model has enough profitable advantages for that customer. The Bangladesh company can seek out those locales where the competition is weak and static, and grow very rapidly in such a situation. The impact on existing companies will be enormous.

One winner employing continual business model innovation can wipe out many thousands of local competitors. That's the future potential of continual business model innovation to fulfill Schumpeter's vision of creative destruction.

Those who lead their industries in continuing business model innovation will initially find limited competition in this critical arena. Most competitors will respond by dropping prices and costs . . . or simply by copying what the innovator has done. Few existing competitors will innovate to seize an advantaged position versus the new business model. Industry leaders in business model innovation will also be the best places to work, form partnerships, lend money, make investments in, sell to and cooperate with.

THE BIG IDEA IS . . .

This book is the first strategy and management process guide based on the successful experiences of continual, industry-leading business model innovators. Using the strategic management process described in *The Ultimate Competitive Advantage*, you can begin to do the things that will make your company a victor in this critical form of competition.

What's the big idea of this book? It is that business model obsolescence is *the* major unperceived opportunity for and threat to all businesses now.

Even the most successful can find themselves challenged. Industry-leader Home Depot is rapidly copying many innovations that provided great momentum for Lowe's. Hewlett-Packard and Compaq merged in 2002 to try to create a foundation from which they can survive and prosper in data processing versus service providers like IBM and EDS on the one hand, and lean manufacturers providing individualized products like Dell on the other hand. Record companies are finding their revenues and profits dropping as more individuals share (both legally and illegally) music stored on their computer hard drives.

Have you ever discovered that you were ignoring an important daily business task? You probably never made that mistake

**EMC Narrows Its Focus to Achieve
Industry Leadership**

Few early examples of continuing business model innovation came under CEOs who were not a company founder. The most impressive example came at EMC, with Mr. Michael C. Ruettgers as CEO from 1992 to 2000. EMC was the fastest growing stock on the New York Stock Exchange during the 1990s. The stock price ranged between $0.06 and $0.12 in 1989 and traded between $82.00 and $10.00 in 2001 (below its high in 2000; it continued lower in 2002). Revenues grew from $132.3 million in 1989 to over $7 billion in 2001, with relatively little contribution from acquisitions. The company went from a loss of $16.6 million in 1989 to a profit of $183 million in 2001, a year when computer products and services companies (including EMC) saw their earnings greatly depressed. During the technology recession of 2001–2002, EMC saw its revenues and profitability fall substantially, while it retained industry leadership in mass computer storage until its competitors, Hewlett-Packard and Compaq, merged.

During the 1990s, EMC passed long-time industry leaders IBM and Storage Technology by making mass computer storage faster and easier to use through a series of four business model innovations. In one of Mr. Ruettgers's first actions as CEO, he focused the company on competing for storage on IBM mainframes using inexpensive, off-the-shelf hardware. Prior to 1992, EMC had a broad product line and market direction. In 1995, the company began to provide mass storage that could connect to almost any kind of computer processor, whether an IBM mainframe or someone else's server, a capability that other manufacturers could not then provide. Later, the company began to offer proprietary software that made it easier to run a data center. Since the software worked only on EMC equipment, this innovation pulled along hardware sales as well. Most recently, the company has been a leader in helping customers tie together existing storage in their networks to get higher capacity utilization with high speed access.[1] In response to the recession, EMC under its new CEO, Mr. Joseph Tucci, is expanding its proprietary software for use with other vendors' storage hardware, yet another business model innovation.[2]

again, but the damage from the cumulative omissions was expensive. Perhaps you failed to perform preventive maintenance on expensive equipment that had to be prematurely replaced. Or maybe you installed new software, but never helped anyone learn how to use it. Some large companies reduced staff during the 2001 economic downturn and later found that key tasks weren't getting done anymore, while everyone sat in endless meetings. You probably wish that you had known about issues you ignored before they became costly. It's what you don't know you're missing that can cost you the most. Right now you are probably ignoring a competitive vulnerability that can literally put you out of business in the next few years. Read on if you want to know what that vulnerability is, and what you should do about it.

Existing business models in most companies changed only after decades, if ever. When we examined the successful innovations that companies made to profitably improve their business models, we noted that the changes could usually have been made decades earlier. What's missing to succeed with business model innovation is imagination and commitment, not opportunity. This underdeveloped potential is another reason why we believe that acceleration in the frequency and rate of successful business model innovation is just beginning.

Continuation of this trend means that improved business models will replace technology as the most frequent and most powerful source of business disruptions. This shift will occur because most business model improvements can be designed and implemented faster than new generations of technology. Most business model innovations require no additional technological advance. Even the fleet-footed companies attuned to the semiconductor improvement cycle (doubling performance as fast as every eighteen months) will have to become faster, more flexible and more effective in their business model improvement focus.

Because of the huge rewards for business model innovation, the vast sums available to back such efforts and the rapid improvements in quickly customized technology, major generations of business models will probably emerge every few months in the future within each industry. In many industries now, such as networked data storage, improved business models already emerge within two years.

Ask yourself if you know what your next two business model innovations are—two that will surpass anything that will become available in your industry over the next five years. If you don't know, you are in good company. Hardly anyone does. However, you will be able to answer that question after applying the lessons found in *The Ultimate Competitive Advantage*.

Which Examples Will Be of Interest to You?

What kinds of lessons can you learn from the companies in this book? We've listed some ideas here. Use the book as a starting point for your own studies of the companies whose experiences are most relevant to you.

If you are planning to start a new business, understanding the experiences of these companies can help you establish a sound foundation for succeeding and later building on that initial success. You can learn from many examples of organizations that started small with few resources and ended up as substantial firms, including American Woodmark, Central Parking, Claire's Stores, Clear Channel Communications, Dell Computer, Education Management, Habitat for Humanity International, Paychex, Virgin Records, and Zebra Technologies.

If you are planning to lend money to or invest in a start-up or if you already operate or work in a small business, you can learn important lessons to increase the safety of your capital and increase your potential rewards. You should pay particular attention to firms like Acacia Research, Business Objects, Cephalon, Cytyc, Red Hat and Xilinx that enjoyed substantial venture funding. You will be helped by examples of what these firms did while they were small and their choices were severely circumscribed. Whether you want to get bigger or better—or both—these examples will show you valuable paths.

If you work in a division of a larger company, you should pay particular attention to Applera, Martin Marietta Materials, QLogic and Sybron Dental Specialties as examples of how great business innovation was established from a base in part of a company.

If acquisitions interest you as a path to growth, look closely at how Beckman Coulter, Central Parking, Clear Channel Communications, Education Management, Iron Mountain, Martin Marietta Materials and Sybron Dental Specialties acquired and consolidated operations.

If customer closeness appeals to you as a way to make faster progress, you can learn a lot from Business Objects, Central Parking, Charles Schwab, Dell Computer, Ecolab, EMC, Huffy, Invacare, Iron Mountain, Jordan's Furniture, Linear Technology, Paychex, Red Hat, Sybron Dental Specialties, Wall Drug and Xilinx.

If technology-driven progress is your strategy, the book is filled with technology companies who pursue their business strategies in dramatically different ways from one another. Most have come to realize that business model innovation combined with technological innovation is far more valuable than technological innovation alone.

If operational excellence is your preferred method for improving performance, you will find that Dell Computer, Goldcorp, Martin Marietta Materials, Nucor and Paychex successfully employed that approach.

If you are faced with a "bet the company" decision where you have to choose one path or another, be sure to look into Acacia Research, Allmerica, Gemstar-TV Guide, Goldcorp, Huffy, PMC-Sierra and Rogers.

(continued)

21

If you want to understand more about being a good corporate citizen and enjoying substantial prosperity, be sure to learn about Cytyc, Habitat for Humanity International, Haemonetics and Timberland.

If you are concerned about corporate culture and values, you should pay close attention to Charles Schwab, Education Management, Habitat for Humanity International, Iron Mountain, Nucor, Paychex and Rogers.

If you are an industry leader and want to get ideas for expanding the scope and growth of your industry, be sure to look into Business Objects, Education Management, EMC, Iron Mountain, Linear Technology, Paychex and QLogic.

If your sales are stagnant, your market share declining and your profit margin drooping, you may find a way to rethink your choices beyond trying to do more of the same with less and less. Six Sigma efficiency won't turn around a company making wall telephones.

If you are a student or someone already working in business who wants to improve your career, you can learn important skills and perspectives that will boost the performance of the companies you work for and help you perform well in positions of responsibility. You can become more adept at spotting untapped potential to shine as a company employee, which, in turn, can help you select the best employer.

PROLOGUE

PROFILES IN BUSINESS MODEL INNOVATION

Work like you don't need the money.
Love like you've never been hurt.
Dance like nobody is watching.
—Mark Twain

Join us now for a visit with seven successful business model innovators to give you a preview of what's coming in the chapters ahead. These companies vary in the duration of their business model innovation experience. Goldcorp and Huffy are new to this activity. Disneyland, Ecolab, Linear Technology and Sybron Dental Specialties have been business model innovators for a long time. Mandalay Resort Group has continued business model innovation over the span of two management generations. We hope that these perspectives will help you appreciate how business model innovation can start and be sustained in a company.

We also present these examples to show you the three most common ways that successful business model innovation usually occurs. Goldcorp and Sybron Dental Specialties eliminate sales-reducing costs to advance their growth and profitability, the subject of Chapter 3. Linear Technology and Ecolab emphasize providing new benefits at the same or lower prices for customers and end users, the topic of Chapter 1. Man-

> **Opportunities abound . . . but we don't know exactly where they are.**

dalay Resort Group and Disneyland use pricing adjustments to improve the affordability and expand consumption of their services and products, the opportunity explored in Chapter 2.

Huffy represents a special case. This company has employed all three primary business model innovation elements: lowering sales-reducing costs, improving benefits at the same price and restructuring prices to encourage more purchases. Although Huffy is new to business model innovation, it is developing its potential much more rapidly than most effective business model innovators have.

Many of the example companies were once small and became industry leaders. To help those who head up small enterprises, almost every chapter includes an example that focuses on business model innovation by a small company, or a larger one when it was small.

GOLDCORP: EMPLOY EXPERT KNOWLEDGE INEXPENSIVELY TO SLASH GROWTH-RETARDING COSTS

Opportunities abound . . . but we don't know exactly where they are. Some stock will double tomorrow, but you would have to know in advance which one to successfully invest and benefit. What if you could summon a magic genie to show you where your best opportunities are? That's not possible, but Goldcorp did the next best thing in this golden tale. Follow its example to grasp more of the opportunities around you.

In the Introduction you read that Mr. McEwen, CEO of Goldcorp, a Canadian gold mining company, asked us whether it would be more effective to improve an existing business model or to establish a better one. We mentioned that he had decided on an experiment to locate an advanced business model. Here's the rest of that story.

Historically, Goldcorp, like most mining companies, kept its geological information secret. Its own geologists and a few others saw all the information. Beginning with the experiment, Goldcorp abandoned that secretive approach.

In March 2000, the company issued a challenge to the world's geologists to find more gold in its Red Lake mine. That gold mine was already tapping into one of the world's richest ore deposits. Everything the company knew about the mine was shared with the geologists through the Internet. Substantial cash prizes of up to $95,000 were offered for the best ideas about where to explore next. This contest came at a time when gold prices were at a near-term low in constant dollar terms. With little else to do in the depressed market, many of the world's best geologists participated. More than 1,400 prospectors registered for the challenge.

A year after the contest ended, the company announced that exploration based on the winning submissions had located six million additional ounces of gold reserves. With further testing, that total may grow. The ultimate revenue from mining the newly found gold will exceed one billion dollars, and profits will probably be several hundred million dollars. The prizes cost only $575,000, much less than the unproductive exploratory drilling that would otherwise have occurred.

To fully appreciate the power of this experience, you should know that Goldcorp's Red Lake mine had been operating for almost fifty years when the contest began. Most would have assumed before the contest that there was little more gold to find in the mine.

Goldcorp laid to rest the ore-finding part of the traditional gold mining business model as a result of this success. The "how" of finding gold is now improved.

To build on that success, the company launched its Global Search Challenge in March 2001 for owners of exploration properties. That contest looked for important mineral deposits worldwide over the following two years and offered two million dollars in prizes. This new contest amounted to a second model change in only one year. This time, Goldcorp will not only leverage its own information, it will leverage that of everyone else as well as their ability to interpret that information. Goldcorp will be able to access every geologist who learned something that a mining company is not yet exploiting. And it can then simply go with the best ideas to select a few new sites for exploration. This approach, combined with the Goldcorp Challenge, changes the "how" and "where" of finding minerals.

Goldcorp has gone from focusing on reducing its mine operating costs to increase profits, to reducing its finding costs to expand its sales and lower its mining costs.

The mining industry can expect that the business model for finding minerals will continue to rapidly change. In response to what it called "the Goldcorp principle," BHP Billiton, the world's largest gold miner, made seven terabytes of data available about its 150 years of mining exploration. BHP Billiton requested joint venture proposals from interested mining companies to further develop its properties. Clearly a new age of monetizing intellectual property is upon us.

No one can say for sure what will happen with Goldcorp in the future. Let's consider some possible results, though, to help understand the implications of successful new business models. If Goldcorp can continue to innovate and find low-cost, high-grade minerals faster and cheaper than anyone else, the company's size and position in its industry will rapidly expand. The company will be able to mine more minerals and earn more profits than ever before. If its stock price follows its mining successes, the company will be able to use stock to inexpensively acquire the resources it needs to do even more mining. As one sign of this possibility, from 1993 to October 2002, Goldcorp shares rose more than twentyfold in price while those of Microsoft expanded eightfold, Berkshire Hathaway sixfold, and General Electric by less than fourfold. Building on this strength, the company sold stock after the first contest ended to pay for more exploration and mine expansion. With further business model innovation, the company could choose to outsource mining to concentrate on finding reserves. By combining more business model innovations, the company could find itself growing more rapidly with higher margins than many high-tech firms do in what is normally considered a low-growth industry.

When other industries hear about and appreciate the cause of Goldcorp's success, we can expect similar challenges to be offered for new information and knowledge to solve problems and find better opportunities. In time, this new model will undoubtedly set off yet

> **How can your business greatly improve its business model by accessing the best experts inexpensively?**

another new model. Companies may acquire lesser-known businesses and properties, following a similar contest to identify these opportunities. A subsequent worldwide contest may then identify the best options for developing and operating the acquired businesses and properties. Such changes will influence the "what" of applying these innovations to acquire helpful knowledge inexpensively.

Such contests should be particularly important for nonprofit organizations. Most could use more volunteers and resources, and contests could help attract attention and ideas for recruiting and employing volunteers. The new volunteers can help create more resources, employ the existing ones more effectively and locate even more volunteers. Foundations are often willing to fund the start-up of such innovations. Costs for operating the challenges can be reduced

> **If acquiring companies survives as a path to industry leadership, how will this activity change?**

by recruiting volunteers to operate the contest and celebrities to offer special experiences (like a bit part in a movie or appearing on stage at a concert) as some of the prizes.

How can your business greatly improve its business model by accessing the best experts inexpensively? In Chapter 3, you'll find another company, Red Hat, that took a different approach to answer this question.

SYBRON DENTAL SPECIALTIES: ACQUIRE PROMISING PRODUCTS, IMPROVE THEM, REDUCE THEIR COSTS AND MAKE THEM MORE EASILY AVAILABLE

Most companies see acquisitions as the primary path to industry leadership. Yet seldom are such acquiring companies innovative with their business models or the businesses they purchase. Will merely acquiring competitors and eliminating redundant costs continue to be a profitable path to improving industry position? If acquiring companies survives as a path to industry leadership, how will this activity change?

The most dynamic and highest potential business models are ones that enable other enterprises to achieve extraordinary results by crossing the boundary from being an independent producer to becoming part of your company, whether through acquisition or joint venture. Many specialized distribution businesses operate with business models that make these combinations possible, so that acquisitions and joint ventures can be paths to much higher profitability and industry leadership. Study this subject well, because it is a secret of creating vastly more growth and more fundamental business model enhancements.

Let's take a look at Sybron Dental Specialties as an example. The firm provides many innovative products used by dentists to serve their patients. Most of these products were added by acquisition. Often the new offerings were developed in start-up partnerships between innovative dentists and people with product development skills. Such start-up companies have low volume and high production and distribution costs. Often, they are too small to be able to afford much marketing. When Sybron learns about a promising new product being offered by such an uneconomically sized firm, Sybron will purchase the company if the price is reasonable. It will inquire about ways to improve the new product and make the necessary enhancements. Being part of Sybron gives the product more credibility, so sales increase. With greater volume, production processes can be improved and scaled up. Being part of

Sybron's distribution network also reduces the costs of getting the product from the manufacturing facility to the dentist. As a result, Sybron can turn a marginally profitable, small market share product into an industry-leading one with significantly lower costs and prices within two or three years of acquiring it. On that increased scale, it can pay to further improve the product, thus enhancing its sales and profits even more.

Sybron's leaders know thousands of dentists on a first-name basis and spend lots of time listening to and sharing ideas with those dental professionals. That frequent and extensive contact increases the likelihood that the company will hear about more promising new companies and products. After acquiring them, Sybron can also use these exchanges to share helpful information about the improvements it makes to those offerings.

> **The most adept business model innovators are those who seek out the most powerful trends to serve and then facilitate their development.**

The company has gone from focusing on efficient distribution to generate profits, to improving the effectiveness of new products developed by others as its way to grow faster and more profitably.

How can your company make others grow faster and be more profitable by either being acquired or by forming ventures with you?

The Beckman Coulter example in Chapter 3 shows another way to create business model innovations through selecting and acquiring businesses that allow you to improve both the effectiveness of the acquired business and your existing operations with the same efforts. The Rogers example in Chapter 4 shows how one company formed effective joint ventures for high-tech product development and manufacturing. You will find helpful concepts about how to create other kinds of symbiotic relationships with larger companies in the Cephalon example located in Chapter 9.

LINEAR TECHNOLOGY: ADD BENEFITS THAT EXPAND MARKET GROWTH AND MARKET SHARE

As nice as it is to have an expanding supply of low-hanging fruit available to harvest, it is even better to have a rapidly growing demand from customers to purchase that fruit. With growing demand, you will have more chances to serve customers and potentially be better rewarded for what you do. The most adept business model innovators are those who seek out the most powerful trends to serve and then facilitate their development. Faster market growth and increased market share follow.

Consider Mr. Robert H. Swanson, Jr., CEO of Linear Technology, an analog semiconductor maker. The company's business model has always been based on having more knowledge than competitors of customer and end-user applications. Mr. Swanson realized that this expertise could be increased by developing higher-performance analog chips to replace commodity ones. To overcome the unavoidably higher costs and prices of its high-performance chips compared to the commodity alternatives, Linear Technology would have to add valuable benefits that the commodity chips did not provide.

In thinking about which benefits to add, Mr. Swanson had an important insight. The company should add benefits that accelerate market growth. The company's customers would receive more economic benefit, as would the company and its other stakeholders. Linear Technology quickly identified that reducing power usage would make cellular telephones and other portable electronic devices (such as laptop computers, digital still cameras, MP3 players and personal digital assistants) more valuable to end users by increasing how long the equipment could be operated between battery charges and changes. With the potential for much Internet and video communication to occur on battery-powered wireless devices, Mr. Swanson thought that he had found a key log jam that his company could help untangle. Improvements in battery technology would make the company's power management chips even more valuable by adding new dimensions to what portable devices can do.

With Linear Technology chips in place, battery life was greatly extended. Portable electronic product designers could either pack more usefulness into the same size package or offer smaller packages with the same utility. Portable devices became more functional.

Aided in part by these improvements, device volume soared. The demand for improved models was further stimulated.

Encouraged by this success, Linear Technology added a new element to its business model. New higher-performance chips were made available exactly when needed for its customers' shorter new product development windows. Linear's development time had to be reduced and timeliness improved. The company was driven by the high cost penalty that lateness imposes. Not being ready on time could cost the company and its customer over 90 percent of the potential profit from a new product.

The company's success has allowed consumers and companies to share information more rapidly and accurately. This sharing has helped create greater prosperity across the whole society. As a result, the economy will grow faster. Linear Technology should be an indirect beneficiary of this increased prosperity, as more people can afford the better performing, ever less expensive, portable products that its technology enables. Even during the technology recession of 2001–2002, sales of most portable devices continued to grow, while purchases of most other technology products shrank. The longer term success is even more

> **Ultimately, the most valuable customer benefits are built on company knowledge that cannot be duplicated in any other way.**

impressive. Company revenues expanded from $64.7 million in fiscal 1989 to $512.3 million in recession-plagued fiscal 2002. Profits climbed from $8.9 million in fiscal 1989 to $197.6 million in fiscal 2002, an impressive 38 percent after tax in a down year. In fiscal 1989, the company's stock traded between $1.80 and $2.70. In fiscal 2002, the range was from $28.58 to $48.08.

The company has gone from being an efficient supplier to a valuable partner who helps stimulate faster growth and higher profitability for its customers.

How can your company stimulate the growth of industry demand and sales of your customers' offerings?

This topic is explored in Chapter 1 though the Central Parking example.

ECOLAB: SHARE BENEFICIAL KNOWLEDGE WITH CUSTOMERS TO REDUCE THEIR COSTS AND IMPROVE THEIR OPERATIONS

Ultimately, the most valuable customer benefits are built on company knowledge that cannot be duplicated in any other way. As that knowledge is built and shared with customers, competitors find themselves trailing behind.

Ecolab provides cleaning chemicals for manufacturers, institutions, restaurants and other service providers. As such a provider, Ecolab learned that it was economically more important to restaurant owners to keep good relations with the health inspectors than it was to simply have effective cleaning supplies. To help its restaurant customers achieve this result, the company expanded its offerings to include the chemicals to sanitize everything in a restaurant. With its knowledge of the chemicals, Ecolab also added ways to improve and better maintain the storage, food preparation, water treatment, cooking, dishwashing, cleaning, restroom and disposal equipment by making better use of the chemicals.

The firm later expanded into the pest elimination, janitorial, floor care, water treatment and management advice businesses because these areas are important to restaurant owners due to their significance to diners and health inspectors. In each area, Ecolab carefully observes and measures its customers' experiences to locate the best practices. Using the expertise gained from analyzing its observations of many similar customers, the company can advise customers on how to save money and get better results while paying normal prices for its chemicals and services. The cost reduction benefits alone are often a large multiple of what Ecolab's products and services cost.

No local provider of any one of these services can hope to provide a more effective combination of solutions than Ecolab does. No new entrant nationally can hope to gain the knowledge that Ecolab has to create valuable, custom solutions while selling its products and services at very competitive prices. As a result, Ecolab is often the first choice of restaurant chains for cleaning supplies and sanitation services. Customers appreciate that Ecolab charges no premium to its products and services for the valuable information it shares about how to operate their facilities more cleanly and less expensively.

Ecolab duplicated this knowledge-based, benefit-development process used for restaurants with other types of customers. Hospitals were an early and natural extension of this concept. Exposure to similar activities in other end-use markets, such as food manufacturing and institutional feeding, created additional knowledge that Ecolab has turned into customer benefits in each market.

The company's revenues grew from $1.3 billion in 1989 to $2.3 billion in 2001. Earnings expanded from a temporarily depressed $3.2 million in 1989 to $188.2 million in 2001. Stock price varied in 1989 between $6.20 and $8.90. The range in 2001 was from $28.50 to $44.20. As you can see, even those serving lower growth industries can prosper with this approach.

> **After your company starts business model innovation, how might that direction be sustained when you and your colleagues are no longer there?**

The company has gone from being an efficient chemical manufacturer to a valuable source of cleanliness and operating best practices for its customers. It is beginning to develop many of the characteristics of an ideal business model, an approach described in the introduction to Part One.

How can your company develop unique knowledge that will make its customers more profitable, without charging for the information? This subject is developed in the Xilinx example in Chapter 3.

MANDALAY RESORT GROUP: IMPROVE
LONG-TERM BUSINESS MODEL INNOVATION

After your company starts business model innovation, how might that direction be sustained when you and your colleagues are no longer there? As good as being a leader in business model innovation is, this innovation should grow and improve if you are going to stay ahead of increasingly effective competitors.

Mandalay Resort Group was the only company we found where rapid business model innovation occurred under two consecutive management teams. Let's examine their experiences to see how harvests from attracting new customers can be expanded beyond the initial series of reinventions.

Las Vegas Strip casinos have always offered entertainment, usually for a fee and definitely for adults. When it opened in 1968 as a stand-alone casino with no hotel or banquet rooms, Circus Circus was an entertainment innovation.[1] Free circus acts performed above the gaming hall. While you played blackjack, a trapeze artist might dangle overhead by her teeth with only a net to protect you. But who normally likes circuses the most? Well, children do. But children are legally banned from gaming areas, so the acts were mostly wasted on gambling adults. Was that entertainment what mainstay drive-in gamblers from southern California were looking for? Probably not, based on the casino's history of unprofitability prior to 1974.

In 1974, Mr. William Pennington and Mr. William Bennett bought Circus Circus and improved its business model based on Mr. Bennett's experience as general manager of the Sahara, a successful hotel-casino on the Strip. The improvements came from adding benefits and charging low prices for them. They emphasized slot machines, providing better payouts than other Strip casinos, and added inexpensive sleeping rooms and food. By covering the gaming area with a new ceiling, the free circus entertainment could continue in a separate area above, where children and their parents could watch without disturbing gamblers. By 1980, Circus Circus was the most profitable hotel-casino in Nevada.

The company's current president and chief financial officer,

Mr. Glenn Schaeffer, was hired in the early 1980s. He improved the business model by adding low-cost bank debt, which had previously been unavailable to casinos. Fueled by these low-cost loans, the parent company, Circus Circus Enterprises, added hotel-casinos rapidly in Las Vegas, Laughlin and Reno, Nevada, and earned $83 million after taxes on sales of $692 million in 1990.

The company profitably added new customer benefits when it opened Excalibur, themed to King Arthur and his knights of the roundtable, on the Las Vegas Strip. Tournaments involving knights on horseback were a regular draw for couples and families, but you had to buy dinner and pay for admission to the show. Excalibur offered a low price point, but not the lowest, while providing more benefits than Circus Circus did in rooms, amenities and entertainment choices.

Despite the credit crunch during the early 1990s, the company used cash generated from its initial innovations to build the gleaming Luxor pyramid hotel-casino themed around ancient Egypt, which opened in 1993 next to Excalibur. Business model innovation temporarily faltered here based on bad execution. Luxor was priced to be upscale, but wasn't. People tried it and most didn't return.

At the same time, Mr. Michael Ensign, former chief operating officer, and Mr. Schaeffer, who'd just left the company, were developing another gaming company, Gold Strike. Following a board battle, Mr. Bennett left Circus Circus and Gold Strike was soon acquired, bringing Mr. Ensign and Mr. Schaeffer back. Mr. Ensign soon became CEO.

The team immediately decided to upgrade Luxor to fit its striking image and higher room prices, spending $400 million. Luxor now offers an upscale experience at a fair price.

Mr. Ensign and Mr. Schaeffer used land next to Luxor to open the company's biggest and highest quality development, Mandalay Bay, in 1999 to rave reviews. Mandalay Bay could serve as a top of the line vacation resort first, and gambling experience second. You choose between two different sleeping room and service quality levels, one delivered by Mandalay Bay, and the other by the foremost luxury chain of the time, Four Seasons Hotels.

The hotel has many fine restaurants and lounges. Outside the hotel is a beautiful recreational area, including a wave pool. A concert theater and an aquarium were later added. As a result, Mandalay Bay provides the best quality but without charging the highest price. The company changed its name from Circus Circus Enterprises to Mandalay Resort Group as a symbol of its latest shift in business model.

At Mandalay Resort Group, business model innovation has continued for an extended period of time. Its core insight now is to offer a full range of resort-based entertainment that includes gambling as *one* of the choices. That's quite an evolution from the company's original core insight of offering the best deal on the Strip for slot machines, rooms and food to inexperienced gamblers.

Las Vegas has changed a lot since 1968. The mainstream visitor now is a well-traveled, high-income forty-nine-year-old with his or her spouse who has flown 2,000 miles. To get there, these people flew over many other casinos. Las Vegas entertainment is the primary draw. Visitors spend half their money at the hotel where they stay and the rest nearby. The closest Strip hotel-casinos you see when you drive away from the airport are Mandalay Bay, Luxor and Excalibur. Only 30 percent of visitors are from California, now that Native American casinos are open there. Where Mandalay Resort Group once got 60 percent of its company revenues from gaming, that ratio is now 36 percent and falling. Mr. Schaeffer predicts that profits from room rentals will eventually exceed those from gaming.

Notice that regardless of how Las Vegas and other gaming resort areas develop, Mandalay Resort Group will be able to adapt and serve the emerging needs of customers through its expanding core insights. If market conditions in Las Vegas revert to being dominated by lots of drive-in customers from southern California, the company will prosper also.

Take a moment to think about how Mandalay Resort Group could serve even more stakeholders.

What are the lessons for extending business model innovation to another management generation? They include the following:

- The company's management team must set an example with at least one successful business model innovation. Otherwise, the task of business model innovation may not be perceived as necessary.

- The management team should establish an accurate core insight for subsequent innovations. Lacking such a core insight, many false directions will be pursued.

- The management team needs to bring in younger managers whose talents and vision are different from and greater than the team's own. Otherwise, innovation will be limited to fine-tuning the past direction.

- The first management team should either be flexible in accepting and following new core insights developed with or by younger managers, or leave. Otherwise, their inflexibility will cause progress to stall.

- The company's core insights must be expanded, refreshed and strengthened. Circumstances change, and core insights have to adjust accordingly.

- Execution must always match the demands of the core insights. The missteps at Luxor probably cost Mandalay Resort Group five years of potential progress.

- Lots of management and employee ownership can provide the necessary insulation needed to pursue progress when business model innovation is temporarily stalled. To emphasize this point, realize that in 2002 Mandalay Resort Group's share price had not yet returned to the levels just before Luxor was opened, despite enjoying higher earnings-per-share since then. Impatient owners could easily have thrown management out during the recovery, even though the right steps were being taken. An incautious management change could have set back business model innovation in the company, following a flurry of slash-and-burn cost-cutting.

What can you do today to be sure your organization is following these important lessons?

An example of launching a new wave of business model innovation is provided in Chapter 7 in connection with Zebra Technologies.

How can your organization change the pricing and benefits of its offerings to appeal to more types of customers in new ways?

You can find more pricing examples in Chapter 2 and more improved benefit examples in Chapter 1.

DISNEYLAND: USE PRICE STRUCTURE AND LEVEL TO ENCOURAGE SPENDING MORE

When Disneyland first opened in Anaheim, California, Mr. Walter E. Disney was concerned that lines not be too long on the most popular attractions. He did what government bureaucrats have often done when supply was limited: he rationed the supply. When you entered the Magic Kingdom, you held a coupon book in your hand. To visit or ride on an attraction, you had to have the right kind of coupon—A through E. Most teens and many adults left the park with extra A and B coupons, good for rides up and down Main Street and attractions designed for small children in Fantasyland, and were soon out of E coupons for attractions like the Matterhorn bobsleds and submarine ride. Parents with young children had the opposite experience. If you wanted more coupons of a certain type, you had to traipse back to the entrance to buy them. After a few years, Disneyland set up kiosks throughout the park where you could buy more coupons. That price structure was expensive for Disneyland and its guests, and made it less attractive to visit Disneyland. Eventually, this awkward system was replaced by a passport that was good for unlimited use of all attractions. However, the change meant that the lines got longer on most of the former E-coupon attractions.

Let's look at Disneyland's pricing structure for those passports in the early 1990s. Visitors were offered the choice of a one-day, multiple-day or annual passport. The highest price per day was the one-day passport, and the least expensive per day was the annual passport (assuming that you visited at least four days a year using the less expensive version). The multiple-day passports were priced at less per day than the one-day passports (assuming that you visited for the maximum number of days allowed by that passport) and were valid for use anytime. If you knew that you were coming back for several days during a vacation trip, you would usually opt for a multiple-day passport. If you lived nearby, you might consider one of the annual passports.

Disney advertised these choices. If you were planning a vacation to include Disneyland from far away, you would often plan the length of your stay to match the longest multiple-day passport available, usually three days. If Disney had only offered two-day passports, many people would not have stayed for a third day because of the added passport cost.

If you lived nearby, you might seldom visit Disneyland on your own, after too many trips to entertain visiting friends and relatives, unless it seemed virtually free. And that's the perception that an annual passport creates. Each entry is free after you have made the annual investment. So, you might even consider stopping by for only an hour or two. In your mind, the cost of the day has dropped from around $40.00 to zero. That's perfect for neighboring parents with small children who soon need naps. Would that change the number of times you go to Disneyland if you lived nearby? Surely.

Why would Disney managers want you to come all of the time? Well, actually they didn't. As we mentioned, there were usually two different kinds of annual passports. One allowed you to come for free admission only on days when Disney expected the park wouldn't be crowded. With that annual passport, you could pay an additional, discounted charge to come on the other dates. For about double the money, you could come every day for no daily fee. The price of the more expensive option was slightly more than buying two three-day passports. The price of the less expensive option was slightly more than buying one three-day passport.

What benefit does Disney receive from having you come on less-busy days? Well, it's almost impossible not to spend some money while you're there. You will probably pay for parking in the Disneyland lot. Even if you don't park there and only spend $2.00 for a beverage, Disney probably made more money than if you hadn't been present that day. Throughout the day, you will be exposed to other Disney products and services, from Mickey Mouse shirts and watches to Disney Channel cable subscriptions. In essence, you are paying to receive increased amounts of Disney advertising. If you have a good time while you're receiving the advertising, you will undoubtedly buy more of those products and services. Also, Disneyland is often operating at minimum staffing so the cost to handle more people is small. Is this pricing strategy a good one for Disney? You bet.

Why did Disney later open a new theme park in Anaheim called California Adventure? Undoubtedly, the company perceived that it could capture vacationers for longer stays and local people for more visits. Also, it had a chance to up the price for an annual passport to include visits to two parks. With twice as many places to entertain Disney's guests when the parks weren't crowded, the chances to increase revenues and advertising exposure were enormous. By the way, a third park is under development there. How do you think the pricing structure will change then?

Will the behavior of millions of visitors be changed in ways that make more money for Disney? That's as certain as the smiles on your face and the Mickey Mouse flower clock greeting you when you enter Disneyland.

Disneyland has gone from focusing on rationing supply of scarce attractions to opening its doors to expanded profitability by encouraging more use during slack periods.

How can your company change its pricing structure to profitably increase the demand for your offerings? Chapter 2 describes a process for finding your best choices.

HUFFY: ADJUST PRICES, ADD BENEFITS AND REDUCE COSTS TO ATTRACT MORE PROFITABLE BUSINESS WITH ONE BUSINESS MODEL REINVENTION

Sometimes, a company's business model inhibits pursuing good opportunities. When that happens, a new business model must bridge the gap to these good opportunity areas with a sturdy base of customer and competitive advantages.

For over fifty years, Huffy designed and manufactured one brand and quality of bicycles, and sold them mostly in the United States. When that business model stopped working, the company didn't adjust.

Under its old business model, Huffy forecasted how many bikes of what sort would be sold. If the estimate was too high, the company lost money. Huffy was accordingly conservative in its sales estimates. If sales took off, that was too bad. Losing sales was better than taking inventory losses. This business model discouraged adding new items. If new bikes failed to sell, the losses were terrible because of development, tooling and inventory costs compared to capacity-constrained sales.

Manufacturing was a source of many other controllable costs. So a lot of attention was paid to factory efficiency. Competitors had moved their manufacturing offshore years earlier. Huffy considered doing so, but saw no advantage over its own domestic manufacturing. Meanwhile, its customer base was shrinking as many new types and qualities of bikes became popular and were increasingly sold through discount outlets.

Led by Mr. Don R. Graber since 1996, the company made a rapid transition into a new, customer-focused business model. Huffy now operates more like Nike, the footwear and apparel marketer, than a manufacturer. Like athletic shoes and sports apparel, bicycles have become more of a fashion item and more specialized. Bike use is diversifying to reflect new concepts of what bikes can do as design, materials and manufacturing improve.

Huffy changed its earlier decision about foreign production. It went further and no longer makes its bikes, relying instead on faster, less expensive and more versatile foreign suppliers to produce its designs. The company has also extended its bicycle offerings to include three more brands in addition to Huffy, its value brand. Royce Union is the trade-up line, and Airborne provides innovative, high-end bikes. Each brand occupies a different market niche. This approach is best exemplified by its new X-Games brand, which emphasizes performance in the popular, televised sport of stunt bicycling. This array of brands and offerings also allows the company to pursue the different distribution channels more aggressively, by minimizing price competition among its retail customers for the same branded item.

An early success with this differentiated, customer-facing approach was in rapidly adding an in-line scooter in 2000. Huffy had had a scooter that usually sold 200,000 units a year. As sales of the new scooter took off, Huffy was rapidly able to expand its supply through outsourced manufacturing. Yet the capital expenditure budget for this ramp-up was zero. Under the old business model, most of the gains would have been missed while the investment would have been significant.

By changing business models, the company's operating focus has gone from inventory risk management to rapid trial of promising new products. The shift has already paid off in better profitability and market share. Huffy plans to expand inexpensive experimentation and make the successes more rapidly available.

As beneficial as those cost and investment savings are, Mr. Graber is far more interested in helping bike riders. As the company listens more to consumers, its ability to notice opportunities should improve. Huffy will promote its improvements at new bicycle events, through word of mouth and Web sites, and with specialized advertising as substitutes for unaffordable network television ads. As its marketing skill develops, the business model can be expanded into related products by employing similar lower-cost marketing methods.

> **How can your company simultaneously improve costs, adjust prices and provide new benefits to create a new foundation of competitive advantages?**

It's too soon to know how well the company will perform under this new model, but shareholders are seeing progress. During the shift in business models, the stock fell to $3.00 in 2000. The company reported record earnings per share in 2000 of $1.62 before falling back to a loss of $0.27 in 2001. The stock price rebounded to trade between $5.30 and $10.60 in 2001, reflecting increased confidence that the new business model would succeed.

Huffy has gone from a manufacturing emphasis involving its

historic product line to being an unbounded designer and distributor of exciting bicycle choices.

How can your company simultaneously improve costs, adjust prices and provide new benefits to create a new foundation of competitive advantages?

Paychex is another example of a company that is making headway in all three dimensions of costs, prices and benefits. You read about Paychex in the Introduction and can read more in Chapter 1.

How can your company organize itself to perform this innovation continually, so that it can have the ultimate competitive advantage? The subject of sustaining business model innovation is developed through processes and examples described in chapters 4 through 9.

PART ONE

THE MOST PRODUCTIVE AREAS FOR BUSINESS MODEL INNOVATION

The purpose of a business is to create a customer.
—Peter F. Drucker

To rephrase Professor Drucker in light of our research, the purpose of a business is to continually develop and employ better ways to create and serve customers, while fairly rewarding stakeholders. Let's look at how two CEOs pursued that imperative.

A beaming CEO greeted us as we entered his office some years ago. He was excited about the opportunity to open a new national market and eagerly shared the details. Through costly cultural contacts, he and his company would be the first American firm in their industry to present their case to Chinese government authorities. He was due to leave in two weeks and asked us to come back to hear the details after his return. Alas, our next meeting found him not so happy. The contacts had led nowhere, and he felt that the whole effort and the company's large investment were wasted. He wished that he had stayed home.

Later that year, another CEO told us of his recent visit to Japan to study the design and manufacturing practices of the com-

> **Blinded by false promises based on spreadsheet illusions of a golden future and the misleadingly reassuring memories of past successes, companies often grope their way into unseen danger and disaster.**

pany's joint venture partner there. He gushed with excitement about what these practices could do for his U.S. products and factories. He learned that the Japanese partner was profitably selling equivalent products for less than his company's U.S. costs. Employing the insights gained on that trip, his company experienced more than a decade of improved prosperity.

Two CEOs leave on trips to the Far East. One returns empty-handed, and the other returns with a gem. What made the difference? The second CEO was better focused. He knew who to talk to and what to ask on his trip. The first CEO was just having a pleasant daydream about his desire to have more business, although he thought he had studied the issue from every angle. You can learn to think and act like the second CEO by using the information in Part One.

Blinded by false promises based on spreadsheet illusions of a golden future and the misleadingly reassuring memories of past successes, companies often grope their way into unseen danger and disaster. At best, they just waste their time and some money, as the first CEO did. Meanwhile, company executives overlook vast, reliable paths to future success all around them. Part One can help you see and follow those reliable paths.

One secret of advancing toward the ultimate competitive advantage is to do more of what works and less of what does not. And the one thing we found that works most often is continual business model innovation developed through an effective process. Such innovations almost always lower the enterprise's needless costs for stakeholders, and, more importantly, they deliver more customer benefits at the same time. Work on improving the performance of existing business models often does the opposite because such performance-improving plans generally call for cutting resources while attempting to keep customer benefits unchanged. In this pursuit, customer benefits usually decline due to disruptions from the change and the reduced resource level.

How does providing a successful business model innovation

create multiplied benefits for all concerned? For one thing, customers like the new model better. Fewer go to a competitor. They tell their friends, which makes it easier to get new customers. Employees enjoy their work more and aren't as inclined to leave you. They also tell their friends, making it easier to recruit top talent. Partners see you as a source of valuable ideas that they have a hard time successfully generating for themselves. Your innovations draw their attention and support. Suppliers get more business and find you more open to new ideas. They bring you their best innovations first. Shareholders like the more rapid growth in revenues and earnings. They will hold their stock and may buy more when prices dip. Potential shareholders will be intrigued and buy in also. Your stock-price multiple will rise. You can use that stock rise to reward employees better through prior grants of lower-priced stock options, and you can sell stock to raise capital less expensively to grow your business and acquire other businesses. You can also sell high-priced shares to retire debt and raise cash to help you weather bad times. The communities you serve will prosper and be proud to support you. When you need cooperation for an improvement such as enhancing local public education to ensure a better future workforce, citizens will seek to speed up the change process because they are in partnership with you. With each successful innovation, these connections and mutual support increase.

What's Required for a Continual Business Model Innovation Process?

Continual business model innovation requires the following four dimensions:

1. *Understanding and following the current business model:* Employing the optimum way goods and services should be supplied now, by informing all stakeholders about what needs to be done to deliver the most benefits.

2. *Understanding and installing the next business model:* Specifying the next innovation to provide more stakeholder benefits

(continued)

---

through goods and services, and how the transition to that innovation will occur.

3. *Understanding and using a business model innovation vision:* The ideal benefits to deliver to stakeholders in your industry, which is used to test the appropriateness of developing future generations of potential business model innovations.

4. *Ongoing design and testing of potential business model innovations:* Vision-defined probes and tests to elicit reactions to providing new benefits and various ways of supplying them.

A more valuable approach to continual business model innovation also describes more than one future generation of innovations in terms of dimension 2.

Already, you are probably thinking that most businesses are weak in all four dimensions. Businesses have usually obscured key points about the first dimension so that some employees, suppliers, partners and customers do not understand what they are supposed to be doing. Even more businesses have left the second dimension undefined and ignored the third dimension altogether. Many companies are pursuing no business model innovation experiments or tests. No wonder few companies are enjoying the benefits of continual business model innovation.

For each of the first three dimensions of continual business model innovation, you need to identify seven key elements—the who, what, when, where, why, how, and how much—viewed from the perspective of all direct and indirect stakeholders. Their combination defines either a business model or a business model innovation vision:

1. "Who?" defines all the stakeholders you are serving or affecting.

2. "What?" describes the offerings and their benefits and negative influences that affect each stakeholder.

3. "When?" captures the timing of offerings' effects on stakeholders.

4. "Where?" identifies the location for delivering benefits and other impacts.

5. "Why?" gives the rationale for providing the stakeholder benefits you deliver.

6. "How?" explains your method of providing your offerings and being compensated for them.

7. "How much?" states the price customers pay and incur.

To improve your understanding that each of the first three dimensions of a continual business model innovation process has seven elements, read the following example of a children's lemonade stand. This example is also the foundation for demonstrating ways to improve business model innovation in each of the introductions to the book's next three parts.

A Children's Lemonade Stand

Assume you are a parent of two children who set up and operate a lemonade stand in front of your house one day. You provide the supplies and help with the preparations. We've picked a children's lemonade stand as our example because almost every reader has either purchased from such a stand, operated one as a child or served as the adult facilitating such an enterprise. We hope that the full development of the example over the book's four parts will encourage some readers to live the example by assisting children to have some fun and to begin learning about continual business model innovation.

As inspiration for you, our publisher shared his own story of having a youthful door-to-door candy business in Jackpot, Nevada. He worked hard but made little because the wholesale price of candy was high compared to the retail price, squeezing his potential profits. Also, many people weren't at home when he came to call.

(continued)

When he decided to change his business model to include selling lemonade at the town's only gas station (which was owned by his father), profits soared. His cost of goods for lemonade was only 20 percent rather than the 50 percent for candy sales, and there was a steady stream of thirsty potential customers. That experience has been a lifelong lesson for him in the importance of business model innovation.

How the Business Model Operates Now

Let's explore the first dimension of a continual business model innovation process, how to operate now, in terms of its seven elements.

Who? The stakeholders include you and your children, the customers, suppliers and anyone whose health or safety is affected by where or how your children operate the lemonade stand.

What? You and your children are providing lemonade to customers as a source of cooling, refreshment and calories. Customers benefit from a sense of helping two children. If the customers are lonely or want to make friends, your children provide companionship. On the downside, neighbors who are distracted or inconvenienced by what you do find the lemonade stand is a nuisance. You want to minimize the downside by keeping noise down, not blocking the street or sidewalk and promptly picking up any trash.

When? The timeframe involved includes the hours you operate and thereafter, whenever any effects occur.

Where? The stand is located in front of your home, but the effects can reach wherever the lemonade and trash are carried or traffic is disturbed.

Why? The reason your children have set up the lemonade stand and that you are helping them is to provide the stakeholder benefits described in the category of "What?" listed previously. In addition, your children enjoy a chance to learn something about business, serve others, make a profit and have a fun experience. You receive a sense of satisfaction when your children pursue a new, constructive interest.

How? Your lemonade is made from frozen concentrate bought at the supermarket, chilled with ice while stored in a portable cooler and served in paper cups. You and your children prepare the materials in the kitchen, carry them out front yourselves and operate from a portable card table that you help them carry to and from the house. The children advertise with a small sign they made from craft materials bought at the art supply store.

How Much? The price is twenty-five cents for the first cup and fifteen cents for refills to the same paper cup.

How the Lemonade Stand Will Operate in Future Business Models

Now that you understand the seven elements of the current business model, let's look at how an improved business model for the future might compare to the existing one. Let's assume that you want to help your children offer a better value at the current price (the subject of Chapter 1). You could improve the quality or increase the quantity. Why not do both? If you as a parent are willing to go along with providing "free" supplies, your children will receive more income. Your children decide to offer fresh-squeezed lemonade as well as frozen lemonade. You serve the lemonade in large ceramic mugs rather than paper cups. You provide sugar that people can add to make the lemonade sweeter if they like it that way. You also provide lemon wedges that customers can add to make the lemonade tarter if they prefer that taste. You've changed "what" you offer as well as "how."

Next, you look into ways to adjust your price structure and prices to increase sales (the issue considered in Chapter 2). Rather than offering lemonade only by the mug, you might offer one price for all the lemonade the customer can drink all day. You could even offer a weekly price for unlimited lemonade. To appeal to parents, you

(continued)

could offer a family price for the week as well. After testing, you decide on the weekly family price approach to complement your per-mug price. You've changed "how much" and "what" is covered by the price. By going past being open for one day, you've also changed "when" you operate.

Then you realize that you had better look into reducing costs that don't help customers (the subject reviewed in Chapter 3). As a parent, you are only going to financially support this venture so far. How can you get your lemonade supplies less expensively? You speak to the manager of your local supermarket and learn about a wholesale grocer who would sell to you at low prices for cash if you pick up your supplies from his warehouse. You've made another change to "what" you do.

Having been inspired by that cooperative experience, you decide to look for ways to make the lemonade stand more beneficial to all (you can read more about this topic in Part Two). You start with customers. Since your children have to be at the lemonade stand all the time anyway, you realize they can offer a limited baby-sitting service as well. This offering increases the incentives for parents to buy the weekly family plan so that their children have something to drink while they are with you. Your "what" has expanded again.

Next you consider suppliers. You are soon tired of going back and forth to the wholesale grocer to get more supplies, so you provide a discounted weekly price on baby-sitting and lemonade for a family that needs to cut back on expenses and would like to buy other low-cost food for themselves while purchasing your supplies. That family becomes your supply network. "What" and "who" have changed again.

Your children are getting tired of spending so much time at the stand, so they decide to hire some other kids to help them. Your children give the helpers unlimited lemonade in exchange for smaller pay. "What" and "who" are further expanded.

Then you offer everyone free brownies if they can give you good ideas for how to make the stand more successful. One of the children that your kids are baby-sitting says he would like to have lemonade at home, not just at your house. So you add a home-delivery service combined with a more expensive weekly lemonade charge. "What" and "how much" have expanded.

Next someone says that those brownies surely would taste good with lemonade, and you start to sell brownies on a regular basis. "What" is increased.

Soon you are testing out other new items. You realize that others may have worked on this problem before you, so you do research on the Internet. You offer additional prizes for the best ideas for improving your lemonade stand. As a result, you are changing your business model almost every month based on successful tests.

Because other kids aren't as good at improving the business model for a lemonade stand as your family is, your children decide to offer the service of sharing your business model through franchising. One of your children likes to do this, so she spends her time helping "clients" get set up and sharing the latest ideas, while your other child keeps fine-tuning the front-yard location. These activities greatly expand "what" you offer.

Suddenly it occurs to you that most people are not in front of your home during the day. How about selling lemonade near workplaces? And what about setting up temporary stands along parade routes? "Where" expands. And so it goes.

While only experience in a local neighborhood can determine whether such a business model scenario is going to be successful, we can point to children who do well offering used golf balls they find in their yards along with lemonade near the tees of golf courses that border their homes.

Now you see how the seven elements play out in defining future business models.

(continued)

Lemonade Stand Innovation Vision

The third component of a continual business model innovation process is a vision to guide future innovation. For the lemonade stand, that vision involves much more than selling products and services to make a profit. The lemonade stand is creating a more supportive and caring neighborhood by helping neighbors find more effective ways to provide for one another. In addition, those who are providing the lemonade stand products and services are undergoing substantial personal development. Future business model innovations for the lemonade stand should be tested against all three aspects of that business model innovation vision.

We hope that this humble example opens your mind to the potential of being innovative with your business model, even if you are starting with one of the best known business models . . . like a child's lemonade stand.

What Is a Good Business Model?

In addition to your business model innovation vision, how else should you assess the quality of an existing or potentially improved business model? Let's begin by looking at the basics for a desirable business model, what we call a "good" business model.

A good business model provides benefits to all its stakeholders more effectively than existing competitors or new entrants can. Here are six common ways to provide a greater array and volume of stakeholder benefits:

1. Help your customers get customers for themselves faster than their competitors, as Linear Technology does.

2. Stimulate industry growth through providing more benefits and fewer drawbacks at the current price level, as Linear Technology also does.

3. Reprice your offerings to encourage using more of those offerings, as Disneyland does.

4. Reduce the resources needed to provide and use these offerings, as Goldcorp does.

5. Reinvest the resources generated by your business model to provide even more benefits and fewer drawbacks in the future, faster than your competitors can, as Goldcorp and Huffy have been attempting.

6. Fairly share excess resources with the stakeholders who have supported and provided the business model's success in a predictable way, so that no other organization can offer these stakeholders as much benefit now or in the future.

By this definition, many businesses have good business models. You can look at Disney's theme parks, Southwest Airlines, Johnson & Johnson's over-the-counter health-care products and IBM's outsourced computer services as examples.

To better appreciate what a good business model is, now let's look at some bad business model characteristics. The worst element of a bad business model is that scarce resources are rapidly drained from the company, harming both current and future performance. Such scarce resources include the time and attention of key employees, time to reach the market with new offerings, stakeholder goodwill and cash. A bad business model will usually favor a few stakeholders at the obvious expense of the rest, causing cooperation to decline. The CEOs of many bankrupt telecommunications companies were such a favored group at these companies otherwise unsuccessful in serving stakeholders.

Kmart is another example. The company's latest discount retailing business model directed its stores against Wal-Mart, but was handicapped by its higher costs and prices and a voracious hunger for borrowing to increase store size and improve attractiveness. Few of

(continued)

its investments helped employees, who experienced low and declining morale. Suppliers saw their sales sag and often had to wait for payment. Shareholders saw their hold-ings erode to nothing. Eventually, Kmart entered bankruptcy in 2001. After enormous investments and efforts, there was little to show for any stakeholder beyond customers.

Ultimately, a bad business model cannot be sustained. A company with a bad business model finds itself wasting time and resources in a blind alley from which it must eventually retreat in a much diminished condition.

What Is an Ideal Business Model?

For new products, becoming just good enough can be the enemy of greatness. The pressure to get to market will often cause a new product to provide fewer benefits than it might have. If getting to market is the key issue, providing fewer initial benefits is a good decision. You can always put more benefits into a "new, improved" version down the road. But, if you lose sight of what should be in that new product as soon as possible, someone else will make the improvements and take some of your customers away.

Business models operate much the same way. Even a small lead can create substantial rewards for getting to market sooner. Yet, without clarity about "what comes next?" what comes next will be "nothing," or worse—a detriment.

In developing ideal business models to help your business reach its fullest potential, our investigation shows there are another four elements to add to the basics required for a good business model:

1. Your business model opens new windows of opportunity for you, while closing those and other important windows of opportunity for current and potential competitors.

2. You find ways to provide more helpful benefits for more types of stakeholders with each round of business model improvement.

3. You serve stakeholders who would normally not be able to meet your minimum standards to become lenders, shareholders, employees, suppliers, partners or customers.

4. Your business model improvements expand your ability to make more types of business model innovations more rapidly in the future.

Many companies discussed in this book portray these characteristics in their business model improvements. Pay particular attention to the sections on Business Objects, Ecolab, Iron Mountain and Paychex for informative examples.

KEY QUESTIONS

These questions, like those at the end of each chapter, are designed to help you deepen, extend and apply your understanding of the key ideas in this book.

- *What is a good business model that you have seen?* In identifying a good business model, consider the elements presented in this introduction to Part One. You will probably find it easiest to consider businesses that you know well as a customer, supplier or industry participant. If you can't think of any examples, consider a consumer service company you like or a store or a restaurant that you frequent.

- *What makes that business model a good one?* Outline your reasons for selecting it. Specifically focus on what provides an advantage over current and potential competitors. In the lemonade stand example, location, availability and neighborhood relationships were key advantages over current and potential competitors. If other children in the neighborhood began offering the same service, the size of these competitive advantages would fall dramatically. In considering why your selection is a good business model, can you also think of any better alternative business models to your choice?

- *How could that business model become more ideal?* If you are like most customers, suppliers or industry participants, you have seen at least some shortsighted behavior by the company you are modeling that appalls and amazes you. How could correcting that shortsightedness be done in ways that would lead to becoming a more ideal business model?

Now, think about your business.

- *What were the last three business models before the current one?* Understanding the evolution of a model often provides valuable insights into improved business models for the future. The forces that made earlier innovations work may still be around today, or may have only been slightly changed. For example, the appeal of costumed performers playing Mickey Mouse at Disneyland and Disney World is limited unless you know about the old cartoon features and comics that introduced most people to Mickey. If you don't know much about the history of your business, find some people who do and ask them about changes in the ways that business has been conducted and benefits received. You can then turn that information into a profile of past business models.

- *Does your company have a process for developing improved business models?* New business models usually emerge from a deliberate process of innovation. If your company has yet to establish such a process, chances are high that you have a substantial backlog of opportunities for desirable new business models.

> **When was the last time your company changed its business model?**

- *If you have had such a process, does it look at business model innovation separately from product and technological innovation?* Many companies see new products and technologies as the only ways to provide increased benefits to customers and end users. That kind of thinking is too limited. It can be easier to add value by turning a product into a service than it is to focus only on improving the product itself. For example, there was no Starbucks in the 1970s.

General Foods' Maxwell House Division could have become Starbucks then, if the division had had a different focus. Maxwell House introduced flavored coffees in the early 1970s, built around flavor concepts like what you get in a coffee bar now. Unfortunately, neither the taste of nor the experiences associated with these canned items are a match for what you now drink and enjoy at Starbucks. Although Maxwell House's advertising agency recommended establishing a Starbucks-like business, that alternative got little attention. A single-minded focus on new business models, which may include new products, services and technologies, can help you stop missing your best opportunities.

- *When was the last time your company changed its business model?* If the answer is more than two years ago, the odds favor the existence of a current opportunity to implement an improved business model.

- *How many times has the business model changed in your industry in the past ten years?* If the answer is less than three times, there is probably untapped potential for a business model innovation now.

- *How expensive is it for you to develop and test a new business model?* Be sure to consider expenses like staff time and physical resources as well as the capital that is required. In addition, think about what else you have to forgo (opportunity costs) while testing new business models. The answer differs from industry to industry. If the costs are low, then you have high potential for developing an improved business model. You will face fewer internal hurdles in performing the necessary early experimentation. Conversely, if the costs are high, you will probably need to create an improved, less costly way to develop business models.

- *How risky is it for you to develop and test a new business model?* For some companies, reputation is so important that it is difficult to test new things until they are almost perfect. Consider launching a new car brand. If the first models run poorly, no one will want to buy the improved version. In other industries, such as those providing new devices used in manufacturing, working with crude prototypes is the expectation. Customers often have pilot lines designed just to test such crude prototypes.

What would you lose if your business model experiment fails in all of the various ways that it could? If not very much, what are you waiting for?

If much is at stake, consider ways to reduce the amount at risk or the visibility of your temporary setbacks and flops so that you can afford more learning experiences. Early experiments should be expected to create learning rather than successful solutions. You need to have a way to learn with affordably low risk.

CHAPTER 1

INCREASE VALUE WITHOUT RAISING PRICES AND COSTS

People go through four stages before any
revolutionary development:
1. It's nonsense, don't waste my time.
2. It's interesting, but not important.
3. I always said it was a good idea.
4. I thought of it first.
—Arthur C. Clarke

Your business grows faster after you give customers something they value more than what the competition offers at the same or lower price and cost. Layer more value on top of what caused you to out-grow competitors, and you will have the beginnings of a sustainable competitive advantage. After a decade of continually applying this approach, your position will be virtually unassailable and the helpful habits well ingrained in your organization. Despite these significant potential competitive advantages, few companies focus on outperforming by providing new forms of value and greater amounts of value at current or lower price levels.

For many years Boston-area radio listeners heard commercials featuring Mr. Barry Tatelman and Mr. Eliot Tatelman on Saturday evenings that began, "It's live. It's Saturday night! It's Saturday night at Jordan's Furniture where underprices begin." The obvious play on the opening lines from the television show, *Saturday Night Live*, amused many and drew attention. The company's single store on eclectic Moody Street in blue-collar Waltham, Massachusetts, was indeed open on Saturday nights until eleven. You were encouraged to come look at furniture with the Jordan's J-Team "consultants." Unlike most furniture salespeople, Jordan's consultants were paid salaries rather than commissions and encouraged to let you browse and answer your questions without sales pressure. Jordan's did actually offer low prices, and many people were pleased with the combination of good value and shopping convenience.

For busy couples, here was a chance to do a little shopping when neighboring stores were closed. You could sneak by on the way to or from a movie, or before or after dining at the many interesting restaurants on Moody Street. We live nearby, and were impressed by the crowds streaming in and out of Jordan's late on Saturday night.

Building on that advertising theme of furniture shopping as entertainment (what Jordan's calls "shoppertainment"), the two Tatelmans, the store's owners, starred in a series of television ads that spoof various television shows and movies. In one memorable sequence, *Field of Dreams* is recreated around a furniture theme. In another funny ad, the owners create visual puns by lounging in baseball uniforms on furniture all over and around Fenway Park, home of the Boston Red Sox. Even Fellini comes in for some good-natured kidding in a satirical ad where a beautiful blonde woman falls in love with the sofa on which one of the store's owners is comfortably seated, while dismissing him.

As its success grew, Jordan's added two other stores in the Boston area and one in Nashua, New Hampshire. Each was built around a different entertainment theme and offered appealing new attractions. The opening of the Avon, Massachusetts, store drew such crowds that people had to wait in line to get in. Jordan's converted its normal ads during the opening into an emergency request that people stop coming to the new store.

At the same time it was adding stores, Jordan's built on its expertise. Soon, you could also be counseled by "sleep technicians" with whom you could discuss your sleep habits and be steered into the right bedding system to help you get more and better rest at night. With its increased purchasing volume, Jordan's could arrange for custom furniture to be created by factories to its own specifications. Taking advantage of this opportunity, Jordan's management learned how to design furniture that would bring even more customer value at the same price.

In 1998, Jordan's opened its fourth store, a magnificent 110,000 square foot shoppertainment complex in Natick, Massachusetts, which commands a hilltop view of competing stores and the largest retail area west of Boston. With that store, Jordan's took the entertainment theme in new directions. That location features a free show in the center of the store not unlike what many have seen at the Country Bear Jamboree at Disneyland and the Magic Kingdom in Disney World. The theme is Mardi Gras on Bourbon Street in New Orleans, and everyone is soon in a party mood. You leave the show wearing Mardi Gras beads and smiling. Before or after the show, you can pick up an ice cream cone or a beverage while you stroll down the Bourbon Street hallway. The show is so good that people travel from neighboring states to view it. At the same time, Jordan's arranged for one of the most popular sandwich shops in the area, Kelly's, to open in the northeast corner of the store. So you can also have a great roast beef sandwich, if you need more fortification before or after you shop. In 2002, the store added a commercially operated IMAX theater featuring 3-D movies to attract even more entertainment-seeking shoppers. You pass through the entire length of the store to reach the escalator to the theater. Hundreds of thousands of viewers were expected annually.

What's in store for the future? Who knows? But it's likely to be big. In 2003, the company plans to open its fifth and largest store in Reading, Massachusetts, which will also host an IMAX theater. Since legendary CEO, Mr. Warren E. Buffett, acquired

Jordan's for well-heeled Berkshire Hathaway after the Natick store opened, money will certainly be no constraint for Jordan's capable management. The Tatelmans have announced plans to double the size of the company over four years.

How does shoppertainment work out economically? In twenty-five years, Jordan's grew from 15 employees to more than 1,000. As a private company, Jordan's did not reveal its sales and earnings, but these undoubtedly soared as shopper visits expanded.

> **Ask most people to think about what a better business model than the current one would look like, and they draw an initial mental blank.**

In the early 2000s, Jordan's had the highest reported sales per square foot of any furniture retailer in the United States. Based on those statistics, the Natick store could be generating around $100 million in annual revenues. At those high revenue levels, many fixed costs should become quite small as a percentage of sales.

What about all of that advertising? Actually, Jordan's spends only 2 percent of sales on advertising while the average furniture retailer spends 7 percent. Most people are coming to Jordan's because of their own successful experiences there and word-of-mouth compliments from delighted customers.

While most furniture retailers turn their inventory over one to two times a year, Jordan's sells its inventory twelve times. That helps return on investment by decreasing the investment.

How does the community make out? Jordan's has been increasingly active in supporting charities in a variety of ways. The revenues from your ice cream and beverage purchases at the Nat-

> **How can you move beyond what you know you should do to create new ideas for better business models?**

ick store as well as from tickets for the featured attraction at the Avon store are donated. Jordan's pays the expenses out of its own pocket. Charities can run fund-raising events for free on Bourbon Street inside the Natick store. A number of other causes benefit from special support.

Does continually providing more value at the same price pay off? It sure did for Jordan's and its customers. Read on to learn how to make it work for you.

USE A DISCIPLINED PROCESS TO FIND
HELPFUL VALUE-IMPROVING IDEAS

Business concepts are only as good as your ability to apply them to your own situation. How many good ideas have you been exposed to that your organization still doesn't use? Since business model innovation is too important to suffer that fate, let's begin our exploration of business model innovation secrets by looking at how organizations learn to be outstanding in adding new and greater benefits at the same price and cost.

If your company's management already agreed it had a good idea for an improved business model, you would probably be working on implementing that idea. Ask most people to think about what a better business model than the current one would look like, and they draw an initial mental blank. The resulting blank stare you see is all the evidence you need that the company's business model innovation slate is empty. How can you move beyond what you know you should do to create new ideas for better business models?

> **Adding value for customers and end users at the same or lower price is a place where relatively few companies search for business model improvements.**

Let's start by simplifying the task. While most minds boggle at coming up with new business models, almost everyone can provide valuable observations about unmet customer needs and ideas for serving them that can be used as ingredients for better business models.

Think about the last time you unsuccessfully looked for a misplaced object. What did you do? Chances are you kept reexamining the same places. If you didn't find it in a particular place the first time, is it likely to be there the second time? Or the third? Your passing gaze may have briefly focused on other areas, but they remained unsearched. When you expanded your search to these other areas, you found what you were looking for. Eureka! You enjoyed your success and a great sense of relief. Drawing on that experience, you will find that your odds of success with business model innovation are also increased if you begin by looking in places where you have not yet searched.

Adding value for customers and end users at the same or lower price is a place where relatively few companies search for business model improvements. Why? A company's quest for improved customer and end-user value is almost always tied by management to either justifying a higher price or a higher profit margin. If neither outcome seems likely to occur, few continue to look carefully at such choices. For example, discount furniture retailers with large stores that are open in the evenings and offer immediate deliveries from extensive inventories have been around for thirty years. Each one wanted more customers and lower costs, yet none added a lot of extra value through entertainment until Jordan's did. The Jordan's approach could probably have worked thirty years sooner all across the United States.

Skipping improvements that don't support higher prices is a mistake because many people who haven't started using your products don't think your value is good enough. By looking at only your current customers, you are missing the larger number of people who could be encouraged to buy. Give some people who don't already use your offerings a chance to try them, and then ask them to tell you how to make improvements to attract their business.

If adding value for customers and potential customers is not thoroughly considered, you can imagine how much less well examined is the opportunity to add value for customers' customers. For instance, if you design jets, how do you go about considering the impact of your design on fragile air freight, such as Central American flowers shipped in a cargo hold?

A good way to stimulate ideas is to spend time with customers' customers, observing how they use your company's and your customers' offerings. Listen to these people describe their needs and problems. Once the jet designers focus on flowers by talking to growers and florists, they can begin to measure how their jet's design might extend or shorten the flowers' freshness. It's normally dry and cold in the cargo holds, but the flowers need high humidity and cool temperatures to maintain their freshness.

And freshness isn't enough; you also have to maintain their attractive appearance. Flowers in cold cargo holds can develop unsightly blemishes.

Take that fundamental evaluation one step further back, and look at customers' customers' customers. For example, how will a cargo plane's design affect the profits of the retail florists who purchase the Central American flowers? There is only the most remote likelihood that much thinking and testing has occurred to consider these customers. For instance, there's a lot of consumer concern about international flower growers applying harmful pesticides that are banned in the United States. To attract more customers for florists, perhaps holds need to be designed to accommodate inexpensive in-flight fumigation, using more environmentally sound chemicals.

Continue this process until you reach the end users. How does air freight transportation affect their enjoyment of flowers in ways not yet considered? For instance, do cargo hold container sizes mean that stem have to be trimmed to shorter lengths than flower fanciers prefer for long-stemmed roses?

Then go to the final dimension and listen to those who are indirectly affected by your offerings through intermediary customers. With regard to imported flowers, this indirect influence might touch those who are harmed by crop-destroying pests and dangerous insecticides that arrive in the flower shipments.

When you perform this analysis, you'll probably see that only a tiny portion of the value-adding opportunity has ever been considered in your company.

So, how do we break out of the mental harness of looking for benefits that "justify" higher prices as easily and as profitably as possible? Well, first you need to know what customers and end users want the most.

> **What are customers already looking for that's hard to find and valuable to them? That question can be hard for you to answer . . . and even harder to deliver profitably. Guessing certainly doesn't work. Leave your preconceived ideas behind when you ask questions.**

FIRST THINGS FIRST—FIND OUT WHAT
CUSTOMERS ARE ALREADY LOOKING FOR

Submerged in a glut of mostly undesirable and unwanted offers for indifferent goods and services they don't care about, purchasers find themselves too often choking on product faults and abrasive service that grate on their nerves and try their patience. Let's look at a better way to profitably serve customers. We'll start by listening to them talk about what they are already looking for.

What are customers already looking for that's hard to find and valuable to them? That question can be hard for you to answer . . . and even harder to deliver profitably. Guessing certainly doesn't work. Leave your preconceived ideas behind when you ask questions.

Professor Martin V. Marshall's marketing management students at Harvard Business School once learned how hard it can be to try to figure out what customers want by trying to answer his question, "How do you think I choose an airline for trips to Europe?" Hundreds of incorrect guesses followed. Price wasn't it because it was similar among airlines. Food wasn't the issue because he did not eat the food. Movies weren't a factor because he never watched them. Frequent flyer miles didn't exist yet, so that wasn't it. Parking at the airport wasn't important to him. He carried on bags, so the checked luggage allowance wasn't his issue. His bags were small, so the size of the overhead bin wasn't significant. Interestingly, the proposed answers were focused on just the sort of characteristics that airlines emphasize in their advertising. Undoubtedly, the market research questions used to create the advertising copy were similar to the students' answers.

What do you think the answer was? You'll never guess, unless you fly a lot by coach to Europe for work.

He picked the airline that had the smallest percentage of customers filling its seats. Why? He was more likely to end up with three seats together in coach that would allow him to stretch out and sleep more comfortably on the overnight portion of the trip from Boston. After a full day of teaching in Boston, his consulting work day would begin shortly after he arrived in Europe. He needed all the sleep he could get on the five- to six-hour night flight. Airline passengers to Europe from the United States have always had this issue, and the airlines feel they have solved it by offering more comfortable, larger and better reclining seats for sleeping in first and business classes. But that solution doesn't help the passenger in coach.

So, airlines that were the least popular and poorest at planning their plane purchases randomly drew Professor Marshall's business. Can his desire be the basis for creating a competitive advantage? Maybe. An airline would have to turn its thinking around to make that happen.

Here's one possibility. You might shift your fare and reservation structure to allow passengers paying full coach fares to block out three adjoining seats on the overnight flights. You could also use planes on those routes that had the highest percentage of three seats together. This offering could be profitable for an airline with a low load factor because it has plenty of seats to fill. In addition, full fares are normally more than three times what the lowest advanced-purchase fares are. You would be providing four seats (three overnight and one during the day), so this deal would be better for the airline than selling out all the seats at the lowest fares. You could redesign the seats in some rows so that they would feel more like a mattress to someone lying across them, and put up notices that these seats were reserved to keep seat poachers at bay. This area could be kept quieter and darker during the flight. You might let other passengers use frequent flyer miles to block out seats after full-fare passengers were accommodated. People who wanted to lie down to sleep in coach would probably favor your airline unless others offered the same service at a lower price. After you successfully accommodate the needs of the coach passengers wanting to sleep more comfortably, other airlines will have a hard time attracting those passengers back with similar offerings. Passengers will remember who looked out for their interests first.

As you can see, a beneficial competitive advantage is possible by focusing on a strongly desired customer benefit. But you have to know what *new* benefits customers will respond to before you can succeed.

WHERE ELSE TO LOOK FOR BENEFIT-BASED BUSINESS MODEL INNOVATIONS

The order of the simple tasks you follow to find a business model innovation is of critical importance. Like a combination used to open a safe, tasks produce the best results when undertaken in the correct order and will not succeed in doing so in any other order. Following the wrong order, you can spend endless amounts of time toiling and never add a successful new business model. The remaining sections in this chapter reveal the correct order for identifying benefit-based business model innovations.

Build on Your Knowledge Advantages

Refer to the material about Ecolab located in the Prologue for an example of how to build and apply unduplicated knowledge advantages to generate more customer and stakeholder benefits.

Build from a Base of Experience and Memory

Because increasing value without raising costs and prices to create competitive advantage is seldom fully explored, you will find that employees' minds are not clouded with negative thinking about what's possible once an important need is identified. They don't know any reason not to explore doing these things, except that you can't get a higher price for them. Remove that mental limitation, and some ideas should be immediately forthcoming. Some of these ideas have been considered and rejected by your company before because there seemed to be no higher price available for providing them. Ask customers how to improve a popular dimension of value for them while they are using your offerings, and you should get an earful about their unmet needs that they feel you should be able to offer. Then ask your customers and employees what can be done to help with these customer issues at the current price and without increasing costs.

Build Fresh Insights

You need to look for as many ways as you can find to add value for your customers at no added cost. Initially treat all ideas you think of as being potentially valuable for the purposes of this task and chapter. You can later evaluate these new ideas before picking ones to test. But now is the time to encourage and collect ideas without applying judgment that can chill creativity and inspiration.

Although your mind is not focusing on ways to add value that cause either higher or lower costs, you will get an unexpected side benefit. Your subconscious mind will pay attention to those other facets. In addition, you will find that focusing on adding more benefits at no more cost is an interesting, creative, self-confidence-building activity. You'll open up the positive emotions that encourage your mind to create its best business model innovations.

Continue thinking in a brainstorming session with people who have many different kinds of backgrounds, ways of thinking and experiences, and you will stimulate one another to do even better. New perspectives and possibilities will fertilize your mind for creating even better solutions. Often, the best insights come from seemingly naive comments by those who are not experts in the field.

There are a wide range of choices and limitations for adding more value. A single organization is bound to be myopic about which choices to consider. For your best chance of success in increasing value without increasing costs and price, you need to stretch your thinking beyond the boundaries of your organization. Your efforts should yield many ideas for improved benefits that can be applied in new business models.

Open Your Horizons to the Many Value Forms

We have met CEOs and senior executives at many companies who have provided sales-expanding extra value at the same price. For instance, Haemonetics helps patients, their families, physicians, blood donors, blood banks and hospitals by providing more ways for patients to reuse their own blood during surgery in order to avoid potential complications. Dell Computer will manufacture a personal computer for a low price, customized with just the components you want and usually ship within a few minutes of receiving your order. Education Management helps students prepare for more successful careers in which they will help their employers operate more effectively and less expensively. Disneyland provides information near the center of the Magic Kingdom on the duration of lines for popular attractions so that visitors can spend more time enjoying their favorites. Consequently, we have been impressed with the large variety of ways that sales-enhancing value can be added. However, even organizations with the most success in adding value at no extra cost ignored choices that others found helpful.

Always assume there are many other productive areas that are not yet known to you. As you act on that assumption, keep an open mind about where to find new customer advantages.

Consider and Expand the Full Reach and Impact of Benefits from a Single Innovation

Who will experience and appreciate an additional benefit? Imagine you're a soft drink ingredient supplier. First, let's look at individual stakeholders without considering the effects on others, the usual way that companies seek to expand benefits. You can make an improvement to benefit the syrup manufacturing customer, such as a faster resolution of billing issues. You can extend increased value to the customers' customers, the soft drink bottlers. This focus might mean making your ingredient so that the syrup works better in bottling equipment. You can go beyond those important people to benefit the ultimate consumers or users. This perspective might mean reformulating your ingredient so it will be healthier to drink.

Or you can create simultaneous benefits for each stakeholder through considering all of their interests at the same time. Hardly any companies think that way. This all-inclusive approach might mean developing a new soft drink formula using your ingredients that is tastier and healthier for the ultimate consumers, runs faster on the bottling lines and eliminates the need for a more expensive ingredient currently in the syrup recipe. Obviously, if you can find benefits that reach all these groups from a single innovation, you have located a most useful opportunity for increasing value without raising prices and costs.

Always address the full reach of new enhancements and their positive and negative interconnections simultaneously along chains of customers through to the final users. As a result, you will probably realize that some potential benefits that you have been choosing not to offer are more important than you had previously realized. For example, your market share growth may be limited because of a downstream customer not being able to sell into an account that has a 70 percent share of its market. Help your blocked downstream customer open up that account, and your volume could go up by as much as several hundred percent. The approach might be as simple as solving a problem that your customer's customer has, but your customer cannot address. In soft drink ingredients, for example, processing methods might be changed to meet religious requirements for people of certain faiths.

Consider book retailing. Prior to 1990, book stores were primarily a place to browse for books you might want to read. Larger stores offered more choices. Smaller stores usually offered more book-knowledgeable staffs. Then newer chain bookstores began to copy some independent bookstores and offer comfortable furniture for people to nestle in while they leafed through appealing volumes. This seating was later expanded to include cafes where browsing could be conducted in even more comfort by providing room to spread out while enjoying coffee and snacks.

Eventually, people who worked at home began to use these locations for brief meetings and work breaks. Bookstore cafes added electrical outlets, and some customers began doing their e-mail there using laptop computers with wireless connections. From those laptop computers, the customers could even choose to order books online at lower prices from the retailer's Web site. As a result, the value of a trip to the bookstore kept increasing and the number of companies benefiting from one person's visit also grew, while the prices for books remained the same relative to bookstores without these new benefits.

For each person who gets a benefit, you also need to consider what type of benefit it is. In our time-crunched society, many people favor products and services that take less time to use. Customers at theme parks have typically struggled with long lines for their favorite attractions. Most of the day seems to be spent winding back and forth in line rather than enjoying the attractions. In recent years, many parks offer the opportunity to secure an appointment for the most popular attractions. When your appointment time arrives, you spend ten minutes in line rather than an hour. After such innovations increase value at the same price, attendance is likely to increase.

FINDING MORE POTENTIAL BENEFITS TO CONSIDER

In the introduction to Part One, we outline some ways that a good business model can be established. Let's look at one of those choices now in more detail, helping customers attract more customers. Then we'll consider noneconomic benefit choices that you may not have considered.

Help Customers Attract More Customers

Helping your business's customer add new customers and more volume with existing customers will usually provide the greatest benefit. For example, in high-technology business areas where new products have short lives, cutting the elapsed time from concept to providing new products and services is often more important than saving the total hours involved in a process. Every month shaved from elapsed development time, for instance, can create tens of millions of dollars of increased sales. As a result, those who help their customers' customers get to market fastest will gain market share. In recent years, those who supply semiconductor design software, technology, equipment, products and services have focused on reducing customers' elapsed time to market with new products.

Sometimes, creating more end-user benefits can accelerate market growth rates and customer and company market shares. For instance, electronic devices are frequently limited by their battery lives. Few people want to carry around extra batteries and replace them, so the devices are often unused when the batteries run down. As described in the Prologue, Linear Technology began to design chips that extended battery life by helping portable devices use less power. Consequently, the company helped accelerate the purchase and use of all the portable devices that employed this new technology. Naturally, the demand for its chips rose, as well.

Look for Noneconomic Benefits, Too

Most people can easily understand examples where time and economic benefits are measurable, but noneconomic benefits can be important, too. When Estee Lauder formulated the Clinique line of cosmetics and toiletries, it provided hypoallergenic relief for those who wanted a better appearance and less discomfort from using common beauty products. Noneconomic benefits can also apply to aesthetics, such as the

> **Begin with direct observation.**

color compatibility of the clothing offered by Benetton. Best of all is when a noneconomic benefit brings emotional or physical pleasure, such as services providing thoughtful personal attention, like a therapeutic massage.

Go Beyond Market Research to Observation and Experimentation

Notice that some of these benefits, like faster time to market, would be obvious from listening to almost any customer. Other benefits, like offering entertainment in furniture stores or a temporary office in bookstores, would probably not have been identified by listening to and talking with customers before anyone began offering those benefits. Because of the relative invisibility of many potential value benefits, such as Professor Marshall's desire to stretch out in coach on a red-eye flight, traditional market research and market analysis methods may be insufficient. That potential deficiency is another reason to keep an open mind as you develop hypotheses. Trial and error on a limited, inexpensive scale will usually be essential to identify new value benefits to offer. Until you have the idea, though, you cannot begin any experiments to test it. You need to expand your sources of ideas. This is a numbers game, and all perspectives help.

Several methods are useful to perceive needs that are not yet being demanded by current customers and competitors. Begin with direct observation. Mr. Disney, for example, is thought to have conceived of many improvements for Disneyland after it opened by observing guests unobtrusively from an apartment located above a Main Street store.

Simply watch how customers and potential customers (and on through to the end user) interact with your product or services. You will be amazed by the awkward ways they go about making your offerings useful to them. As an example, watch people trying to work on drop-down airline trays in the coach cabin. Everything is just set for a productive work session and then the person in the seat in front of them reclines, taking away most of the vertical work area. Providing a way to drop the tray lower or to pull it out further away from the seat in front would solve the problem for most people. Then, watch the passengers in the seat in front of those using laptops on a tray grit their teeth in exasperation as the keystrokes vibrate through their seats. Disconnect the tray from the seat, and the vibration could be reduced. Designing and providing such a tray for a reconfigured cabin could probably be done for no more than the cost of existing trays by substituting less expensive materials.

> **Pretend for several hours that you are a specific person who doesn't buy from your company (or even your customer's customer).**

For another example, let's revisit book retailing. As mentioned previously, prior to 1990, you would have seen people in bookstores camped out on the floor and leaning awkwardly against bookcases, reading books while they sipped from take-out coffee and soft drink cups. When their cramped bodies couldn't take it any more or they found the right book, they left. In many cases, the sore body was the limitation to selling more books.

Think about metaphors.

You don't have to sell many more books in a year to pay for a chair and a table and the space they rest on. Additionally, if customers get their take-out coffee or beverage from you, you save them the time to go to a take-out outlet and increase the time they have to shop for and read books.

You can usually experience the lives of your customers and potential customers. Go out and walk in these people's shoes as you follow their paths. Try to do what they do in the best ways you can. Then imagine how you could change what you offer and provide to make their lives simpler, easier and better.

You can also imagine that you are them. Pretend for several hours that you are a specific person who doesn't buy from your company (or even your customer's customer). Once you have totally immersed yourself in that mind-set, think about why you don't want to do business with your real company. Imagine what it would take to get your attention and keep it so that you would try a different offering. While in this potential-customer role-playing mode, also ask yourself how your current supplier could change to keep your business.

Imagine that you can totally customize your products, services and the ways that you market and deliver them to quickly match what any one person wants.

Think about metaphors. You will probably find it easiest to start with ones that personally inspire you and will probably inspire others. Questions can help you find helpful metaphors. For example, what was the best product or service you ever bought? Think about that offering as a metaphor for what you might offer. Bookstores could have used a five-star European hotel staffed to provide service and comfort as a metaphor for their business. Con-

> **Extend this questioning to include suppliers, customers, shareholders and partners through the Internet, and you will experience a geometric increase in richness of ideas and refinement of promising directions.**

sider why you enjoy the experience of certain products and services while you dislike others. New metaphors can emerge from this pondering.

Imagine that you can totally customize your products, services and the ways that you market and deliver them to quickly match what any one person wants. This capability is very important because one secret of achieving competitive advantage is to individualize products more effectively than anyone else. Having identified a method, how can you employ that method in ways that do not increase your costs, but do improve value? Many companies following this approach have been able to add customizing processes that lower costs. For instance, Amazon.com created a listing service for new, collectible and used books offered for sale by its customers. This service is easy to add to its existing marketing pages, complements its own inventory and access to stock to improve availability, draws more potential customers and reduces customer costs. Amazon.com's service also provides a very high profit contribution similar to what eBay enjoys, because most of its selling and all handling and delivery costs are eliminated in the process.

By this point, you will probably have exhausted a lot of what one person can learn from exploring these questions. If you have encouraged others to follow these same steps, you can now have more effective brainstorming sessions with them about the questions. Your individual ideas will strike responsive chords in the minds of others to produce better ideas than any of you could have developed individually.

With work document shareware, you can post questions and observations on a company intranet and encourage everyone in the company to post their own ideas and comments. Extend this questioning to include suppliers, customers, shareholders and partners through the Internet, and you will experience a geometric increase in richness of ideas and refinement of promising directions.

ONE THING LEADS TO ANOTHER

As you consider the type of value you want to add, you should pay special attention to potential longer-term consequences. Other-wise you may create short-term solutions that offer limited benefits. For example, adding new variations to a fad toy, like a hula hoop, will extend its life. Yet, at some point, the fad will be over no matter what you do. The rewards of offering those variations will have a limited life. In this section we look at creating longer-term advantages.

> The most far-sighted companies consider how a benefit for customers in one area can be used to create an important benefit in another area.

Other improvements may have a geometric effect over time, especially in rapidly growing markets. As mentioned in the Introduction, EMC decided in the mid-1990s to make sure that all of its computer storage products and software would work with any server platform or operating system at no extra charge. This change made it easier for customers to attach EMC's storage to their existing servers, and made it less likely that EMC would lose a customer account when a new server vendor made a temporary or even permanent inroad. During the period when most other electronic storage was not so flexible, EMC rapidly gained market share while charging higher prices for its products because its customers valued this flexibility.

The most far-sighted companies consider how a benefit for customers in one area can be used to create an important benefit in another area. As described in the Introduction, Paychex began as a company that provided reliable, low-cost payroll services for small employers. In the beginning, Paychex gained a competitive advantage by streamlining communications. Most computerized payroll services then required that their forms be filled out by employers. Paychex eliminated this step by filing out the form for employers when bookkeepers called in their payrolls. Because of this simplification, no customer had to learn how to fill out the form, errors were reduced and the computer form did not have to be sent to the employer or returned to the processing company . . . saving time and costs. Paychex then mailed the checks to the employer, while others hand-delivered them, saving more money. If a mail delivery was late, a Paychex service operator could save the day. The employer could call Paychex, which would immediately provide the necessary information over the telephone so the employer could write and deliver on-time, accurate pay checks for the few employees involved.

Paychex's leaders began to realize that many other employee-related services for small companies depend on having accurate payroll records. Whoever provides good payroll records can save employers time, money, aggravation and government fines in these other areas. It's also less expensive to provide services in these other areas if the payroll records are already in the correct data processing format. As a result, Paychex now offers a whole range of record-development and record-keeping services based on the payroll database that was its initial product line. An increasing percentage of the company's customers buy some of Paychex's newer services because of the accuracy and time-saving benefits its integrated systems provide. Paychex is also able to price these services competitively with what other suppliers charge and what it costs small employers to do the tasks themselves.

Value and Honor More Individual Preferences

Think about something you buy frequently. Think about how you would change that offering if you had complete control over what was delivered. The result would look a lot different, wouldn't it? Your customers feel the same way, as do their customers, and so on.

Let's expand on the idea of individualizing what you offer. This important subject may provide many pleasant and unpleasant surprises. To begin with, you probably don't know what choices each potential customer will make. Overall market research estimates the percentages of the whole market favoring various options. Better market research may even segment the market and tell you preference percentages by category. Be wary of the answers, however, because market research approaches can be misleading for identifying the right new benefit choices to add.

Instead, look at your customers in a different way. Use economic analyses of your company and your competitors to segment your current and potential customers in the following manner. Begin by locating customers where you could or do earn a higher profit margin than any of your competitors would by serving the same customer. Then consider one by one how you could add valuable benefits to each of these high relative profit potential accounts. Begin by observing how they and their customers (and so forth through to the final user) engage and respond to your and your competitors' products and services. Then follow up by discussing what you learned with those you observed. Ask them what else is important that you did not mention. Your sensitivity to their problems may help them uncover resentments and problems repressed or withheld because they assume you can or will do nothing to help them.

Why do we start with accounts where you can earn a higher profit margin than competitors? First, because you will be more eager and interested in finding new benefits for them. Second, you are more likely to create customer-specific solutions for them because of the profit potential (even though all of your potential customers may have this need). Third, the potential rewards for your company from adding these benefits are large. Your successful experiments will add the resources you need to deliver a better business model.

After you have done all you can with this set of customers, look at the current and potential customers (one by one again) where your total account profit margin will be similar to your most effective competitor in supplying or helping that account. Follow the same fact-finding process. In addition, you can discuss and offer to add improvements that you have identified from your first experiences.

Having worked with these two groups, next think about how each benefit can be efficiently customized to reflect individual customer's needs. Rather than giving each new benefit to all customers (whether or not they need or value that benefit), explore how you can change your business model to provide just the right mix of new benefits that a particular customer wants. In many cases this customizing may include doing less than you do now in some areas for certain customers. For example, many PCs used at home were purchased with a CD burner because it came as a standard item. A home business computer user may seldom need that capability, and a custom-built PC for a user who didn't need that feature could omit that equipment and software while reducing the price charged.

Consider Dell Computer again. Each of its corporate accounts can opt to be treated like an individual by completing an online profile that tells Dell what configurations of hardware and software the company wants for computers and servers. The profile for each customer is different, based on the customer's preferences. When a person at a large Dell corporate account orders a piece of equipment, the equipment will be sent preloaded with the exact capabilities and software that work best for that company. No further action or input is needed from the customer's information technology staff. Compatibility across equipment allows all tasks in a given application to run faster and more reliably for their intended purposes.

Can your business model be improved to go from providing consistent potential benefits to all customers to tailoring those benefits specifically to individual customers, and still sell at today's prices and profit margin? The odds are pretty good that you can, because many people don't want expensive-to-provide aspects of your current offerings. At the same time, others will be willing to pay a premium over a reduced price level to receive those features. The cost of acquiring and responding to the right information for what to provide is likely to be a lot less than the cost of providing

Get people involved who have expertise in other disciplines that you are not currently using, and who have no experience in your industry.

the wrong combinations of features and services for almost every customer. If you find the customizing challenge insuperable, many contract manufacturers and outsourced service suppliers have the skill and experience to help you put processes in place or to do those processes for you in order to fulfill these individual needs.

Borrow New Expertise You Have Not Thought of Using Before

Could you personally rewire and replumb your home or business? Probably not. You'd get expert help to do those things. The same principle applies here, except that expert help often resides in places you don't think about.

Suppliers and partners, as well as potential suppliers and partners, can find many more ways to add benefits at the current price than you would otherwise notice or consider. If your company doesn't look very much at how customers' customers are affected, you will only be able to make rapid progress if you request help and pay attention. As just discussed, direct observation followed by open-ended questions and careful listening is a great way to start. You will find such collaboration more beneficial if you have already established credibility with your customers by providing attractive new benefits that your own people have identified. Having come up with valuable innovations will also help make it intriguing for potential suppliers and partners to get more closely involved with you. You have to make the collaboration easy, relevant and interesting before you will fully engage their top minds.

When you think you've exposed everyone you can to the problem, think again. Chances are that fields you consider disconnected from the problem can make valuable contributions. In most companies, "industry experience" is the test of whom to get involved. Now you want to do the opposite: Get people involved who have expertise in other disciplines that you are not currently using, and who have no experience in your industry. If your head of research and development is a knowledgeable scientist, she or he should be able to lead this part of the effort. Your chief scientist will be able to think of potentially related fields that your company has never explored and know how to involve top people from those fields who lack experience in your industry. Be sure that your budget and objectives allow for time and money to pursue these exploratory efforts. Most research and development groups will tell you they get little direct access to the problems and inconveniences that customers and customers' customers are experiencing. Be sure to include experts in knowledge transfer if you don't have that skill internally. Otherwise, an improved understanding of your customers will reside only with those who have worked with them, rather than your whole organization.

Central Parking provides a good example of creating an improved business model around such investigations. When the company first started, most commercial property developers didn't see that parking could help them sell buildings and rent space, while charging higher prices for both. Central Parking developed the necessary expertise and then educated major developers about how to work with the company to obtain these benefits. In the process, parking went from being a minor revenue source for developers to a key tenant benefit that enabled them to be much more profitable. Its innovative approach permitted Central Parking to grow rapidly with limited competition.

Anticipate the Implications of Trends

How many times have you started doing something new and found out that the environment changed in a way that made your new activity inappropriate? That happens all the time in business. Successful business model innovators often avoid this problem by considering what could happen before the business environment shifts.

A minor irritant or opportunity today can become an enormous factor tomorrow. Forecasting is seldom accurate for anticipating these shifts. The problem is even greater for predicting trends. On the one hand, the only thing we can accurately say about the future is that it will come, and it will probably be different from what we expect. On the other hand, we can make important progress toward being prepared for unexpected changes by thinking systematically about their potential impacts in advance.

Design four to seven extreme scenarios (*not* forecasts) of what could happen in the future. A forecast is what you think the future is most likely to hold. A scenario is an imaginary future designed to stimulate your thinking about the implications today of what could happen.

If the subject is potential regulation of corporate behavior in reaction to the 2002 scandals, scenarios should include far more intense regulation than you expect from your forecast. That's because in creating alternative scenarios, you gain by considering both greatly more and much less of each potentially significant factor than has occurred before. Consequently, these scenarios include also looking at alternative futures where new regulation, like CEO and CFO certification of financial results, is eliminated.

The primary reason for using scenarios is because your forecast is likely to be wrong. Scenarios are designed to prepare you for the unexpected, so their range of circumstances needs to be wider than your forecasts. In developing your scenarios, be sure to examine the same topics of possible value discussed earlier in this chapter.

There's another major benefit that scenario-based thinking can provide. As a result of examining these scenarios, you will eventually see choices for adding value that work across all of your scenarios. Those value-adding ideas will turn out to be especially beneficial because

> **When you feel as if you've exhausted all of the important kinds of value that you could potentially identify, you are ready to repeat the process described in this chapter for finding new kinds of value.**

they will leave you better off, no matter what comes next. For example, regardless of what the regulations are, a company needs to have accurate financial results to run itself properly. How can that accuracy be obtained? You might conclude that the only effective way to have clean, accurate books is by having all accounting officials in the company and external auditors personally verify the financial results, without reservation, to the company with unlimited, uninsured liability. If people have their whole financial worth and reputation on the line, accounting looks a lot different and will be more accurate. (For more explanation of how to use this scenario process, see Part Two of our book, *The Irresistible Growth Enterprise.*)

Repeat What You Have Done, but Differently

Champion chess players report that the key to winning is to start looking for a better move as soon as you have found a good one. Then repeat the process by looking for a still better move until time runs out. Naturally, you know you don't have time to repeat yourself in very much of what you do. In business model innovation, however, repetition is essential to building the ultimate competitive advantage.

When you feel as if you've exhausted all of the important kinds of value that you could potentially identify, you are ready to repeat the process described in this chapter for finding new kinds of value. Otherwise, your belief that there is no more to find will become the cause of future competitive disadvantages. You'll stop looking for new benefits. That's a problem because many more opportunities are still waiting out there. You just haven't found them yet. And remember that it's important that you find them before your competitors do. So keep looking in new places!

Your challenge is to find different ways to repeat the innovation process so that your company's thinking will move into more productive paths. A great way to do this is by changing the participants. Undoubtedly, some people will have chosen not to participate the last time, new people may be available now and some people who were considered unlikely to help remained on the sidelines. Each new person will bring different life experiences and perspectives. They will also be stimulated to have new thoughts from seeing what was just identified.

Another prime opportunity is to ask different questions. For example, a good role-playing alternative is to perform the same analysis . . . except from the perspective of imagining that you work for each of your competitors and potential competitors. You can profitably do something similar by imagining that you work for complementary companies that you might acquire.

The most effective variation may be to change the nature, scope and dimensions of the scenario assumptions from the ones you used last time. Make the scenarios even more extreme and confining. Or do just the opposite.

The science of this art is to systematically examine potential circumstances along many different dimensions. With each repetition, you will notice that the opportunities just identified are heavily bunched in certain areas. In planning the next repetition, ask yourself how you can identify more of the opportunities in other areas by looking more carefully at different aspects of future circumstances.

After you have repeated this process a few times, you may also find it valuable to change the basic premise of this chapter. Only consider adding benefits that you could offer profitably at a *lower* price. That sounds like a paradox, but it will force you to identify how to trade off supplying less-costly, more-valuable stakeholder benefits for existing more-costly, less-valuable ones. When you feel you have exhausted this dimension, start to consider benefits that will spur growth, but require small price increases.

> **A good way to make the right benefit choices is to find simple, cheap and easy market tests that excite your organization.**

SELECT THE RIGHT INNOVATIONS TO DEVELOP AND TEST

Selecting the right benefits to offer is like deciphering an encoded secret message. Use the right key, and you can learn valuable information. Use the wrong key, and you still have gibberish. Waste your time on fruitless decoding paths, and all you have to show for your effort is a wastepaper basket full of scribbled-on paper. The key is to pick the right benefits and develop them in the right order. You will enhance your competitive position in the process.

A good way to make the right benefit choices is to find simple, cheap and easy market tests that excite your organization. Few people will probably want to work on developing a business model innovation when it first becomes a company priority. Many will see the work as likely to be a career dead-end. The challenge is great because one of the scarcest resources in many organizations is people who like to work on new ways to expand demand for your offerings. Even rarer are the people who are good at this demand-expanding work.

Some companies have responded to this limitation by attracting talented people who find this work rewarding. Semiconductor innovators Linear Technology and Xilinx report almost no employee turnover in their research and development staffs, primarily due to the powerful intellectual challenges of doing their work on world-class problems with the top people in the field. Both companies have work cultures that emphasize achieving volume breakthroughs through technology solutions that provide customized adaptations for individual customers.

Your best bet is to appeal to curiosity and passion to draw your organization's challenge seekers forward. Share the potential opportunities that have been identified and ask for proposals to test the ideas. Make it clear what recognition and rewards will be provided for developing and conducting these experiments. Ideally, you want good work in this area to pave the way for promotions and significant compensation improvements as well as recognition for simply doing the testing well, regardless of the results.

> **During the tests, the unexpected will frequently provide clues to breakthroughs.**

Monitor the Tests to Validate Assumptions and Learn about the Unexpected

You want to get into the market fast with your improved business model. Freeing up resources from tests that are failing can help you do that. How can you speed up the process of making those resources available again?

Some of the tests will falter as soon as you begin them. If that's likely to continue, the correction is to stop the test unless something more valuable will be gained by continuing.

During the tests, the unexpected will frequently provide clues to breakthroughs. Especially pay attention when a customer buys a great deal more than you would have ever thought likely and where customers ignore something that looks like a great deal. In the former instance, you may simply be seeing test contamination. For example, in a test in a small locale, a local unit of a national organization may be buying into your new offering for its whole company. That result means that your test is working, but not as well as you thought. Of even greater significance is the possibility that customers have found a better way to use your offering. Ray Kroc's introduction to McDonald's came from his curiosity about why one hamburger stand in San Bernardino, California, was ordering so many more milk shake mixers than any of his other customers. When he arrived, he saw a fast-food business model that could be improved to cover the globe. He chucked the milk shake mixer business to buy into McDonald's. The rest is history. When customers ignore something you think will expand their use, you also have the opportunity to learn something valuable. What were you missing when you decided to run the test?

With only a few successful experiments, you won't get far in creating an improved business model. You need to diagnose why you have had few successful tests. Most likely, you are not running enough tests. Few organizations are. If you have lots of ideas to probe, you may not have enough people with the skill and interest to run the necessary experiments. If so, you need to change staffing and assignments to create more time for these critical innovation tasks.

Some companies find that they are running lots of tests, but don't have any successes. This dead-end usually means that the quality of the testing is inadequate. You need to see if good ideas are being poorly implemented. Finding this problem is usually a sign of an organization that is overloaded with tasks or has people without all the necessary skills running the experiments. Examine what went wrong, and figure out how you can fix it. If you have concerns before the testing starts but are uncertain about what remedies to apply, have an expert help you evaluate the proposed tests and the availability of skills and tools to execute those plans.

One way Paychex ensured its ability to make many successful business model changes was by bringing in top management executives who are experienced in many different functions. Mr. Golisano, the company's founder and CEO, looks for people with greater breadth of experience and psychological flexibility than is usual for the functions they head. In many cases, these executives came to Paychex after having succeeded in much larger organizations. As a result, each senior executive has the ability to put together world-class tests and make them work. The difficulty of implementing a successful test throughout Paychex is always on their minds during the testing. Top management executives spend a lot of time together developing business model innovations. As they do, each functional head becomes more aware of how expanded customer demand affects all of the company's operations.

If you don't have this sort of team, especially in a small organization, consider recruiting an unpaid board of advisors comprised of recently retired executives with varied functional backgrounds to play the same role.

KEY QUESTIONS

These questions can help to keep you focused on locating sales-expanding choices to provide new or more benefits to stakeholders at current prices and costs. If these questions inspire you to add other questions that you find helpful, that's good. They are designed to stimulate your thinking, rather than to totally guide you. Be sure to answer them before beginning the process described in this chapter. This is important homework that can smooth your progress.

Innovation-Creating Questions

- *What is the funniest thing we do to hurt the purchase and consumption of our offerings?* We all like to laugh. And when we do, the creative juices flow best. One of our favorite examples of an answer to this question is a recent book about making your business more accessible that came in a shrink-wrapped plastic wrapper that was hard to remove.

- *What is the stupidest thing our company does that reduces the purchase and consumption of our offerings?* In answering this question, take the viewpoint of an outsider to your organization. If you find yourself having an easy time answering this question, also answer the following question: *What is the second stupidest thing our company does . . . ?* You can turn this exercise into a whole string of such questions, as long as they help you. If few answers occur to you, then be sure to ask customers, suppliers and other stakeholders. For example, for how many years did ketchup makers only use bottles from which it was hard to remove the ketchup, before introducing wide-mouth jars? Some touted the thickness of their ketchup in ads demonstrating how hard it was to get the ketchup out. No wonder salsa outsells ketchup. It always came in wide-mouth jars.

- *What is the most embarrassing thing we do to hurt the purchase and consumption of our offerings?* The human desire to avoid feeling embarrassed is very strong. Realizing that we are (or could be) embarrassing ourselves and being less successful in the process will stimulate lots of creative thoughts. The results of some restaurant research indicated that consumers are very sensitive to the cleanliness of fast food. Yet in many fast-food restaurants, you will see the cashiers who handle the money also touch unwrapped food. You'll also see customers cringe when that happens. How soon do you suppose they return? Certainly, the health inspector wouldn't be pleased, either. Or visit a rest room the employees use and find that there's no soap. Go figure! Would you be embarrassed to be the CEO of that business or store manager of that restaurant? Could you find a solution to avoid that embarrassment?

- *What questions are most likely to stimulate and motivate you to locate better benefits that cost no more?* Make a list of questions as you think of them. Experience with answering the preceding questions will help you think of similar questions that you would rather answer. Shift to those questions.

- *In what physical setting are you most likely to think of new benefits that don't cost any more money?* Some people think best while soaking in the bathtub, others while resting on a blanket in the park and others in a comfortable chair in the library. Whatever that setting is, be sure to make it available to yourself. Repeat this question with your group before establishing the site of brainstorming sessions.

- *What incentives would motivate you the most to find better benefits?* Many of the most desirable incentives only you can give yourself. It might be as simple as sleeping in one morning when you're tired, or as complicated as taking time to imaginatively stretch a limited budget to cover an ideal vacation. If your organization is willing to provide special benefits for working on business model innovation, let those who establish these incentives know what would be most meaningful to you. Well-run companies have a lot of flexibility in providing small rewards, like extra time off and recognition.

- *How can you find business model benefits to add or expand that are the most consistent with your personal values?* In business, much creativity is blocked when people feel that they are being asked to do something inappropriate. If you specifically address that concern, huge amounts of creativity can be released.

- *How can you help other people in your organization to see this work as stimulating and rewarding?* Observers can often coach others to perform better than the participants or observers can direct themselves. Start by asking each person about their initial reactions to the work. Then find out what has to change in order to inspire them. Keep at it until they glow with excitement. We often encourage client team members to begin by developing their personal life objectives. Once those objectives are identified, we ask them to write down how the current task can help meet their objectives. Then we ask questions to help them see even more important personal benefits from performing the task well.

- *How can you help other people working on this question find it easier to locate great benefits?* You probably have some observations or knowledge that no one else has. You may not know how to turn your insights into benefits, but suspect that others could. You might simply need to circulate your information to unleash enormous progress. Find a way to help that leaves you feeling comfortable.

Experimentation and Test Questions

- *What went wrong with the last ten volume-building experiments and tests your company ran that did not work as well as you expected?* Organizations, like individuals, often show consistently good and bad habits. Start by understanding what your roadblocks have been, and you are likely to notice patterns. If you don't have documents that capture this information, simply spend some time talking with those who were involved or were affected by the experiments and tests. Be sure to include at least the company employees, customers and suppliers who were involved.

- *What are the patterns, if any, for problems that were encountered in implementing the experiments or tests?* Botched implementation is usually present in volume-building tests. One company found that it spent so much time writing plans that it had too little time to execute them. One problem was that it didn't have the resources to do all of those tests, but management insisted. When the company cut back on the number of tests and monitored the implementation carefully, the results improved dramatically.

- *How can you overcome the habits that caused the unsuccessful patterns?* In the case described in the preceding paragraph, testing was transferred to a new executive who didn't insist on too many tests, but did insist that tests be well executed. Performance immediately improved.

- *Where could each experiment or test go wrong?* In deciding which tests to pursue, you will notice that some tests have dozens of items that could trip up the test results. Others, meanwhile, will have few. Be cautious about taking on tests that require perfect execution in many areas. Chances are that you won't be able to implement them well enough to learn what needs to be done to expand volume. For example, a fast-food restaurant chain decided to test candlelit steak dinners served by waiters in the evenings. Can you guess the result? That's right—it failed. Neither the food nor the service was worth the price because of execution mistakes.

- *What's likely to be your success rate for implementing the key changes involved?* Here is where a lot of people fool themselves because they don't do the numbers. They rely on instincts alone. In other cases, they misanalyze the risks and take on too much.

Let's say that a new business model requires doing fifteen things where you are successful around 90 percent of the time in each one. Do you feel confident that you can pull off successfully accomplishing all fifteen things? Most people would say so because they believe their chances of success are 90 percent. They would be wrong. Each element separately affects the success of the test. Because that's the case, your likelihood of success is less than 20 percent (0.9 to the 15th power). As an example of this flawed thinking, a well-known consumer products company thought it had a 95 percent rate of success in filling orders on time. Actually, the company was measuring its error rate on all the separate tasks needed to fill an order. The average rate of success in filling orders on time was actually less than 60 percent. They had a lot of improving to do and didn't realize it!

Let's test your understanding by evaluating another case. You are 90 percent likely to succeed in two key tasks, and 20 percent likely to succeed at the third necessary element. Is that test a good idea? No way! Because all three tasks are needed, your likelihood of success is not 67 percent (the average of the three) but less than 20 percent again (0.9 times 0.9 times 0.2).

If you have a low likelihood of success with a test because of one or two implementation vulnerabilities, what can you do to improve the odds? Sometimes the solution is as simple as getting some outside help in these areas. If your overall opportunity to make millions is at risk, it should be worth spending extra tens of thousands on the test to give it a decent chance to succeed. Otherwise, you may well be better off not doing this test.

- *Have you eliminated conflicts of interest in the experiments and tests you are considering?* Experiments and tests are delicate things and often involve a lot of extra work for little recognition or reward. If you cannot eliminate these harmful conflicts with an individual's self-interests, you will have to obtain individual commitments that the individuals honor above their own interests. The classic problem is that you rely on your regular sales force to make the new offer. The sales force is mostly paid on meeting its overall volume quotas that are little impacted by your test. Without changing compensation methods or commitments from individual salespeople, you cannot expect much help from them.

- *Have you reduced the conflict with "standard operating procedures" for the experiment or test?* Experiments and tests usually require fast response, agility and good communications. Most companies foster just the opposite way of operating, wanting to make it hard to make an inappropriate change. Unless you loosen up the normal rules for the experimenters and test operators, they will be stymied and stifled by some of those rules. If you cannot create the necessary flexibility in any other way, a potential solution is to set up a temporary stand-alone organization that is exempt from the usual rules to run the experimentation and testing. Lockheed established its world-famous "skunk works" to develop experimental aircraft for just this reason. Normally, any change to an aircraft has to go through lots of checking and rechecking before anything is tried. You have to rely more on trial and error, however, to create new airplane concepts. The skunk works was very good at meeting its time and budget targets because it was freed from the normal procedures to do the necessary trial and error in the early conceptual stages, like the experimentation this book advocates.

CHAPTER 2

ADJUST PRICES TO INCREASE SALES PROFITABLY

In the market economy, the price that is offered is
counted upon to produce the result that is sought.
—John Kenneth Galbraith

*Most companies set prices to optimize profits at similar selling vol-
umes. That pricing strategy is a mistake in markets where either
volume is sensitive to price or a company's added costs to produce
more are low. Further, many companies look only at their own
prices rather than at what it costs a customer or end user to
acquire and employ the offering. Some offerings are much more
attractive at a lower total cost to the customer or end user. Companies need to greatly increase their testing of new price structures
to lower costs incurred by customers and other stakeholders.*

In 1931, a young married couple, Mr. William and Ms. Dorothy
Hustead, bought a store in a small town near the South Dakota
Bad Lands. They chose that location for their new home because
they wanted their own business, preferred small town living and
wanted to be near a Catholic church so they could attend daily

Mass. For almost five years, they struggled through the Depression, serving the town's 326 impoverished residents.

Then on a hot and dusty day in the summer of 1936, they made one of the most famous pricing decisions ever for a small business. While trying to rest at home during that hot afternoon, Ms. Hustead was disturbed by the sound of cars on the nearby highway heading for Mount Rushmore. Instead of just being bothered by the noise, she was stimulated to think about how the Husteads might take advantage of the traffic to attract more business. She suggested to her husband that he put out signs on the highway to draw visitors to their store, making a unique appeal. The signs said, "Free Ice Water . . . Wall Drug."

Thirsty travelers stopped for ice water and frequently stayed for ice cream. The rest is history. By the time Mr. Hustead returned from installing the Burma-Shave-type signs, the store was busy.

Years later, Wall Drug made a second price innovation. The Husteads offered free signs to anyone who wanted one. In a typical year, customers take 14,000 small and 8,000 large ones. The signs appear all over the world thanks to peripatetic customers, including such unexpected places as the South Pole and the London Underground. Each one tells how far it is to Wall Drug. Many people who see the signs decide to visit Wall Drug. These signs also draw free publicity in articles and books.

These pricing decisions have been supported by friendly service, even if all you want is free ice water for your thermos. On a summer day, Wall Drug will host 20,000 visitors in its 76,000 square foot emporium. By adding more retail items, Wall Drug continued to innovate.

> **The business advice that many give is "buy low, sell high." A better strategy is "buy low, and set prices to increase profits through increasing volume with good margins."**

As a recent business model innovation, you can take a virtual tour of the store and buy products without visiting Wall, South Dakota, by logging on to www.walldrug.com. The lessons? "You can reach out to other people with something that they need." When the price is right, that reaching out works even better. The third generation of the Hustead family still owns and operates Wall Drug.

SET PROFITABLY APPEALING PRICES

There is an enormous appeal to getting something you want for nothing. Any company with a deep pocket, however, can give products away. How can you turn low price appeal into profitability? Only a few experienced, price-based business model innovators fully understand how to use more attractive pricing to expand their customer base and profits. We look at many ways to accomplish that attractive result in this chapter.

> You cannot improve your business model through price structure and price levels until you find a concept that expands your competitive advantage, regardless of what competitors do.

Remember first that lowering prices may fail to attract more purchasing when the offering is cheapened in the customers' eyes and experience. For instance, if the Husteads had provided poor service to those who wanted the free ice water, their story would have ended up quite differently. Raising prices without providing more benefits predictably discourages buying in most circumstances. How can adjusting prices help create a more profitable business model?

The business advice that many give is "buy low, sell high." A better strategy is "buy low, and set prices to increase profits through increasing volume with good margins." To follow the more effective advice, you need to know a lot more about where your costs are or could be low, and how price structures and levels affect consumption. Combining these cost and demand perspectives can greatly improve your competitive position and profitability.

Locate Where Lower Prices Are Profitable

With a stroke of your pen or a few taps on your computer keyboard, you can change your profits by adjusting your prices. That's a lot easier than finding and implementing all of those subtle value improvements at the same price that you read about in Chapter 1.

Do you know what price adjustments you should make? A spreadsheet can tell you the profit impact . . . if you know what the volume and cost effects can be. However, you know that most of your volume estimates will be way off the mark. To overcome those potentially expensive errors, you need to test new prices first. But you already test prices. How can you test differently to improve your business model?

First, reconsider how your prices affect your volume and costs. Here's an example of what we mean. Assume you efficiently produce a particular kind of bolt. You now sell these bolts at a dollar for a standard quantity. You want to find ways to increase your profits. You would normally test a slightly higher price in one geographic market to see how it goes. That price might be $1.05. The average of all your costs for this product is $0.80 per unit. If sales in the test area stay about even with what you expect, you will probably apply that price increase to all territories. That apparently profitable change in price could be a major missed opportunity, but you'll never know it unless you think differently about your pricing choices.

We'll continue with this example to demonstrate other possible ways to adjust prices. Let's consider an alternative to raising the price to $1.05. Making more of an item is usually much less costly than a company's average costs. In this case, assume it would only cost you $0.25 per unit to produce more bolts than you do now. You decide to test a price of $0.80, your average cost, instead. Obviously, you have to sell a lot more to make this price as profitable as the $1.05 price. If the volume you sell in-

(continued)

creases by at least 50 percent, you do make more money [($1.05 - $0.80) (old bolt volume) < ($0.80 - $0.25) (0.5) (old bolt volume)]. If you don't have to invest in more equipment or much more working capital and you are the lowest cost producer, capturing a 50+ percent volume increase at $0.80 is a better deal than raising the bolt price to $1.05. Competitors will probably assume they cannot afford to match you, and may not. If the expansion of your test is successful, they will have a more expensive and harder time making inroads against you in the future. Your costs will be lower, while their average costs will increase as they lose customers and volume to you. In addition, they will have to spend more for marketing to overcome the new preferences for your product and price offering. By improving your relative cost position, you can turn this change into a lasting competitive advantage.

If you started as a high-cost producer compared to competitors and expand the new pricing after running the same successful test, you will probably set off a price war instead. With a new price that's still above their average cost, competitors will see potential profits in fighting you. In that case, your "successful" price test will lead to lower profits for you when lower-cost competitors react. Further, if competitors ignored your test, the volume increases you experienced then were misleadingly positive. Lower-cost competitors are unlikely to ignore a full rollout of the lower price by you. Their price cuts will lead to lower market prices and much less increased volume than in your unchallenged test.

Now consider a second alternative to see if we can find a better choice. The bolt's price stays at $1.00 to a customer for the volumes purchased in the last twelve months, but for purchases increased above that quantity, the price is $0.70. If your total volume increases by at least 15 percent, you make more money than with the $1.05 price [$0.05 (last year's quantity) < (0.15)($0.70 - $0.25) (last year's quantity)]. Again, if you don't have to invest much more to earn this money and you are the lowest-cost producer, you are ahead. As before, the price war risk is much greater if you are not the lowest-cost producer.

Next, look at what else these customers purchase to find a better choice. It turns out they almost always need a special nut to go with the bolt. The nut costs $0.10 to make in increased volumes and a unit now sells for $1.00. You sell the same quantities of both products. In this third alternative test, you price the bolt at $1.00 on existing volumes, and increased bolt purchases at $0.40. If the purchased volumes of both products go up by at least 5 percent, you make more money than by increasing prices to $1.05 on both items, before considering required changes in investments {$0.05 (existing bolt and nut volume) < [($0.40 - $0.25) + ($1.00 - $0.10)](0.05)(existing bolt and nut volume)}.

Since customers need both products, you also should consider how price sensitive the volume of the bolt is versus the nut. You may make more money by cutting the price of the nut for incremental volumes and holding the price of the bolt. This price structure would work better if you have some customers who buy their bolts from you and their nuts elsewhere.

Before acting, realize that these test evaluations could easily be faulty due to measurement errors. Why? Well, the customers may simply be storing the increased product purchases in warehouses, and there is no real increase in consumption by end users. If they were, the benefit of your better prices goes solely to increase profits of the customers, rather than to encourage the customers' customers. Another potential measurement problem is that well-conducted tests will work out better than poorly executed, full-scale price changes.

If you have a small market share and low costs compared to competitors, the strategy of one of these price reductions might be the right one. One of these price reductions can help you gain share of customers' total business.

(continued)

However, if you are a large market share competitor, price reductions are less likely to work well because of limited potential to add more volume. The last bolt and nut pricing alternative is a good choice for both large and small market share competitors because only 5 percent more volume is needed to earn more money.

Instead of influencing your customers with price changes, you could aim your incremental price reduction at the end users. For instance, you could offer a rebate to consumers who haven't tried your customer's product before and are likely to find their product desirable. Or, if your product is superior enough to attract end users to your customers, you might share the cost with your customer of providing reduced-price orders to your customers' potential new accounts for an introductory period. If the end users are more price sensitive than your customers are, either alternative could be a good idea.

Imagine that we are talking about services instead of products. In some cases, the extra cost of supplying more services is extremely low, such as an Internet service provider offering unlimited connection time to light users. In this case, the usual price for upgrading to unlimited use might be $5.00 a month, while the actual cost of providing more might be as little as $0.50 for the typical light user. In many cases, one service also affects the usage of another service. As with the bolt and nut example, you want to look at the total profit potential. For instance, when you stay in a hotel, you might also spend money for the restaurant and parking garage. In such a case with lots of empty rooms, the correct room price to optimize profits (before considering increased investments) could be much lower than what it is today, assuming that you could supply all of the demand that your new room price stimulates. If you make your change quickly in peak market conditions, competitors might not be able to respond at a time when they are out of capacity. A hotel might do this to attract business conferences and other events involving overnight stays and extensive use of the hotel facilities. With lots of increased volume at low added costs, you may also grasp large relative improvements in average costs at the same time.

Do you still think that keeping the current pricing structure and testing small price increases is the way to go? We hope not. The rest of this chapter can help you understand what kinds of tests you should design and evaluate.

ADJUST PRICES TO CHANGE THE WAY YOUR OFFERINGS ARE USED AND TO EXPAND CONSUMPTION

You cannot improve your business model through price structure and price levels until you find a concept that expands your competitive advantage, regardless of what competitors do. In this section, we show you how to locate such advantaged pricing.

We have already demonstrated the potential value of conducting the right pricing tests. Realize the limitations, though. Such tests are difficult to do well. Only if purchased volumes vary widely will you be able to tell the advantage of one pricing structure over another. Measuring the results can be costly. Also, beyond a certain point, you cannot effectively run any more tests at the same time.

Why do tests, then? Well, they are still the best route to verifying the effectiveness of price-based business model innovations, and most business model innovators do eventually locate a price-based business model advantage.

Long before you reach your testing limits, you should first do a lot more thinking about how pricing could expand demand. Be sure you always do more thinking about pricing than actual testing. Such thinking can help you identify better opportunities for tests, define better tests and save you time. For example, notice how each subsequent way of adjusting prices for bolts offered more profit potential for the manufacturer. If the bolt manufacturer had stopped thinking about price after designing the first test, much potential profit would have been lost. As you do this thinking, focus on how changes in your pricing structure could change your customer's and an end user's behavior. Refer to the material in the Prologue about Disneyland to appreciate how pricing can encourage using more of a service and its related offerings.

Now let's see how your customers' price inhibitions can be reduced.

Locate What You Can Deliver at Low Cost

First, you need to identify situations in which having customers buy more of your products and services would cost you very little. Consider what your actual costs for increased consumption would be, rather than what your standard costs tell you they average now. Unless you have already done Activity-Based Costing (ABC, a more accurate way to understand product and service costs), finding out the answer will require some investigation.[1] In the earliest examples of the bolt priced at $1.00 in this chapter, we assumed that there would be little increased investment to handle additional volume. Actually, there usually will be more investment than you expect. You should find out how, when and under what circumstances increased investment will occur. Your decision to change pricing needs to be made in light of the profit *and* cash flow consequences.

As part of this evaluation, think about how you could change the way you provide your products or services. You have thought a lot about how to add benefits in the context of the current price and cost levels based on the material in Chapter 1, but the potential of making products and services available at much lower prices will improve your perspective on adding benefits. With the value-improving ideas you have already conceived, the minds of those involved in business model innovation should now be ripe to see even more opportunities.

By combining both the benefit and the price-based perspectives, you can assemble even more effective innovations. Let's look more closely at that combined approach.

As you reduce your price as a disincentive to purchasing, you may realize that your offerings have more fundamental limitations that must be addressed. For instance, how could you offer attractive new benefits in addition to a lower price to encourage purchasing? As an example, if you sell macaroni, could you add to your package more appealing, easy-to-make, inexpensive recipes that delight a family on a budget so that they would want to eat macaroni more often? Could you go one step further and provide a free packet of tasty powdered spices that would inexpensively dress up the macaroni and further increase your sales? How does the profit effectiveness of providing the new benefits compare with the price adjustments alone?

Structure Price Out of Increased Usage

Second, focus on profitable pricing structures that will make increased purchases of your offerings as close to free as possible. Such structures will often have much lower prices for higher volumes and higher prices for lower volumes. In some cases, there may be an annual charge, such as the membership fee for a warehouse club that permits access. Such a charge can allow you to drastically drop the prices on the goods you offer, so that their value and the value of the membership will both seem higher. Sometimes, a similar result is achieved by having a minimum charge. Paychex uses this price structure by having a minimum payroll processing charge. The smallest employers see no increase in their monthly costs from Paychex when they add one more employee. Some retailers and online merchants require a minimum-size purchase in order to qualify for free shipping. Security analyst reports frequently mention the success of such policies in stimulating sales growth. After people purchase the quantities required to overcome the minimum charge, all shipping is free.

Change Price Perceptions

Third, understand how the cost of your offerings affects the way your customers think about their costs. Most companies are very careful about adding new expenses. They focus on producing at least the budgeted profit amount on expected revenues. However, many costs never affect that profit number. For example, one reason that investment bankers get paid such enormous fees is that the cost of those fees rarely reduces the reported profits of their clients. Usually, accounting rules permit the investment banking fees that are paid to be capitalized as a cost of the transaction that has taken place. The fees are counted on the balance sheet, rather than running through the profit-and-loss statement. Can what you do be capitalized in some similar fashion rather than being a reported profit-reducing expense for customers? Work with your accountant to develop ideas for eliminating the profit impact on your customers from your prices.

If you can't eliminate the profit impact of your prices on your customers, you may still have some influence over which fiscal years the expenses are counted in. There may be more budget in a future year (if a company is coming out of a weak period, for example), and pricing that allows the costs to shift between years may well be critical to changing behavior. Technology companies often take advantage of this timing opportunity by providing equipment for free during a "shakedown" period. The invoice is then issued a number of months later, even though the equipment has been in service during the second half of the customer's prior fiscal year. Some companies even delay the start of their own fiscal years so that their earnings from such sales are not delayed too long. Again, discuss this subject with your accountants to develop appropriate choices for your customers. Encourage your customers to do the same with their accountants.

MAKE YOUR OFFERINGS SEEM MORE DESIRABLE IN BOTH PRICE AND NONPRICE WAYS

In many product categories, having a somewhat higher price is part of establishing a quality image in the minds of those who buy and use the product. Companies that price their products based only on considering costs will often miss this point, and may hurt sales volume by having prices that are inappropriately low. How can you use price and nonprice methods to enhance the sales and profits of your offerings?

In the 1970s, Kentucky Fried Chicken usually offered two

kinds of chicken. One was produced according to Colonel Sanders's original recipe. The other was made like standard "crispy" fried chicken found throughout the southern United States. Both products were priced the same. KFC's competitors usually sold their crispy products at lower prices, and KFC felt that the less attention paid to the price differential versus competitors the better.

The original recipe was actually less expensive to make than the crispy product. Colonel Sanders had done his homework. He designed the product to taste better and to be easier to prepare than the competitors' offerings. Some people in the company considered cutting the price on the original recipe chicken to lessen the price disparity with competitors.

Talking to customers showed something quite different. Customers felt that the original recipe product was a better offering and was worth a premium price. They reported being confused about why KFC's crispy and original recipe chicken products were priced the same. Customers also had some concerns about the quality of the crispy product, which sometimes created doubts about the quality of original recipe chicken when it was sold at the same price.

A pricing test was conducted by charging a 5 percent premium for original recipe chicken, along with printing a blue ribbon on the original recipe packages. During the test, volume increased significantly for both original recipe and all sales in the KFC store. When queried, consumers reported that the original recipe quality rose, and it may well have. Knowing that customers had to pay more for it, managers and cooks may have paid more attention. Research results often show that employees achieve higher quality for premium-priced goods and services, even when the same processes are used within the same facility. KFC's successful repricing program ran in the company-owned stores for several years before parity pricing between the two products was reintroduced by a new management team.

Introducing a premium-priced, higher-quality brand that shares the company's low cost base can make a similar positive impact on adding profitable market share. Black & Decker found this out when it introduced the more expensive DeWalt line of portable power tools. While many people who do home improvements want the least expensive product that will get the job done, others take pride in their work and enjoy the feel and look of top-quality tools. Some tool lovers will happily pay a hefty price premium for higher quality tools. By offering both brands, Black & Decker can be more competitive on parts and distribution costs for both, allowing lower prices for the Black & Decker brand and a higher quality image and better performance with the DeWalt brand for those who are sensitive about those factors. As a result, the company was able to gain market share and expand profits faster.

USE PRICING TO REDUCE YOUR COSTS

Lower prices instinctively feel to most managers like an inevitable path to reduced profit margins and a cash flow squeeze if volume does increase. You certainly need to be careful whenever you lower prices. An offset to the risk of lowered profits and negative cash flow can come from price adjustments that reduce your costs more than your prices. In this section, you can learn how to find these cost-reducing price adjustments.

You can use pricing as either a carrot or a stick to influence which offerings your customers and end consumers will choose.

An example of a carrot has been the kind of discount dining offers that restaurants provide for those who eat early in the evening, before most patrons arrive. The stick approach is employed by credit card companies when they impose large penal-

> **Southwest Airlines uses pricing as both a carrot and a stick to reduce costs.**

ties for late payments. Whether you use the carrot or the stick in a particular circumstance depends, in part, on your fully analyzed current and potential costs and the relationship you want to have with customers.

From one offering to another, adding volume has widely differing impacts on average costs and your costs for just the increased volume. These effects also vary over both the short and the long term. You should consider both time perspectives and the two key dimensions of costs (average and those on just the increased volume) in selecting when and where you want to shift demand. For instance, a restaurant's costs are little different between a dinner at 5 P.M. and one at 8 P.M. If customers who would have normally paid full price at 8 P.M. all arrive for the 5 P.M. special, no cost improvement or volume expansion has occurred and revenue has been lost. A better approach is to limit the 5 P.M. specials to smaller portions and to offer them on a senior menu. In this way, costs are reduced for the food, and the risk of all diners shifting from the full-priced menu is reduced. Seniors are a good choice because many do eat smaller portions, are more flexible in when they eat and have tighter budgets for dining out.

Consider how Southwest Airlines uses pricing as both a carrot and a stick to reduce costs. The airline specializes in lean operations that incur lower costs than all other major U.S. air carriers. This cost advantage enables the company to use the carrot of lower prices for vacation travelers and others who can book flights well in advance. Such discounted prices are usually about 10 to 20 percent less than competing airlines for the same routes. As a result, a passenger can fly Southwest coast to coast today for the same price paid for a similar discounted flight thirty-eight years ago. Those low prices attract lots of customers, and the airline often has a higher percentage of seats filled than its competitors. Increased popularity drives down costs while driving up profits because the extra expense to add another passenger is very small. As Southwest might say, "It's just peanuts." Most of the increased revenue turns into profit contribution.

Like other airlines, Southwest also employs the stick of charging more for people who buy tickets at the last minute. However, Southwest's prices are based on a much smaller percentage increase from the discounted fare than its major competitors charge. This policy adds the element of a carrot for the stick and provides a large advantage versus competitors for these more profitable tickets. Thus, a business traveler may be able to buy a last-minute ticket for as little as 25 percent of the price of a competing airline. This pricing drives a lot of last-minute travelers to Southwest at premium prices, further lowering costs while fattening margins.

Now, consider an industrial example. A commodity manufacturer of building materials studied the mix of its products to see how customer buying patterns affected profits. Compared to competitors, the company had a unique manufacturing process that made it less costly to produce higher volumes of identical items, but much more expensive to produce smaller volumes of those same items. This cost difference occurred because every order above a minimum size was produced on demand by mass production methods, rather than being shipped from existing inventory maintained by long production runs. Smaller orders than the mass production minimum required expensive hand crafting. The ideal solution for this company was for customers to split their orders, buying unit quantities below the minimum from competitors and the larger quantities from this firm. The manufacturer prided itself on being the low-price supplier across the board and wasn't sure how it could add profitable volume based on this cost analysis.

Using sophisticated research, the company determined that a high percentage of current and potential customers would be willing to split their orders if a price disincentive, a stick, were provided for lower volume orders. The manufacturer raised prices on small volumes of individual items and kept low prices on the higher volumes. Its business mix quickly shifted toward its lowest-cost products and volumes, and its profit margins soared. This happy result occurred despite having just lost most of its low-unit-quantity orders.

A Hewlett-Packard unit investigated how its customers used its various service capabilities in the mid 1990s. Products were priced as though every customer used each service offering equally. In fact, some customers used most services while others did not. The profitability of an account that did not use the services was naturally much larger than that of a similar volume customer who used most services. The services presented another problem. Providing them often tied up the best research and development people at Hewlett-Packard because customers wanted help in creating custom solutions that no other customers needed.

Based on a financial and market analysis, the Hewlett-Packard unit began charging for most of the services that were not used by the bulk of its customers. At the same time, it lowered the base price of the product. This adjustment lowered the total price paid by those who used few services, and Hewlett-Packard gained market share with those customers. Services that were hard to supply or were too intrusive on the time of key people were priced at a substantial premium to their cost to discourage anyone using the services who didn't really need them. Consequently, Hewlett-Packard saw its costs drop as the required service levels declined, while revenues and market share rose due to more competitive prices for those who didn't need much service. The increased volume also helped drive costs down.

CONTROL THE TIMING OF DEMAND TO IMPROVE CUSTOMER BENEFITS

Nearly everyone has had the experience of being disappointed by a new restaurant after reading great reviews. Immediately after the reviews appear, the waits for reserved tables may be long and the service can be compromised by having too many diners. Pretty soon, few may want to go there again. A similar problem occurs with excess demand for many superior new offerings or when demand surges unexpectedly for existing ones. How can you protect the integrity of what you offer while establishing a good foundation for the future? One possibility is to use temporarily higher prices to match demand with your ability to deliver high-quality production or service. Our next example looks at how demand for a new consumer service was controlled.

In 2000, Gilat Satellite Networks, an Israeli company, announced a technical breakthrough. You could receive high-speed, broadband Internet service on your personal computer without being connected to the telephone network or a cable television box. Gilat did this by fine-tuning its technology for very small aperture satellite dishes. The personal computer uses wiring to the dish to communicate by bouncing signals to and from a satellite in space, which the satellite relays to and from a ground station connected to the Internet by high-speed transmission lines. This technology means that people in almost any locale can access the latest computer communications technology. Service companies now provide this breakthrough access for out-of-the-way places around the globe.

One of the first sites for this service was the Havasupai reservation on the normally hard-to-access floor of the Grand Canyon. This new service was initially provided by StarBand Communications Inc., a joint venture among Gilat, Microsoft, EchoStar and ING Furman Selz Investments using Gilat equipment and technology. StarBand's service was the first of its kind to provide consumer two-way satellite broadband Internet service for always-on, high-speed access all across the United States. Ordinarily, the Grand Canyon location would have been one of the last to have such top-notch service. StarBand made the service available as part of a technical test and to help establish credibility for its offering.

StarBand wasn't sure how to price this unique service initially. For many people, this service was going to be the only way to get high-speed Internet access for several years. On the one hand, that situation argued for charging a very high price. On the other hand, if the company could charge a low enough price, the sales potential would be greater. In that case, more customers with the choice of using competing telephone lines or cable connections for their high-speed Internet service would purchase StarBand's service.

A further complication was that a key Gilat component supplier would only be able to make a limited number of its products during 2001. After that, volumes could scale up into very large numbers. Realizing that it would make many people angry if it could not supply them, StarBand temporarily set the price high to match its limited satellite dish capacity from Gilat in 2001. In this way, the company could establish the technical quality of its service, create a premium image for the service through pricing, add a lot of accounts that would probably be loyal in the future (because they would have no alternative) and maintain a future option to price more competitively in new and existing accounts.

A similar problem often arises near the end of recessions and economic slowdowns. During such times, prices are often low and falling. To cover overhead and fixed costs, companies may aggressively add contracts at low prices for the next several quarters.

This aggressiveness will often be a mistake. If demand comes back quickly, prices will rise even faster. The provider who did not sell out capacity will be able to accommodate old and new customers and get the best prices. In fact, temporarily "shuttering" the capacity during weak periods can often be a more attractive strategy. A classic example of that opportunity arose in 2000 during a period of weak aluminum prices, when a severe electricity shortage arose in the western United States. Aluminum smelters are large users of electricity, and many of them could earn more money by reselling their fixed-cost electricity than from the aluminum that they could make with that power. As a result, many western smelters chose to shut down. At the same time, with so many U.S. smelters not operating, the price for aluminum from smelters located elsewhere was higher. Profitability was doubly aided.

Strategically Manage the Growth of Emerging Technologies

If you are like most executives, you're doing some work to create the proverbial "better mouse trap." A lot of companies succeed in designing the mousetrap, but don't catch too many customers with it. Somebody else usually removes most of the customers first. How can better pricing be used to control that situation?

In Silicon Valley and in technical companies everywhere, stories are told about how Apple and Microsoft "borrowed" from the Xerox Palo Alto Research Center. We remember that time well because our company was a beta test site for the first Xerox in-office computer networks. The salespeople kept asking us nervously about whether we minded paying the very high prices that Xerox was asking for the STAR system. We kept responding that the quoted price was no problem, as long as the technology worked. The salespeople looked at us incredulously. But we were serious.

When the network began to crash whenever it rained (and it rains a lot in Cambridge, Massachusetts, where our offices were located), the price suddenly became much too high for us. The equipment was thoughtfully taken back by Xerox.

Attractive new technologies that can be the basis of improved business models are usually very price sensitive. When new technologies are first available, often the only people who can afford them are customers for whom a vastly improved way of operating is made possible for the first time. As others see the technical promise being fulfilled, it simply becomes a substitution pricing decision. How do the benefits and costs of the old technology compare to the new alternative? Most customers will prefer the new technology only when their cost to perform a key activity becomes enough lower than the older choice to justify the time and investment to change. A good example of this need for lowering prices can be seen in the transitions from one generation of personal computer microprocessors to the next. When it is first available, the fastest, most capable chip may sell for as much as $200 while the price for the chip that is two generations old may have dropped to $30. Yet the old chip also once sold for $200—just about three years before.

Most new technologies have about as much volume sensitivity to price as the older technologies that they replace. But occasionally a new one comes along that is more price sensitive. Then a changed pricing strategy becomes critical to controlling the pace of market development. If prices are kept high for too long, the market growth declines. The innovator misses the chance to make more profitable sales. If prices are too low, the market grows explosively, demand cannot be fulfilled by the technological innovator and competitors are encouraged to enter by the dozens. Market share is dramatically lost under such conditions by the original supplier.

By controlling the rate of price reduction along with the timing of its own capacity additions versus competitors, a farsighted company may be able to seize large quantities of market share. Although product innovation is clearly part of its success, Nokia appears to have used this pricing approach in part to manage the demand for its digital cellular handsets during the 1990s to rapidly gain market share. Nokia timed its market-expanding price reductions to coincide with times when competitors' excess capacity was limited for digital cell phones, and Nokia had just finished large capacity expansions. Competitors felt they had to match Nokia prices, which further stimulated market growth.

Be sure you know what value you are delivering and how your pricing will affect consumption of a new technology. You will probably have to be fast on your feet with those prices. At a low-enough price, that Xerox network would have stayed with us despite its water problems. We would simply have used the work-stations for stand-alone word processing and desktop publishing, and hand carried floppy disks to and from the shared laser printer that was inaccessible over the wet Ethernet cable connections. How might the world have turned out differently if the price for the network had been a lot lower and the reliability a lot higher? Certainly, Xerox's performance since then would have been brighter.

Use Temporarily Low Prices to Encourage Customer Trial of New Business Models

Several times a day, you probably get a telephone call offering you some new product or service that the telemarketer claims will be really helpful to you. You don't have time to listen or to try out all of these things, so you probably avoid whatever is being offered. Your potential customers may see your new business model's price offers the same way. How can you overcome that barrier to attention?

Sometimes the benefits of a new business model just have to be experienced to be appreciated. Customers are naturally suspicious of what they haven't seen or tried before. They don't want to waste their time and money. Temporary price cuts can sometimes overcome that

> By developing price-based introduction methods as part of your new price-adjusting business model, you enhance its effectiveness.

resistance and help establish credibility faster and less expensively than other methods. When you are using this approach, you should be sure that everyone understands that the low price levels are a temporary way of introducing what's new.

This approach has been highly effective in helping retailers with new concepts build initial traffic into the store. Take trusted brands and offer them at a price that is unlikely to be repeated. Advertise those offers all around, and you will soon experience wall-to-wall customers. Make their visit an enjoyable one, and many shoppers will be back even when the prices are raised to sustainable levels. For the best results, price the bulk of your items normally during the introductory period so people can get a sense of what they will pay when they return.

By developing price-based introduction methods as part of your new price-adjusting business model, you enhance its effectiveness. Returning to Southwest Airlines, the company is still expanding its national availability on a city-by-city basis. In doing so, Southwest doesn't want to be in just any airport. It only wants to be in airports that are not crowded, have few flight delays and are near large metropolitan areas. These circumstances are essential to the low cost and high performance parts of Southwest's business model.

When the company initiates flights near a new metropolitan area, it offers extremely low fares to entice people to try its no-frills, good-service features. These fares usually trigger a price war from competing carriers and draw a lot of attention. Southwest performs well during this period by temporarily importing experienced personnel and soon will have 30 to 40 percent of all the traffic at the new airport. At the same time, the price war usually leads to permanently lower prices at that airport. Flyers develop a new habit of traveling to that unaccustomed airport instead of closer ones, and the volume of the airport may increase by more than 50 percent in a year. Traveling has been reshaped in favor of Southwest in a way that is consistent with the company's normal, low-fare philosophy. When cost leadership allows it, that's a good concept for you to apply as well.

PREPARE PRICE TESTS

As mentioned earlier in this chapter, you need to test improved price structures that lower costs for customers and other stakeholders before changing your business model. Naturally, your test results can only be as successful as the quality of the ideas you test. Developing excellent ideas and properly evaluating them are critical elements for the continuing business model innovation process.

Develop Better Pricing Concepts to Test

Focus first on having your organization produce solid price-adjustment concepts. A good way to start is by rereading Chapter 1, because you'll think of more pricing opportunities when you consider a more appropriate price structure and price levels as simply being benefits. Since you have now had experience with thinking about adding benefits, progress will be faster if you also use the same process to explore price adjustments.

You will probably get more innovative proposals if you employ a slight twist in the process from when you developed ideas for more benefits at the current price and cost level, such as by involving different people this time. When you do, watch out for a tendency to defer to those in sales jobs for their thinking about price-adjusting concepts. Although salespeople are certainly a good source, they often don't know about key operating and financial issues that should also influence your thinking. Seek out those who can round out the perspective on the operational implications.

We strongly recommend that you build multifunctional teams (at least one person from each function) to develop new price-adjustment concepts. The more people who can contribute their thinking to these teams, the more you will learn. But don't make the teams too large, or they will get bogged down. Having five to eight people on the team is a good size. You can bring others in to discuss specific issues without permanently involving them with the team.

You should be sure to hold discussions with customers to understand the problems that pricing causes them now. If you have good relations with partners and suppliers, involve them as well. If you don't have such helpful relationships, work on improving them.

In considering pricing, think about the implications of your pricing methods, as well as the prices themselves. One business-model-innovating company found that its detailed pricing scheme (not its prices) was by far the biggest barrier to improving customer relationships. A typical product installation came with more than forty pages of invoices. How would you like to check through all that detail looking to see if you got all the little bits of wire that you were being charged for on an invoice? More inclusive and simpler prices were very welcome to this company's customers. In the process, costs were reduced for customers and the company.

Once the team thinks it has a good concept, they should turn it into a test proposal.

Evaluate Pricing Test Proposals to Find Ways to Improve Them

Let's look at how a company should consider these proposals for pricing tests. A regional franchisee of a well-known fast-food restaurant chain wanted to add more business on Monday nights, the slowest time of the week. He thought that a price cut on that night just might do the trick. Let's look at this idea prior to testing. Several analyses can be helpful.

First, find as many things that can go wrong in each proposal as possible. Although no list on this subject can ever be exhaustive, here are some questions to consider:

- Will the test results provide reliable guidance for what to do for the customers who were not part of the test? Yes, the franchisee planned to test the new pricing in every store he owned.
- For which product and service offerings will the test results provide reliable guidance? It will be accurate for all products because this is a broadscale, ongoing test.
- Will competitors respond to the test or a full-scale implementation of the test in ways that are harmful to your company? The franchisee had no competitors in the same product line, so this potential vulnerability was not a problem.

- Will customers and end users be upset by the test? Saving money hardly ever upsets fast-food customers.

- Can operations provide the needed support for the test? Business is light on most Monday nights. The current minimum staffing could handle a big increase in business.

- Will those who have to implement the test do so happily and with the necessary time and attention? Because the electronic registers can be programmed to automatically adjust the prices, employees should not be distracted. Since they aren't busy on Monday nights, they may even welcome seeing more customers to help the time pass more quickly.

- Can the company's or the offering's reputation be tarnished by the test? Only if quality slips. Managers can plan to work that night to be sure performance is top-notch.

- Will suppliers or partners respond unfavorably? They would love more volume being sold.

- Will the test or its results have any negative impact on the company's profitability or stock price? Here's where the test had a problem. Sunday night was the busiest and most profitable time of the week. If customers waited until Monday night to buy the same quantity of food at lower prices, profits would drop a lot. The franchisee's business value could decline as well.

Second, think about how any faults can be overcome. Jot down your initial ideas about whether the faults can or cannot be eliminated, and share those ideas with whomever proposed each price-adjusting test. If the franchisee ran his price reductions far away from Sunday, the profit risk was greatly reduced. Perhaps Wednesday or Thursday would be a better choice.

Third, consider how the test could be combined with other proposed tests. One successful method for combining tests is to add elements to the test sequentially in time, after an initial success. For example, Disneyland could have tested a two-day passport on a few quiet days before offering any other choices. When that two-day passport test was working, a three-day passport could have been tested while the two-day test continued. Again, the new choice could be offered on just a few slow days. After the testing of multiple-day passes ended satisfactorily and was added as a permanent change, tests of an annual passport could be limited to people who lived in certain zip codes through direct mail. A measurement panel could be set up to analyze the visits and spending patterns of those who took the annual passes compared to those who did not buy the annual passes. Then the economic case for the change could be considered.

In the fast-food case, profitability would be enhanced if the customer who was lured away from higher-priced Sunday purchases spent more money on the test night than on a Sunday, but got a lot more food . . . rather than buying the same quantity of food for less money. A second-stage test could increase the quantities involved in the discount offer, if the initial test generated enough added weekly volume to be profitable.

Fourth, look at how one new structure suggests other changes. For example, most people come to Disneyland by car and there is a charge for parking there. The logic of the annual passport suggests that you want visitors to think of each trip as being free during the year. Perhaps you should also test annual parking passports. In fact, Disney offers these as well. If annual passports for entry to and parking at Disneyland are a good idea, what about offering multiple-year passports?

In the fast-food case, you might attract even more volume by offering limited quantities of attractive, novelty dishes only on the discount night. These could be prepackaged items like pies so that the food spoilage and labor costs can be kept low. So a third-stage test might include such items.

Fifth, evaluate the tests for how well each one is likely to work under a variety of future business environments. Beware of those structures that are tightly linked to one view of the future. For instance, replacing passports for individual theme parks with passports for two theme parks at a premium price could backfire if many people did not particularly like one or the other park. Why pay more money for the privilege of doing something you don't want to do?

In the fast-food situation, you would have to consider if there are times when any weekday night normally does a lot of full-priced volume. For example, if the local towns run free band concerts (as many do) on Wednesday evenings, families may pick up fast food to take to those concerts. So Thursday might be a better choice, because it is remote from Sunday and volume is rarely high then.

Sixth, consider where competitors can disrupt your test results. During the 1950s and 1960s, Procter & Gamble (P&G) was famous for extensively testing any change in the quality, packaging or price of its offerings in limited geographic markets. Competitors learned that they could profitably disrupt those tests with unsustainable levels of low pricing, high advertising and extensive promotion. Although the competitor lost money fighting in the test market, the amount lost was less than what it would cost to face a successful rollout of the new P&G offering. In fact, in some cases, P&G would give up on an idea if enough tests failed. Later the company realized that competitors could be more easily overcome by implementing good, low-risk ideas nationally in one fell swoop without any testing. For choices where tests can be disrupted, you need to consider how you can correctly decide whether or not to implement the new structures without testing. What is the potential loss if you do? If that potential loss is small, affordable and comfortable compared to the potential gain and your total resources, go ahead.

Although the franchised company had no fast-food competitors in its product line, it had plenty of restaurant and fast-food competitors selling other products. Could those competitors offer their own specials and disrupt the test? They certainly could. The company should carefully check for what programs competitors regularly offer on Thursday nights that might encourage counteractions against its test.

KEY QUESTIONS

The following questions are intended to simplify your search for price-based business model advantages.

Innovation-Creating Questions

- *How can you change your price structure to encourage customers to purchase and consume more volume from you?* In answering this question, focus on making price disappear as much as possible from purchase and usage decisions. You may want to revisit Disneyland's use of multiple-day and annual passports to encourage people to return more often each year. What can you do that would work even better?

- *How can a new price structure reduce your costs?* Answering this question requires understanding how your current pricing policies affect your costs. For example, many public companies offer large specials at the end of fiscal quarters, especially the fourth one. Operations incur extremely high costs to handle these volumes while sitting idle during parts of the early weeks in the quarter. How would your costs change if you had a steadier operating load? You may also offer expensive customer benefits that everyone doesn't want or need. If these benefits are strongly preferred by some customers, can you charge extra for them and drop the base price for those who don't need the benefits? Again, remember that your standard costs will not tell you the story. You need to look at the economic reality of how your operations will be affected. Activity-Based Costing is designed for this measurement purpose.

- *How can changing your price structure make your offerings more attractive to customers in nonprice ways?* Can changed pricing make it more convenient to work with you? If people won't be charged every time they call you, you may get more sales opportunities while providing ongoing service. Can changed pricing make scarce resources more available to those who need them the most? Can pricing improve your image?

- *How can an improved price structure help you make better use of your resources?* Almost every organization has necessary, but under-used, resources. Think about how you can use pricing to attract customers and provide offerings that need your underused resources.

- *How can a better price structure expand the market faster?* Answering this question requires understanding how your offerings fit into each customer's and end-user's business or personal life. At some points of their potential use, the way you price your offerings inhibits purchase and consumption. How can you turn that effect around so that pricing encourages purchase and use? For example, could you offer discounts that reflect such low marginal costs that almost everyone would take the offering? When America Online (AOL) first shifted from a time-related charge to a fixed fee for unlimited usage, the market expanded so rapidly that AOL struggled to keep up with the demand. AT&T's cellular services created a similar rapid demand expansion with its One Rate plan through which AT&T charged a uniform price-per-minute for cellular-based calls.

- *How can you use the timing of price changes and price structure to assist in gaining market share?* One option is to time such break-throughs to occur when you have plenty of spare capacity and your competitors don't. Companies that shift to more appealing pricing models are often surprised by how much their volume increases. If you aren't prepared, you will have unhappy customers and higher costs, as occurred both at AOL and AT&T.

Experimentation Questions

- *How do the tests potentially impact your customers' relationships to their customers?* Have you ever provided customers with an incentive to buy more, watched them respond to that incentive and then suffered as they reduced future purchases to work off excess inventories? Most companies have had that experience. For example, many consumer products companies offer quarter-end sales incentives to sell extra products during the current accounting period. These incentives usually mean that customers don't buy very much in the subsequent two months. The higher customer inventory means that what consumers receive isn't as fresh. In many cases, the customers never reduce their prices to consumers. At the same time, volume is unchanged or even reduced compared to price structures that help consumers, such as by temporarily lowering consumer prices when alternative products are more expensive. For example, discount coupons for lemon concentrate could expand consumption when fresh lemon prices are at their highest.

- *How would delays help or hurt your ability to test different structures?* Have you ever raised prices at the start of a weak economic period? It didn't work very well, did it? Or lowered prices, just as the economy took off? You ended up with a lot of less-profitable volume than you needed to, didn't you? Timing and circumstances are important. Today's best pricing structure may be a foolish one tomorrow. As you look at proposed pricing structures and levels, you need to think about how well each one fits into the various types of business and economic environments that are likely to occur. At the same time, you want to be consistent in your pricing stance, as Southwest Airlines is in always being a low-price alternative.

You may have to expand the results of your test very rapidly, depending on what customer and competitor reactions are. In the context of that requirement, you may not yet be prepared to undertake some of these tests. For example, if you don't have enough capacity to handle potential volume increases, you may lose much of the advantage that you would gain from the new structure.

Alternatively, some of these tests, such as a price structure that would become obsolete if any of the other tests worked, may make no sense unless they are done right away. A potential spot pricing test for occasional purchases faces that issue, when a company's other tests all involve long-term contracts for every customer.

A developing trend's expansion may mean that a new price

structure, such as increasing premiums for offerings and features made more valuable by a continuation of the trend to a minimum level, will be more appropriate in the future than today. Keep those ideas ready for the right time. Gasoline prices have to rise quite a lot, for example, before they trigger increased, sustained demand for fuel-efficient cars. If gasoline prices stopped rising before a high enough level was reached, it may never be timely to make a change in fuel-efficient car pricing. If gasoline prices were to spike briefly, many products (such as SUVs) would probably see their volume hurt while products that required less gasoline (like compact cars) might temporarily increase in volume. But, with consumers knowing that gasoline prices can be volatile, changing price structures to profit more from compact cars than SUVs could be untimely, unless the floor price for gasoline rose permanently. Such a long-term gasoline price increase would occur if gasoline taxes were increased to the levels in Europe, where government policy uses such taxes to reduce oil imports.

Further, many tests can be done more safely by first lining up partners and making acquisitions. Realize that establishing those relationships takes time. Your tests may have to be delayed by three to twelve months to allow for developing those relationships.

CHAPTER 3

ELIMINATE COSTS THAT REDUCE CUSTOMER AND END-USER BENEFITS

We might as reasonably dispute whether it is the upper
or the lower blade of a pair of scissors that cuts a piece
of paper, as whether value is governed by utility
or the cost of production.
—Alfred Marshall

Reduce your unnecessary costs faster than competitors, and you can afford to deliver additional benefits at more attractive prices to customers. Reduce those costs more quickly, and your potential for volume expansion soars. Eliminate costs that harm customers and other stakeholders, and even better results will follow. Fail to apply the savings from major cost reductions for customer benefits, and you have lost most of the potential to make your business more profitable and successful.

Most companies feel that they already have their costs near the lowest potential level due to ongoing budgeting and cost-reduction efforts. However, many missed opportunities remain. These firms have probably ignored many of their biggest cost-reduction opportunities, such as reducing the cost of investment capital from shareholders' equity and doing more outsourcing to efficient suppliers. Some companies also have reduced costs in ways that harm the value of their firm's offerings. Changing the business model to be more effective for all stakeholders will provide the best results when managements look to new places for cost reductions that help people. To find better cost-reduction opportunities, you have to move beyond looking at spreadsheets, standard costs and optimizing specific processes, activities and functions. Instead, you need to look at each stakeholder individually to see what needless and harmful costs can be removed and what benefits can be improved or added at a lower cost.

Have you ever wished for a dry cleaner that was always open? Wouldn't that be handy for times when you really need some cleaning done right away and long work days preclude a trip to the cleaner? Some dry cleaners offer pickup and delivery services . . . but the cost is enormous and their prices are high. Staying open twenty-four hours a day would also be costly, and that expense would inevitably show up in higher prices. Imagine our pleasant surprise when Mr. Marc Rosenthal of award-winning Jaylin Cleaners in Newton and Wellesley, Massachusetts, offered his VIP service. VIP customers can drop off their dry cleaning and laundry anytime! He provides three heavy-duty bags for dirty clothes and a key to open a special depository. Customers can place any special instructions on a tag so the cleaning is done properly. VIP customers also have their credit card numbers on file. When arriving for pickup, these pampered customers use a separate line and find that their cleaning has already been charged to their credit card accounts. The laundry bag is returned with the cleaning. So pickup takes only a moment or two. The staff gets to know all of the VIP customers by name, which makes the experience even more pleasant. And . . . the price is the same for VIP service as it is for regular service. So it's great for the customer.

How does it work for Mr. Rosenthal? He cuts costs! His staff can process VIP orders when no one else is in the store, allowing Jaylin to handle its customers with less counter help. He gets paid as soon as the work is done, even if the cleaning isn't picked up for months. That arrangement means better cash flow and less investment in the business. VIP customers are more likely to stay loyal, meaning more cleaning business over the years. The counter staff likes it better, too. They face fewer impatient customers waiting in long lines to drop off and pick up their cleaning.

Mr. Rosenthal is also a progressive cleaner in other ways. He uses more environmentally friendly chemicals. He controls emissions. And he recycles plastic bags and wire hangars. Customers who favor those practices are more likely to do business with Jaylin Cleaners. Customers and neighbors especially appreciate the cleaner air, as do those who work for Mr. Rosenthal.

We had another surprise when we joined an organization for small company leaders, CEO Roundtable, LLC, based in North Andover, Massachusetts, that is directed by Mr. Loren Carlson. One of the leaders was Mr. Douglas Ross, president and CEO of AristoCraft in Oxford, Massachusetts, Mr. Rosenthal's source for many dry cleaning supplies. Mr. Ross recounted that his company provides ways to eliminate dry cleaning costs for his customers that improve service for their customers. Both the VIP program and some of the environmentally friendly practices were suggested to Mr. Rosenthal by Mr. Ross's company. Not all dry cleaners who buy supplies from AristoCraft use these customer-friendly programs, even though Mr. Ross charges nothing for the ideas. He just wants to help his customers be more successful and to cement a relationship with his company. Stay involved with AristoCraft and other good ideas will be made available to you. These days dry cleaners can buy their bulk supplies very inexpensively from importers who sell through catalogs and on the Internet. Mr. Ross delivers and takes orders several times a week with his own trucks, so his prices and costs are bound to be higher for commodity items like wire hangars. But by helping eliminate unnecessary

> **Look back at the costs of operating your business several years ago. What indispensable costs from those days do you easily do without today? What prevented you from eliminating those once-indispensable costs sooner?**

costs that harm his customers and their customers, Mr. Ross's business continues to profitably gain market share.

Regardless of your business model, you should eliminate costs that reduce customer and stakeholder value and harm stakeholders. In pursuing this goal, you will abolish what is directly harmful, like features or materials that cause injuries. You will also eliminate what is annoying for customers, such as time wasters like complex telephone menus and lines for service. Finally, you will eliminate what is unnecessary, such as features that

> **The biggest challenge facing cost reducers is obscure to them: They don't know where to look!**

make a product or service less efficient to use like warranties requiring lots of record keeping and difficult to complete claim forms. When you make these changes, you will have saved money that you can use to stimulate sales by adding more benefits, adjusting prices and holding those prices longer without an increase.

Look back at the costs of operating your business several years ago. What indispensable costs from those days do you easily do without today? What prevented you from eliminating those once-indispensable costs sooner? If you are like most people, it is that you assumed that your business model should be unchanged. Improve that business model, and costs suddenly become redundant in unexpected places. For example, when a business goes from full service to self-service, the number of face-to-face, service-providing employees you need drops. Improve point-of-sale product information at the same time, and customer satisfaction may rise. Encourage your employees to solve problems for prospective customers, and your volume can increase.

The biggest challenge facing cost reducers is obscure to them: They don't know where to look! Like the person who has misplaced his or her glasses, they keep squinting and groping in all the same places. In this chapter, you can find ideas for looking in new, high-potential places that have routinely produced business-model-based improvements for others. Because these sources of cost reductions have not been mined as thoroughly as the ones you look at all the time, you may find ways to reduce costs that you have not considered before as you design your new business model using the concepts and questions in this book.

Few are reluctant to reduce costs except when the human price is high in terms of cutting jobs or making working conditions less tolerable. At the same time, few are excited about seeking out ways to lower cost levels. To many, this activity is as appealing as participating in a fire drill on a cold, rainy day when there appears to be little likelihood of a fire. In addition, finding new, large cost reductions is often a more difficult task than locating more benefits at the current price or creating new price structures that stimulate demand. In part, this lack of enthusiasm for cost-reduction searches happens because costs are continually scrutinized. So it's old hat. And people can think of fewer stones to turn over for the first time. In part, the difficulty relates to misconceptions about how to find large cost reductions. In addition, focusing on reducing costs for the current business model is like looking for dark-colored items while wearing dark glasses on a moonless night. You won't see most of the possibilities without imagining improved business models. Replace the dark glasses with night vision goggles, and everything is clear. This chapter provides you with new business model innovation perspectives and questions that will operate like such vision-enhancing goggles.

> **Converting business model cost gains into new, substantial customer benefits is one of the most important secrets to gaining and retaining competitive advantages.**

USE COST REDUCTIONS FIRST TO EXPAND CUSTOMER BENEFITS AND PROVIDE MORE ATTRACTIVE PRICING

So far, we have discussed the substantial challenges of finding better cost-based business models. These challenges are much smaller in scope than are the difficulties of redirecting the bulk of the new benefits from cost-based business model innovation to provide still more desirable and attractively priced offerings. This latter point is poorly understood in all but a few companies, yet its importance is paramount in establishing a better business model and improving upon it. Converting business model cost gains into new, substantial customer benefits is one of the most important secrets to gaining and retaining competitive advantages.

Let's consider General Motors in the period from World War II to 1993. GM started this period with the highest market share and the lowest costs of any major auto maker in the world. The company saw its cost opportunities as avoiding strikes, reducing head counts, making fewer production errors, designing for greater parts commonality among car lines, acquiring high-technology businesses that could help GM and investing in computer technology and automation. In pursuing those cost-improvement opportunities, GM probably spent more capital than any other company in the world. Yet GM ended up with costs that were substantially higher than most of its car manufacturing competitors and a much reduced market share.

What went wrong? Several books could be written on that subject. For our purposes a few areas deserve special attention because they represent common problems with the ways many companies pursue and exploit cost reductions.

First, the bulk of the benefits from GM's cost reductions were shared with only two stakeholder groups: employees and shareholders. Labor unions negotiated better wages, benefits and work rules than were provided in most other unionized and nonunionized industries. During the entire period, these costs also rose much more rapidly than for most worldwide competitors. Because Ford and Chrysler produced fewer of their own parts, these high-cost labor contracts affected the General Motors cost structure more than anyone else's in the United States. In addition, a high percentage of GM earnings went for dividends to shareholders. Such paid-out funds were not available to reinvest to lower costs further, or to create more customer and end-user benefits, or more attractive pricing. Companies that consume cost-reduction gains in ways other than serving customers and end users may lose ground to competitors who do more, or more effective, cost-improvement reinvesting.

Second, the company did little to create new business models for its automobile business until the Saturn experiment began offering cars in the 1990s. During those same years, Toyota pioneered the "lean manufacturing" process that provided customers with higher quality cars built to their specifications in just a few days, while Toyota's required investments levels and costs were slashed. Although GM did some experimentation in this same area by partnering with Toyota in California, the lessons of Saturn and lean manufacturing were not widely disseminated throughout the company. As a result, most of GM's investments supported the company's outmoded, high-cost business model. That approach does about as much good for customers as gold-plating an obsolete piece of electronic equipment to make it look better. Chrysler's developments and enhancements of the minivan and SUV from truck technology were also new business models that GM was slow to follow, although GM has now become competitive in those products.

Third, the focus on cost reduction at GM sometimes led to paradoxically higher costs for customers and GM relative to competitors. In the 1970s, for instance, GM was slow to shift to the more expensive systems that dipped parts in paint baths to help cars resist rust and reduce the need for repainting. People who were disappointed in these cars were reluctant to buy new GM offerings. To GM, it was cheaper in the short term to use the traditional spray painting process that created the spotty results. Yet the reduced automobile sales increased costs per unit over millions of cars by reducing GM's economies of scale. At the other extreme, GM spent billions in the 1980s to put robots into its factories. Observers noted that these robots were not always less expensive to employ than the people they replaced, and using robots made it more difficult to shift to the less costly lean manufacturing processes that could quickly provide individualized cars. In addition, a purchasing-driven focus on expanding economies of scale led to a mandate to make all GM car models share as many parts as possible to limit part and assembly costs. Because of this design consolidation, GM car shoppers noticed that brands as different in image as Chevrolets and Cadillacs were often physically very similar . . . yet sold at quite different price levels. As a result, sales often shifted away from the more profitable brands and the most common GM design platforms to the offerings of other manufacturers. With reduced sales volume, costs were increased on a per car basis.

Fourth, the company acquired its cost-reduction capabilities expensively. For instance, GM became interested in more modern computing that management could use to reduce costs and improve effectiveness. It purchased Electronic Data Systems (EDS), then headed by Mr. H. Ross Perot, to pursue a proprietary advantage in this area. Would EDS have been willing to take on GM as its only car and truck manufacturing customer without being purchased by GM? Probably, because having GM as a client would have been a bonanza, more than doubling EDS's revenues and profits. However, GM's investment in EDS probably yielded no special operating benefit to the company over having EDS as a supplier. In fact, knowing that the GM business was not a "lock" might have led EDS to perform even better for GM. Ultimately, GM did gain something from its EDS purchase when a portion of the company's shares in EDS were used to pay unfunded auto worker retirement benefits in the late 1990s.

> **Most of the announcements you read about companies slashing costs amount to running in place on a hamster-cage wheel of new industry practices.**

Fifth, the company was slow to make structural changes in its costs that would permit GM to shift its business model. For example, despite much public and private hand-wringing about its high-cost parts operations, the company waited many years before making those activities independent of GM. The company also had problems with Oldsmobile for many years before announcing a decision to suspend production.

Let's look beyond GM's experience. Despite all the attention that cost reduction receives, it is clear that normal cost reductions rarely cause a company to gain much ground on its lowest-cost competitor. Most of the announcements you read about companies slashing costs amount to running in place on a hamster-cage wheel of new industry practices. After lots of activity and pain, companies usually end up staying in about the same cost position relative to competitors as they were a year before. Most companies come to think of this effort as a necessary part of staying competitive.

How can a company gain significant, beneficial cost advantages over competitors?

FIND AND MAKE GOOD USE OF THE BEST COST REDUCTIONS TO HELP CUSTOMERS

New business models can create large cost reductions that boost margins and profit growth in sustainable ways. Historically, most of these new business models have come from entrepreneur-led start-ups, funded by venture capitalists who believed that there was a better way of serving needs that the current suppliers were ignoring. Let's look at some ways that new business models have helped.

Build Cost-Based Business Model Innovation from Knowledge Advantages to Create Stronger Competitive Positions

Consider the advantages that mighty Microsoft has had in software for personal computers. Microsoft's muscle is so great that it lost its antitrust trial concerning the way it competed in the Web browser market. Netscape, the early industry leader, had been all but wiped out even though it literally gave the product away for free. To compete as a new entrant, Microsoft's Explorer product was not only free, but it came already loaded on new personal computers so consumers saved time by using the ubiquitous and unavoidable Microsoft offering. How could anyone hope to develop costs low enough to vie with such a tactic?

Red Hat, another software company that competes with Microsoft, hopes to do so by accessing superior knowledge inexpensively. Red Hat shows signs of creating a still lower-cost business model than Microsoft's for personal computer and server operating systems. To do so, Red Hat's software is only partially developed by the company itself. The software kernel of its offerings was created and is now maintained by programmers who did not and do not now charge for their time and effort. The operating system, called Linux, has drawn on the talents of hundreds of the world's most innovative software designers. In the process, many customers find that Red Hat's version of Linux (an improved version of the original UNIX software) works better and is easier to customize for new applications than the Microsoft alternatives.

Why do these talented programmers provide such a favor to Red Hat? Primarily because they want to be able to have access to operating software source code so they can create applications that are more pleasing and effective for their own use. Microsoft refuses to allow such source code access. Whether Red Hat used their work or not, these programmers would have continued to help one another to improve Linux.

> **Many companies have installed changes intended to be cost reductions that ultimately led to higher costs.**

While it is too soon to know, it may be that basing one's business on the concept behind open source software is a superior business model for producing the best products and services at the lowest cost. Yet few companies even consider how to access top talent in such inexpensive ways. Instead, they compete to hire these people for top dollar as full-time employees.

For another way that top talent can be inexpensively attracted to create profitable competitive advantages, refer to the Goldcorp contests in the Prologue.

Look for Total Company Cost Reductions as They Relate to an Attractive Customer Rather Than to Maximizing Individual Activity or Facility Cost Reductions

Many companies have installed changes intended to be cost reductions that ultimately led to higher costs. How does that boomerang effect occur, and how can it be avoided?

Avoid Conflicts of Interest

In marketing their offerings, vendors of all kinds of products and services may describe enormous potential customer cost benefits . . . but rarely do these vendors offer guarantees that the indicated cost benefits will occur. Beware of potential conflicts of interest where the seller's offering may not help you! *Caveat emptor* (let the buyer beware) is still true.

In addition, consider that outsourcing has proven to be a new business model that can eliminate this vendor problem. Properly engaged, the outsourced supplier gets paid for pre-agreed-upon results. If the vendor makes a mistake in putting the deal together, the vendor has to solve the problem and usually can. Compare this relationship to the old cost-plus arrangements for specialized out-sourcing. In those relationships, suppliers made more profits by increasing the customer's costs!

Conflicts of interest within a company can also be a problem. Operating executives sometimes find that using new computer systems fails to deliver improved costs, despite being recommended by the corporate financial staffs to provide operations with more cost and production information. However, the new systems do increase the overhead costs of the business. The financial staffs are usually pleased by such investments because they often provide better control tools for the internal accountants and external auditing firm. Unfortunately, more financial information about doing the wrong thing (such as operating an outdated business model) seldom helps. If you could have rearranged the deck chairs on the *Titanic* faster, would that have helped matters while the ship was sinking? As a result, most such systems are a bad idea compared to working on improved business models. Yet most companies make adding computer systems a top priority, while improving business models is largely ignored.

Another problem can arise from who does the cost-reduction work. Computing systems to provide more financial information are often developed by a company's external auditing firm. In some cases, systems vendor selection may have had little to do with reducing the company's costs. Instead, the spending may reflect a desire on the part of the company's senior financial management to have more financial clout with the firm's auditors whenever questionable accounting treatments and issues arise. Should such senior financial managers later lose their jobs, such a favored accounting firm will do more to help them find a new one. There's a lot of turnover in senior financial positions, so be careful.

So conflicts of interest can arise in many different directions related to attempted cost reductions. Watch out!

Expand Your Cost-Cutting Focus to Look at the Whole

Even when conflicts of interest are not involved, too narrow a focus can be deadly to cost-reduction progress. Many companies retain a mental model of only looking at the pieces of what a company does rather than considering the whole effect. That method of cost reduction doesn't work well enough. You not only have to learn new ideas to become an effective cost reducer, you also have to eliminate old ideas that are ineffective or wrong.

Some readers may be familiar with Adam Smith's 1776 description of how ever more specialized tasks by many workers led to less expensive pin manufacturing compared to one person doing everything, as recounted in *The Wealth of Nations* (Modern Library, 1994). With task specialization and mass production, the cost of making many items similarly falls. While true, however, the relevance is usually limited to situations where customers want and need lots of identical, low-cost goods and services.

In today's world, more and more people want just the opposite—something made just for them. Motor vehicles, personal computers and clothing can now be quickly and inexpensively customized to fit the purchaser's needs in unique ways. As a result, the company that offers one type of product or service with little or slow customization will find itself at a big disadvantage compared to companies that provide lean manufacturing or services, two effective rapid customization methods.

Not only are standard offerings less attractive to customers, they usually cost producers more money by the time all is said and done. There is a risk that some of the standard items produced will not be sold, thus wasting finished inventory and the unsuccessful efforts to sell those items. In addition, the investment in creating large volumes of standard items is usually much higher per item for specialized production capabilities and working capital. Further, customers often don't want or need parts of the standard offering, which makes all of the costs involved in adding them a waste of time and money. For instance, imagine a customer whose employees take the low-cost, mass-manufactured straight pin and bend it slightly in the middle to create a pin that holds tags to clothing more securely. Any efforts or costs by the manufacturer to make the standard pins even straighter and more resistant to bending are of no benefit to this customer. Also, optimizing the costs of producing your offering isn't the only cost issue. You also have the costs of marketing and distributing the product. Lower your marketing and distribution costs enough, and you can still have a lower total cost even if custom-made offerings are somewhat more expensive to produce.

In fact, most companies don't measure or think about total costs and profits for an account when considering how they might establish an improved business model. That oversight is a key mistake. Any control process that optimizes the costs of individual company activities will create significant inefficiencies for the rest of the system that will raise overall costs.

Here's an example of this problem. Imagine an independent copier service company offering one type of service contract to its customers. You pay so much per year or per visit, and you get a certain type of service. Independent copier service companies often combine maintenance services and toner sales with a minimum annual charge. Let's assume that's the case.

As copiers became more reliable, fewer and fewer copier customers bought maintenance agreements on their smaller machines. A copier customer that finds it needs maintenance infrequently sees this service supplier's maintenance and toner combination as an expensive way to buy toner. If a customer later finds it has an unreliable machine instead, buying an annual fixed price maintenance agreement for that machine is a great deal for the customer and a disaster for the service provider. Cost-conscious customers with machines needing lots of repairs will solve their problem by buying annual fixed-price maintenance agreements, while those who have high-performing copiers will pay for service on a per visit basis and buy their supplies from the lowest-priced provider.

As a result, the independent copier service company sees its cost per customer rise to reflect the more poorly designed and manufactured copiers. Yet the standard contract certainly does limit selling and administrative costs (which was probably the purpose), an area that is far less important to the service company than how many maintenance visits and parts must be supplied to a customer.

Not only does a company have to think about total costs of an account, it needs to do so in terms of specific customers. Using this approach, one commodity maker of building materials became the profit margin leader in its industry despite having a small market share. While competitors offered all products to all customers and shipped them from each plant, the savvy small producer looked at which potential and current customers were the most attractive to gain and hold. The small company focused its attention on those where it could gain a large cost advantage over its most effective competitors. Then the small producer examined how it could increase its relative cost advantage even further by optimizing its total costs versus those competitors for these accounts.

The company's analysis showed that it should become a specialist in certain types of products and not produce the rest of its customers' needs. The company should also locate its facilities so that each one could be specialized to make even fewer products than before, to allow even longer production runs (following Adam Smith's advice about specialization) to cut costs and improve quality. The company should add facilities to increase this specialization in locations that reduced the shipping costs and time versus competitors for the most attractive current and potential customers.

As a result, the company was able to develop high market

share positions in selected low-cost items. Using that cost-effective base, it made an acquisition to expand geographically to help lower relative shipping costs, further enhancing its cost position versus competitors. With additional strategic acquisitions and subsequent plant expansions, the company was able to duplicate this success in other territories.

Another example of this customer-centered, cost-optimizing approach is Martin Marietta Materials, a producer of rock products for construction. While the company was owned by Martin Marietta (Martin Marietta Materials is now an independent public company), its management was encouraged to see its business as a total system to be optimized, much like the parent company did for its government clients in providing complex engineering solutions. For example, the parent company's CEO thought of a way to automate loading and billing so that trucks could be expedited through the company's facilities. This method saved time and money for both the customer and Martin Marietta Materials. Similar to the building materials company, the company has analyzed how to produce and deliver its rock products differently for each customer to capture the greatest combined raw material and shipping cost advantage over competitors. For a particular customer, quarried rock may come by ship from Nova Scotia, crushed rock from a neighboring state by rail car and sand by truck from a local gravel pit. A similar customer located 1,000 miles away would receive the same type of products from totally different facilities through other, more appropriate transportation methods customized for it. Optimizing when to use the three forms of transportation allows access to lower-cost rock sources than local competitors have while meeting customer delivery requirements.

> **Typical cost-reduction thinking stops at the shipping dock.**

You can see the problem with many cost reductions focused on particular operations. In either the building materials or rock products examples, the optimum company-wide cost solution for a single customer is to make complementary use of several company facilities and different transportation methods. In traditional cost analysis, each facility would be straining to deliver as much volume as possible itself to the customer in order to spread the fixed costs of that facility. In doing so, the operation would often be using higher-cost materials and transportation, and charging customers unnecessarily higher prices to cover those costs. No one would be looking at reducing the cost of serving individual customers while improving customer benefits through using other facilities and transportation means.

> When a company reaches out to reduce the customer's total costs, great things can happen.

LOOK TO REDUCE THE CUSTOMER'S TOTAL COSTS IN DEVELOPING THE OPTIMUM SOLUTION FOR A CUSTOMER

Have you ever lost a customer because your offering didn't work very well for that customer? Most people have. Undoubtedly, you were given several chances to improve the effectiveness of your offering before the customer cut you off. Had you been focusing on that customer's total costs from the beginning, you might have avoided this costly loss of business.

Typical cost-reduction thinking stops at the shipping dock. If a company's offerings cause customers to incur avoidable costs, most companies aren't aware of the issue. As a result, they don't work on eliminating those avoidable costs.

Naturally, if the product is so bad that the customer has to send it back, the manufacturer will pay attention. However, the focus will be on avoiding a repeat of the problem that led to the rejection. In dealing with that problem, it is unlikely that the supplier will look to how the product can be improved in ways that will reduce the customer's overall costs. This latter area, however, would be a more productive one to focus on.

When a company reaches out to reduce the customer's total costs, great things can happen. Xilinx designs and provides programmable semiconductors that can be used to operate electronic products. The company's customers are usually firms that make subassemblies or total electronic products with fairly short market lives. The costs of such electronic products decline rapidly with increased manufacturing volume. Often, the first reliable manufacturer will garner the bulk of the industry volume. As a result, reducing time and increasing effectiveness from beginning a product's design to reaching the market are critical. Xilinx's base technology helps by allowing a company to customize semiconductors with software, reducing the time needed to create the product design by simplifying the semiconductor design task. Xilinx also realized that its own engineers could write custom software faster than many customers, and began offering this service along with its products. Xilinx's service-enabled products can cut months from development time and save many millions in lost sales for the customer, while improving effectiveness and lowering the costs of the ultimate electronic products.

> **Why stop at the customer in this search for lower costs? Helping a customer's suppliers, partners and end users can be even more valuable.**

Create Cost Benefits for a Customer's Stakeholders

Why stop at the customer in this search for lower costs? Helping a customer's suppliers, partners and end users can be even more valuable. That's exactly what Business Objects discovered with its business intelligence solutions.

Business Objects makes it possible to extract more information from large databases to find business growth and cost-reduction opportunities. Previously, the person with an information need had to work with a programmer to translate a business question into programming language to obtain vital information from corporate systems. Simple requests such as "show me product profitability by region, where profitability is less than x %" can actually be quite complicated for a computer to process. Business Objects reduced that difficulty by creating a patented "semantic layer," basically using a set of standard business terms to shield questioners from the complexity of the underlying computer systems. The advantage is that questioners now have "self-service" access to all the information they need, when and where the information is required. Business Objects improved on its business model by creating ways for suppliers, partners, designers, distributors, customers and many end users to query each other's data. Naturally, this access only occurs when prior agreement to share information has been reached, and strong security is employed. As a result, each authorized person can enter the combined databases to find more ways to optimize the total cost solution. This kind of perceptual expansion will be standard in encouraging and directing cost-reduction questions in the upcoming years.[1]

Open the Door to Alternative Technologies That May Offer Cost Advantages for Your Entire Business System Extending from Suppliers to End Users

Increased benefits from an existing technology eventually run out. You couldn't get more letters from an electric typewriter handled by a fast, accurate typist until electronic typewriters with memories were invented. Then you could reuse parts of letters and merge lists with customized letters, producing far more while employing less-talented typists. Now a personal computer you use yourself can launch hundreds of millions of customized e-mails during the blink of an eye.

What we have been reviewing reconfigures the current state of the cost-reduction art into more effective system solutions for customers and their stakeholders. Technology advances can play a role in creating such improved business models. The potential benefits of such advances are often limited by a too-narrow focus on how the particular performance of a certain technology compares to the existing alternatives in terms of a company's costs at a point in time. Such comparisons are flawed for many reasons. First, the current performance of a new technology will often be far below its future and potential performance. Second, many technologies can substitute for one another. As a result, a technology with lower performance may still win in the marketplace if its costs are low enough. Third, performance that makes the end user more productive is what ultimately counts. Achieving that desir-able result can sometimes make higher costs sensible for the producer. As a result of their narrow focus on adding technology-based performance capabili-ties, technical experts are often in the worst position to consider the cost-reduction potential of their technologies. Those who look at applications from the end-user's perspective usually see the best opportunities.

> **Find acquisitions that allow both companies to create an improved business model that adds many new dimensions of customer and stakeholder benefits and cost reductions.**

QLogic is a company that understands the significance of the end-user's costs. As a result, the company's first priority is to locate technologies that reduce end-user's costs for employing mass com-puter data storage. The company's products enable communica-tion between individual computers and mass storage. Over time, the company has evolved from providing components to deliver-ing bundles of technology, as solutions to rapidly changing end-user needs. In testing the potential of such technologies, QLogic considers not only end-use effectiveness but also how the tech-nologies will affect time-to-market for the intermediary suppliers to the end users. Exceptional ability to evaluate and master new technologies has guided the company to unusually rapid growth, quadrupling its revenues between 1997 and 2000 before the stor-age industry "bust" of 2001–2002 arrived. During the bust, QLogic had a much smaller and briefer decline in revenues and profits than the average storage technology provider.

Locate Partners and Acquisitions Who Benefit from Being Part of Your Company's Business Model

Refer to the example of Sybron Dental Specialties in the Prologue to see one way acquisitions can be used to eliminate harmful costs from both the acquiring and acquired company.

Here's an even better way to acquire. Find acquisitions that allow both companies to create an improved business model that adds many new dimensions of customer and stakeholder benefits and cost reductions. Beckman Coulter has successfully pursued this business model innovation approach. The company was formed by the merger of two companies with complementary product lines in the biomedical testing industry. While many companies would have primarily examined the opportunity to reduce costs by consolidating headquarters, sales activities and manufacturing, Beckman Coulter's CEO, Mr. John P. Wareham, saw those areas as only the beginning of the cost-reduction possibilities.

Mr. Wareham had headed Beckman Instruments, Inc. before its acquisition of Coulter Corporation. Beckman Instruments was well known for its expertise in simplifying and automating tests to make them more reliable, faster and less costly. He dreamed of putting all of the Beckman and Coulter tests into the same automated equipment and processes. Because of the merger and this business model vision, such automation equipment is now being offered and provides a biomedical lab with broader

> **Do you spend much time finding ways to satisfy your needs for almost free?**

testing capabilities in ways that reduce both Beckman Coulter's costs and the costs of the laboratory running the tests. At the same time, physicians and patients get their tests done faster and more reliably.

Not content with that set of improvements, Mr. Wareham has now expanded the business model vision to focus the combined operations of the two formerly independent companies in a new way. Beckman Coulter is creating a linked set of technologies and tests that begin with fundamental medical research and end up in patient diagnosis and treatment. By conducting all the biological measurements for a disease with consistent processes and chemical reagents, illnesses can be more easily and inexpensively studied, diagnosed and treated. An example comes in the company's technology for detecting prostate cancer (the PSA and free PSA test). Once a tedious manual test, the test is now automatically processed on the firm's analyzer in fifteen minutes. As a result, many lives will be saved while medical costs drop. By expanding the company's line of testing technologies through acquisition, Beckman Coulter is now in a position to provide similar benefits as the new generations of genetic and protein-based tests are developed.

RATHER THAN GET IT WHOLESALE, ACCESS WHAT YOU NEED FOR CLOSE TO FREE

Your company probably puts a lot of effort into getting the lowest prices for what you need. But do you spend much time finding ways to satisfy those needs for almost free instead?

Savvy companies are increasingly developing and providing knowledge-based advantages for customers and end users as part of their business models. Usually this knowledge can be applied to reduce customers' and end-users' costs or increase the attractiveness of their customers' offerings. In developing and providing knowledge-based advantages for customers and end users, you have a choice. Your company can either study how to optimize that value-adding activity for customers and their stakeholders as part of an improved business model, or you can ask the most expert suppliers to help you create that better business model. Chances are that the latter approach is not only free, but will lead to a more effective solution. For example, if you are designing a new restaurant concept, Ecolab's expertise in cleanliness best practices can help you design a building and locate your equipment so that your restaurant will be easier to maintain in optimally healthful ways.

Companies have often relied on suppliers for cost-improvement advice. Increasingly, firms are looking to their customers to provide the same sort of help. After all, who is a better judge of their own needs than the customers themselves? The Web site eBay asks its customers to rate sellers so that customers can improve the service they receive through their selection of a more reliable seller. Online retailers like Amazon.com and Barnesandnoble.com get free product reviews from their customers, which are then used to help other customers find products they like. These ratings also allow the retailers to suggest other items that have most appealed to customers who have tried both.

Shareholders can likewise be a powerful source of free expertise. By providing discount coupons or reduced rates to shareholders, some companies get reviews of their operations from concerned customers with a stake in the outcome. Marriott has been a good

> **Whom do you trust to help provide for your customers?**

example of this approach in providing discounts on hotel rooms for all shareholders and encouraging feedback from these investors.

As we have touched on before, outside professionals can also be attracted to provide free or low-cost inputs if you can make the tasks appealing enough to them. Combinations of making the activities fun, intellectually rewarding and prestigious can be helpful in this regard. For instance, our publisher, Berrett-Koehler, has a network of outstanding business professionals who review each new manuscript and receive a modest honorarium for their efforts. These reviewers add a lot of value in making the books more accurate, interesting to read and simpler. The reviewers benefit by seeing new material sooner than it is available in book stores and enjoy the satisfaction of helping knowledge advance more rapidly and well. At the end of the process, reviewers are invited to have lunch with the

> **Companies are learning that the only thing that works better than focus is . . . even more focus.**

authors, an occasion enjoyed by all. One reviewer told us that she enjoys the contact with new ideas, being part of the Berrett-Koehler community and the small gifts she gives herself with her honoraria. The potential to do much more in this area remains for most companies.

Outsourcing as a Core Part of Your Business Model

Whom do you trust to help provide for your customers? Many companies only trust those who work on the company premises and receive company payroll checks. While that approach increases the potential access to information, it may also create higher costs than being more trusting of deserving outsiders. Studies of best practices show that larger companies operate in most activities somewhere around the level of average, with some serious advantages and deficiencies in a few areas. Smaller companies often have more deficiency areas. Why not turn your challenges over to caring world-class people and organizations instead, especially where it is important to be as good as possible? In the process, you will undoubtedly lower your costs. Your effectiveness in delivering customer and stakeholder value is also likely to improve.

Companies are learning that the only thing that works better than focus is . . . even more focus. Outsourcing is an important way to help achieve greater focus. Well-chosen specialists in those outsourced activities can often produce levels of effectiveness and timeliness that your company could never match. Data storage giant EMC's use of outsourcing suppliers is a good example. While the firm spends billions on hardware and software development tied to improving the performance of mass storage for its customers, EMC's manufacturing is a simple activity. The company puts together a few subassemblies that are produced by others, and then places its attention on a rigorous, days-long testing process. The assembled products are run twenty-four hours a day in very hot and cold environments, and put through heavy vibration to simulate shipping to find if there are any loose connections. If a component fails a single test, it is replaced by one that has already gone through the entire test cycle. As a result, EMC's customers get great reliability based on the firm's outstanding component suppliers and EMC's own "torture-testing" methods. If instead EMC made and assembled all of its own components, product costs would be higher and reliability would be lower. In a recent move, Dell Computer has hired EMC to design some of its new storage products. These products will undoubtedly benefit from both Dell's superior manufacturing skill and EMC's design experience.

Most companies doubt that they can use very much outsourcing. Yet Cisco Systems, one of the world's largest technology companies, outsources everything it can, including the development of the new technologies it relies on to upgrade its products. This approach allows the company to be more flexible in creating and delivering new solutions for customers. By accessing helpful new technologies faster, costs are lower for customers and Cisco.

Reduce Your Cost of Capital to Get an Additional Discount on Everything You Buy

How would you like it if you could get an additional discount on almost everything you buy, after having negotiated your best deal? That's what reducing your cost of capital (especially your cost of equity) can do for your purchases.

Most CEOs are delighted if their company's common stock can sell at around the industry average price/earnings ratio. If they do better than that, they are even happier and will usually avoid using the stock to buy anything in order to protect the current price/earnings multiple. Both views are major missed opportunities. As a result of these limited perceptions, almost all companies today lack the fundamental skill to create and sustain a stock-price premium that can be used to lower the company's cost of providing offerings.[2]

For a sustained price/earnings premium, a company must use its stock in ways that shareholders approve. When that happens, paying with premium-priced stock then provides the equivalent of a discount compared to competitors on everything the company purchases, from other companies to compensation to supplies. For example, one company may be looking to purchase another for cash by borrowing the money. If the company that is purchased earns more cash than the after-tax interest charges on the money borrowed to buy it, the acquiring company sees its cash flow per share rise. If not, the acquisition is a cash-flow drain. If a competing acquirer has a high stock-price multiple, that firm can afford to exceed its borrowing-based, cash flow per share breakeven and profitably pay a much higher price for the acquired company. Stock-based purchases also can defer capital gains tax bills for the sellers. If shareholders like the idea enough, the acquirer's stock-price multiple may even expand because of the acquisition. Who's more likely to succeed in making and operating the acquisition? All other things being equal, the premium-priced stock acquirer has the advantage.

Companies with rapid growth in stock price can turn this advantage into cash cost savings on their key employees' compensation. Employees are often interested in getting low-priced stock options (such as were available in the fall of 2002) rather than cash both because of the upside potential and because tax rates are lower on this income. Further, stock options historically didn't affect company reported earnings as much as cash payments do, unless a company chose the option to expense the options. Many people advocate requiring all public companies to expense employee stock option grants, and some companies began to do so voluntarily in 2002. Regardless of the accounting rules, however, when a company purchases its own shares at prices far enough below the option price, the stock-option grants can be a source of cash profit for the company on which no taxes need be paid. That's the law. Since most stocks are volatile, quick-witted managements with extra cash can dramatically reduce employment costs during temporary stock-price swoons.

Of the companies in our study base, Cisco Systems was the most effective in building an industry-leading position through spending low-cost capital during the 1990s. Competitors were often bowled over by the seemingly limitless prices that Cisco paid with high-multiple stock to acquire new technologies and management teams. Naturally, during the technology bust, the value of the stock Cisco paid with shrank. But the company continued to benefit from its high-priced acquisitions by gaining market share during the industry decline.

Most important, companies can simply issue stock to get the cash to make other kinds of investments and purchases. When your source of cash is cheap enough, it's like getting a discount on whatever the money is used for.

Privately held companies can get some of these benefits by creating performance-based incentives for employees and suppliers to purchase equity. Unless the incentives are too large, such investments can also help align stakeholder interests in more positive ways.

Borrowing costs can often be reduced by providing lenders with options to convert debt into equity, or by securing guarantees and contracts from more creditworthy companies.

Some financially driven efforts to reduce costs routinely create harm instead. These setbacks occur when companies unsuccessfully chase what appear to be cost reductions for the old business model and waste resources that could have gone into business model innovation. For example, public companies seeking to lower capital costs should be careful to avoid the aggressive tax schemes that many accounting firms and investment banks promote. These "smoke and mirrors" structures are often legal under the tax code, but are just as likely to be overreaching in terms of accounting and financial disclosure rules. Such schemes

> **Spend ten hours examining the potential sales impact of any cost reduction for every hour you spend considering how it will improve your business model.**

may temporarily pretty up profits and the balance sheet, but are also likely to destroy credibility and the value of securities when disclosed. Prime examples of such manipulative structures were Enron's loans from money-center banks that were packaged to look like profitable energy trades, temporarily boosting publicly reported corporate profits and cash flow in a deceptive way.

AVOID THE MOST HARMFUL MISTAKES AND BREAK BAD HABITS

Like a mountain climber ascending a challenging peak, business model innovation progress is usually slow and more likely to occur on some routes than on others. Danger needlessly dogs your progress when you choose some routes over others. Regardless of your route, trial and error are essential to progress. Make the wrong mistake on the right route, though, and you can have a disastrous fall. In this section, we focus on which mistakes to avoid . . . and how to do so.

Spend ten hours examining the potential sales impact of any cost reduction for every hour you spend considering how it will improve your business model. The most valuable cost reductions will be those, like Beckman Coulter made following its merger, that lead to better quality, more effective performance and greater benefits for customers, end users and other stakeholders.

If you are careful, you can find sales-expanding ways to establish lower-cost business models almost as easily as methods that harm profitable sales. Care in selecting the right sales-expanding cost reductions is a key secret of the most successful companies that routinely improve their business models. Choosing correctly makes all of the difference to your long-run success!

Each time you look at ways to use cost reductions to improve your business model, you will benefit by reinforcing a focus on adding profitable sales in a variety of ways. For instance, consider how cost reductions can help you be more attractive to certain customers where you have competitive profit margin advantages. On another occasion, you might consider cost reductions that can help increase sales to the most important trend-setting customers. At another time, your attention might focus on customers whose volume would fine-tune your operations to become more efficient.

Chess masters warn against the dangers of too much emphasis on attacking their opponents. While constructing a seemingly potent offense, great care must be taken in examining their own vulnerabilities or they may leave themselves unguarded from counterattacks. Similarly, although you're looking to help profitable sales, you can easily make a mistake while doing so that costs you valuable benefits. To avoid those most harmful mistakes, shift the burden of proof in your thinking. In examining each potential innovation, require that the proposed cost improvement overcome these presumptions:

- Profitable customers will be lost.
- Unprofitable customers will be added.
- Costs squeezed out in one area will reappear elsewhere in larger amounts due to mistakes in estimating system effects.

- Top-performing employees will be lost.
- Weaker-performing employees will be attracted and retained.
- Quality and performance of your offerings will drop.
- Cash flow will be harmed.
- Regulators will investigate and find you in the wrong.
- Taxation will be adjusted to penalize what you are doing.
- Customers and end users will sue and win large judgments against you.
- Partners will be lost.
- Good suppliers will stop providing their best ideas to you.
- Lenders will be concerned and alienated, causing interest costs to rise.
- Negative publicity will occur.
- Stock price will drop.

> **For a typical manufacturing company, a 1 percent sales decline will offset the profits from a 6 percent reduction in payroll costs.**

Be sure to add to this list other negative results that you've experienced in looking to cut costs to expand your profits.

Avoid the Big Mistake—Hurting Sales

When is a cost reduction always a profit decrease? When the cost reduction drives away too many profitable customers!

Whenever you read in the financial press about a company making a large cost reduction, check whether the same firm has made such a move before in recent history. Chances are that the announcement you read is just the latest in a series of such cuts. If current layoffs and facility shutdowns are such a good idea, why didn't the company make all of the changes during the last round of layoffs and shutdowns? The usual answer is because the company's sales have since fallen below its budgets. By examining these cases, you'll be reminded of the customer-reducing effects of many cost cuts.

Most ways companies cut costs now will eliminate some sales. In fact, some of these so-called cost reductions will permanently lower earnings because the profit impact from lost sales will more than offset lower costs. For a typical manufacturing company, a 1 percent sales decline will offset the profits from a 6 percent reduction in payroll costs. Think about that ratio the next time someone in your company proposes cutting back on customer service personnel.

While cost-cutting ideas are being generated, more analysis goes into examining how they will affect costs at budgeted or estimated sales levels than into how the sales levels themselves will be affected. This emphasis should be reversed.

Layoffs, for instance, can mean delays in providing existing and new offerings, poorer service and worse quality. Do those degradations in performance help sales? Usually not. These harmful effects occur as many productive employees choose to leave for better opportunities with generous severance payments in their pockets, and processes are disrupted as work is reassigned to those with less experience in the key activities.

> **Some other cost-reduction practices are so harmful that you need to stop them immediately or avoid beginning them.**

Why do companies take such actions, even when the actions haven't worked in the past? Usually the board of directors and lenders want to see short-term costs reduced when profits lag below budget. Company executive bonuses often reward layoffs, because the bonus calculations for a given year look at this year's profit rather than future lost revenues and earnings. Executives also keep their own jobs safer this way in the near-term. They've done something that looks like it may help, even when it doesn't. As an example of this harmful approach, a well-known CEO once advised his people when profits were under budget: "Do something. It doesn't matter what. There's always time to fix your mistakes later."

Focus on Cash-Based Accounting

Some other cost-reduction practices are so harmful that you need to stop them immediately or avoid beginning them. How costs are measured is one such area of required reform. Begin by being sure to look at cash-flow rather than accounting costs while working on business model innovation. Business people usually agree that their job is to earn a profit above the cost of the capital they use. To do that, you often have the choice of spending an accounting dollar to save a real one or vice versa. Which should you choose? We favor reality over the imaginary in calculating profits, as most people do. Cash is the reality, and accounting is the imaginary when it comes to the profit and loss statement.

Profit and loss accounting is a homogenized, convenient way to learn how a company did in overall profitability between two points in time. However, the more detail you examine using accounting-based costs, the more likely you are to draw the wrong conclusions. For instance, accounting "standard costs" to provide an offering will not match what your actual cash costs are. If you improve the throughput of your system, for instance, you will often see your average accounting costs per unit rise as more standard costs are incurred while actual cash costs per unit fall. That paradoxical result occurs because the standard costs are based on earlier assumptions about your business process rather than on your current experience. For an excellent discussion of how to avoid being misled by this phenomenon, see the business novel, *The Goal* (2nd revised edition, HighBridge, 2000), by Eliyahu M. Goldratt and Jeff Cox.

Another problem is that if you want to remove out-of-date equipment from service and start using more effective equipment, you often have to take an accounting charge to the profit and loss statement. Actually, you already incurred the cash cost when you bought the out-of-date equipment. You are being required to take all of the remaining capital expense deferred by accounting rules on your profit and loss statement now, because you don't plan to use the equipment any more (that's probably part of the reason why GM was slow to replace its spray-painting processes).

Business thinkers now find Activity-Based Costing an improved way to comprehend the cash costs you incur if you operate in one way versus another. Performing ABC analysis can be helpful to you in understanding the cost potential of different business models.

KEY QUESTIONS

- *How can your business model be changed to increase revenues and cut costs much faster than your competitors?* By starting with a focus on expanding revenues, you are less likely to fall into the trap of working on profit- and volume-reducing business model alternatives.

- *How can we get suppliers to pay us?* This question is a more aggressive variation on asking yourself how to get resources for free. If the connection to your organization is valuable enough, people will pay you to have an association. For instance, cookbook authors are usually expected to agree to buy a large number of books before a publisher will take them on. And these authors seldom receive advances from publishers because there is an oversupply of both cookbooks and those who wish to write them. Open your mind to places where free or lower-cost resources can be made available to your company.

- *How can more people productively work on finding cost-based business model improvements for you?* Innovation in this area is in part a numbers game. An organization that has more people thinking about cost-based business model innovations should come up with more and better alternatives. Obviously, if everyone is only working on this question, basic business doesn't get done. Start by having a reputation for wanting these ideas, and recognizing and rewarding those who produce them. Go on to make it clear that both business model improvements and daily operations need to be done well, or the quality of your operations may falter.

- *How can the search for cost-based business model innovations be separated in peoples' minds from unappealing and ineffective past cost reductions?* Basically, you won't get much attention, enthusiasm or creativity if people feel that the activity is simply designed to lead to another layoff or painful restructuring. What promises can you afford to make and be sure to keep that will make everyone feel more secure? For example, are you in a position to promise that there will be no layoffs for the next year? If you can't, can you promise more aid in helping employees find new positions?

- *Where can you find expertise to reduce costs in areas where you know little?* A good example of such an area is creating a stock-price multiple premium that can be used to reduce the cash costs of compensation, new assets and cost-reducing acquisitions. Chances are that neither your company nor your company's investment banking representative has enough expertise in this area. Where can you find help? Begin by talking to executives in other companies who have been successful in this activity. Ask them how they developed their expertise, and how they would advise someone to do so now.

- *What cost-reduction business models would most effectively reinforce the positive personal values of those who work in your company?* Cost reduction is often pursued in ways that cause people to feel they are selling out their values. If you can turn that feeling around, you can unleash creativity as people find congruence between new cost-reduction-based business models and their own lives. Beckman Coulter succeeded, in part, because people in the company are excited about helping more people avoid illnesses and recover from them more rapidly. The organization shares a common belief that better, faster and less costly biomedical tests are one of the best ways to overcome disease.

- *How can your company make it easier to find new business model advantages based on cost reductions?* Many people report success through creating teams to work on these concepts and questions. Teams can help people feel more comfortable and gain experience faster. By combining many different perspectives, knowledge and skills in a single team, you enhance the scope of what can be appreciated and effectively considered. Visiting companies with more experience in this arena can also help.

Spend enough time to understand what they do differently from your company to find better cost-reduction-based business models.

- *How can cost reductions greatly expand your company's ability to provide more benefits and pricing that customers and end users desire?* Cost reductions are seldom considered as the launch pad for more benefits and desirable price structures. Like all new perspectives, this one can be fruitful for you. Many people find the question fascinating, which helps to generate useful initiatives. A good example is the innovation of charging double tolls in one direction of a bridge or tunnel, rather than the regular toll in both directions. You only need half the toll collectors, and travelers save time in one direction.

PART TWO

PROVIDE SUSTAINED BENEFITS FOR ALL STAKEHOLDERS

Lack of money is no obstacle.
Lack of an idea is an obstacle.
—Anonymous

The first sweet flush of business model innovation success can create a giddy urge to celebrate the completion of a difficult task. But viewing one success as an end to your business model innovation process can threaten to dismantle the foundations of that success.

If profits and scarce resources are then unwisely consumed, crucial new investments may be postponed or become unaffordable. Lacking these investments, profit growth will eventually decline.

> **Viewing one success as an end to your business model innovation process can threaten to dismantle the foundations of that success.**

After installing a successful business model innovation, another new danger arises. Some stakeholders may begin to satisfy their wants and needs at the expense of others, causing cooperation to break down. Performance declines . . . and competitive advantage ebbs away. Profits soon fall into a trough.

Alternatively, an initial business model success can lead to another pitfall: overexpanding by taking on too much financial risk, especially through excess borrowings. Aggressive growth usually means taking on more business risk, as well. Combine lots of financial and business risk, and you have created a dangerous company environment that can leave you without firm footing in turbulent times and prone to experience painful falls. Wise leaders focus on reducing unnecessary business and financial risk. They rely instead on future rounds of business model innovation to stay ahead of competitors, grow and improve financial performance.

How can these potentially vicious, downward-spiraling cycles be turned into virtuous, growth trajectories? Let's look more closely at the lemonade stand to answer this question.

As a parent of the two children who own and operate the lemonade stand, you encourage your children to ask customers about their needs. In these conversations, your children learn that people would like to spend more time at the stand conversing with others. There's a problem though. While the children have lawn chairs to sit on, there are none for customers. Standing quickly becomes tiresome for older customers and parents carrying younger children.

Although your household has two additional lawn chairs that could be pressed into service, more are needed. Yet the cost of a single lawn chair is equal to the profits from many days of operating the stand. What should your children do?

As you learned in Part One, it's good to test the potential value of an investment or an action before spending much money. You can add the two extra lawn chairs from your household and borrow some others from neighbors or relatives. If that's not enough, you can spread beach towels that customers can sit on. If sales and profits increase enough as a result of making more lawn chairs available, your children can save from their profits to gradually purchase lawn chairs. By doing so, they will eventually replace the borrowed lawn chairs with ones they have bought. Notice that borrowing money to buy the chairs without testing could be harmful to the stand's cash flow if the additional chairs did not expand sales and profits. Also, if customers prefer lounging on the beach towels, no more chairs are needed.

After any needed chairs are purchased, your children should think about the future. Lemonade sales are likely to be lower in the fall, winter and spring than in the summer, when they started the stand. Totally different products, like hot cider, hot chocolate and coffee, may be needed in those seasons. These beverages may require different equipment, such as thermos jugs to keep the drinks hot. Unless your children save and prepare for the lean times for lemonade sales and necessary future investment needs, they may see their profits disappear until the warm weather returns. Like the lemonade stand, all businesses have to reinvest in further business model innovations and build a buffer against lean times.

In the meantime, your children must be considerate of others as they operate the lemonade stand. Otherwise, they will have no customers. When that happens, almost nothing will save the business.

A sound grounding in ethical values and morals is a good beginning. Your personal example and your family's moral heritage will help create the right kind of concern for others and behavior toward them. Youthful lessons will become good lifetime habits. Years from now, these same values will remind your children to make the choices that better business leaders and good citizens should make.

Pursuing business model innovation in constructive ways, providing for required investments, building a buffer for lean times and establishing a good ethical base for your company are discussed in Chapter 4, along with ideas for how to apply these important activities in your company.

As the lemonade stand operates, you may discover that some of the initial ways of rewarding stakeholders are a mistake. For instance, some parents and children may balk at unlimited lemonade as a substitute for higher pay to work at the stand. Parents and children may prefer a trip to a local theme park as an end-of-summer treat for workers. If making that theme park incentive available will improve the morale and performance of those working at the stand, your children would do well to persuade you to help them organize the trip.

Also, since parents are paying for most of the lemonade, they may want a lower price for their whole family if their children are also working at the stand. Otherwise, these parents may feel that they are subsidizing outsized profits for your children. Naturally, their situation needs to be addressed in a fair way.

You and your children tentatively agree on a formula to set fair prices and wages, sharing the cash flow benefits of the lemonade stand. Your children should freely explain their thinking with customers and workers, and give them a chance to comment and suggest improvements. You want to use a process that makes everyone feel respected. You also want to pick a formula that leaves everyone feeling fairly treated.

> **Our interviews with business model innovators persuaded us that they consciously attempt to reward all stakeholders fairly and in ways that the stakeholders prefer.**

Your children should also ask about how to share the benefits with neighbors. Perhaps some time should be spent picking up litter from the stand that ends up in neighboring yards and gutters. While there, why not pick up any other litter so that everyone has a cleaner environment?

We live in a time when CEO compensation can be measured in hundreds of millions of dollars paid in a single year when long-held stock options are exercised. As a result, you may feel that this notion of fairly sharing the benefits of a business among stakeholders is out-of-date and unrealistic. Did you know that there's little association between companies paying huge CEO compensation and their stakeholders receiving rich benefits? In fact, some studies have suggested that too much financial incentive for leaders is harmful for a company's long-term performance.

What did we learn about the leaders of business model innovating companies? Although many of these company leaders are wealthy, most got that way by founding the company and owning company shares that were paid for with their own savings and sweat. Sure, they got good salaries, bonuses and stock options over the years, but these payments were usually minor sources of their wealth. Our interviews with business model innovators persuaded us that they consciously attempt to reward all stakeholders fairly and in ways that the stakeholders prefer. In most cases, they demonstrated more interest in making their business model innovations work for everyone, than in their own financial rewards. In Chapter 5, you can learn more about how these CEOs rewarded all stakeholders fairly in ways the stakeholders prefer, and why that is important.

CHAPTER 4

FURTHER IMPROVE YOUR BUSINESS MODEL AND BUILD A BUFFER FOR LEAN TIMES

The toughest thing about success is that you've
got to keep on being a success.
—Irving Berlin

The first round of successful business model innovation tests will show you a variety of ways to create new competitive advantages. Implementing the results of those tests will impel you forward, like a rocket sled on a test track, toward a stronger industry position. You will be so busy once you deploy these innovations that many important tasks may lack attention. How can you be sure that needed innovation experiments are conducted? How can you prepare for lean times ahead? This chapter shows how leaders can build an improved business model innovation foundation by employing a healthy vision of future innovation and encouraging solid values. Leaders also have to prepare for temporary setbacks by avoiding unproductive investments, keeping business and financial risk at levels appropriate for troubled times, and building the right organizational focus.

Good business models generate more resources than are needed for the company's future innovations and growth. They also expand stakeholder resources. What does such a business model look like? We immediately thought of Mr. Richard L. Sumberg, head of The Financial Advisors, another CEO whom we met through Mr. Loren Carlson's CEO Roundtable.

Founded in 1991 by Mr. Sumberg, The Financial Advisors organization is based in beautiful Andover, Massachusetts, home of Phillips Academy. Mr. Sumberg had owned and operated a tool distribution business for fifteen years before obtaining the education that a financial advisor needs. He next worked in the field for six years before founding his company. Starting from a small base, the firm now has eight professionals who provide financial planning and investment advisory services to hundreds of individuals, families, businesses and charitable organizations. The firm has expertise in almost every area where a client may need help, and knows of specialists who are available to supplement its knowledge.

The essence of Mr. Sumberg's business philosophy is earning trust and caring about stakeholders. Why get financial advice if you don't trust the person providing it? Why get advice from people who care more about their own income than your best interests? Working with Mr. Sumberg is like being with a helpful, knowledgeable older brother who's looking out for you. Even when he just listens, you feel better.

These professionals do more than just dispense honest, useful financial advice. They help people with any of their problems in a thoughtful and respectful way. A client may call to discuss a parent who is ill or a child who is in trouble with drugs. On occasion, they have found criminal attorneys to help a client's family member solve a problem. Such helping is emotionally rewarding for those who work at The Financial Advisors. Trust and mutual understanding are deepened in the process.

That trust and helpfulness translate into continuing relationships, expanded assignments and referrals to other family members and friends. Even when the economy or the stock market is doing poorly, Mr. Sumberg's business grows because people know that they can trust him and his colleagues to provide knowledge-able, caring service.

Mr. Sumberg realizes that providing the highest quality of personal service is critical to his business's success. As a result, he carefully recruits new professionals from among experienced people who share his values. He also realizes that he cannot grow the firm faster than he can provide outstanding service to all clients. Otherwise, clients might have their trust and financial resources needlessly put at risk.

After a few years of operating this business, Mr. Sumberg began to think about how to make the firm's expertise available to more people. He realized that most people cannot afford to get objective financial advice. He thought of a way that simple financial advice could be provided inexpensively for people whose financial circumstances are uncomplicated. The firm's business model innovation for these people was the NET.Worth program. For $375 or less, an individual or family can get a year's worth of financial advice on the telephone from a personal advisor. Mr. Sumberg was assisted by his son, Alexander, in developing this service.

Having a business model that provides a growing cash flow and emotional bounty has given Mr. Sumberg and his colleagues the chance to enhance the many lives they touch. At the same time, clients see their financial security grow . . . along with their peace of mind. As a result, clients can better care for their families and their favorite community concerns.

Compare this business model to the one used by many brokerage firms. Trainees are brought in to sell their friends and relatives on their stock-picking expertise, when they may, in fact, have little. When those contacts are exhausted, the neophyte brokers start calling hundreds of investors who have accounts at other firms. The advice is almost always to "buy" what the firm is pushing. Often, that "buy" recommendation of a NASDAQ stock for an individual investor matches what an institutional client (pension fund or mutual fund) of the brokerage firm is selling or the brokerage firm itself owns too much of. When individual investors can be attracted to buy what the institution is selling, the brokerage firm makes money on both the buyer and seller as the market maker without having to put up any capital of its own. How much caring, unbiased advice can you expect in such a situation?

Most people would prefer Mr. Sumberg's caring, objective business model for obtaining their financial advice.

GET READY TO CREATE
BETTER BUSINESS MODELS

The largest harvests only occur if farming practices improve, the weather cooperates and the necessary investments are made in obtaining better seed, applying fertilizer, controlling weeds and pests, and providing the right amount of moisture during dry spells. On this firm base, surpluses will be harvested that can be used to acquire and bring more land under cultivation. Some of the surplus should first be kept for lean times, when crops are ruined or prices are low. The farm's lessons should be applied to building your company through continuing business model innovation.

> The sooner you begin to imagine the best ways to pursue ongoing business model innovation, the better.

Before implementing this chapter's concepts, you will probably have made innovations that either generated added customer or end-user benefits at the same or lower prices, improved price structures, or lowered customer and end-user costs as well as your own. Most people will then wait until the new business model has been in place a while before starting to design the next innovation. That instinct, while understandable, is misguided. The sooner you begin to imagine the best ways to pursue ongoing business model innovation, the better.

Consider an example of what's involved in successfully making a major change. Let's look at a group of campers getting ready for an unusually long hike in a remote locale. Each person needs to be in good physical condition for the hike. Getting in shape might mean an exercise program, following a physician's examination and testing for health and fitness. Depending on what sort of hiking is involved, special equipment may need to be purchased. Hikers without experience using this special equipment will need training and practice. Those who don't have proper hiking boots will need to purchase and break in the boots. If the hike is to take place in an area where hiking is restricted, such as Yosemite, special permits may be needed. If you want to stay overnight at campgrounds with limited capacity, like at the bottom of the Grand Canyon, you may need reservations months ahead of time. If airline travel is involved, buying tickets well in advance secures lower fares. You'll also need to find the best way to ship the bulkiest hiking and camping gear. Airlines don't let you take very much baggage any more for free. Many more steps have to be planned and executed well in advance if you want to have the best possible experience. Skip those steps or leave them to the last minute, and your hike will be impaired in otherwise avoidable ways. As a result, investigation into such details should begin early. Similarly, the best business model innovations spring from advance investigation, thinking and preparation. The most important area is establishing a vision to guide future innovation.

THINK ABOUT CREATING AN IDEAL VISION TO GUIDE YOUR FUTURE BUSINESS MODEL INNOVATIONS

Successful innovation experiences are necessary, but not sufficient, to take you to a powerful, new vision. What's missing? First, you may not have the resources to implement all of your successful tests immediately. In that case, what is the right combination of improvements to emphasize first? Second, varying combinations of successful tests can have remarkably different meanings and potential for directing future business models. Choose a combination of features that creates a powerful new vector for a long time to come. This chapter can help you anticipate how to do that by selecting which competitive advantages to continually

> The best business models create more stakeholder resources than are consumed in a higher ratio than competitors provide.

169

emphasize. Third, expanding some innovations may create cross-purposes and harmful effects among stakeholders. How can those limitations be understood and avoided? Business model visions are very helpful for this purpose. Fourth, some innovations will stimulate opportunities for later business model improvements. Those innovation combinations are best that generate the most resource-creating new opportunities. How can opportunities for future business model innovations be identified sooner and more clearly?

The best business models contain elements we earlier described as ideal in the introduction to Part One. Now is a good time to review and explain more about those concepts. These elements can guide you to choose and implement better future innovations. Incorporate these principles into your business model innovation vision to stay focused on the most productive innovation opportunities.

Expand Resources Faster Than You Consume Them

The best business models create more stakeholder resources than are consumed in a higher ratio than competitors provide. Think of this effectiveness as creating more financial and nonmonetary benefits for all those who come into contact with the company. The greater the ratio of benefits provided to stakeholders compared to the resources required, the better the model.

> The best business model impresses each stakeholder that she or he will benefit more by encouraging the success of this company's business model than by supporting any other, or by ignoring the company.

Cytyc is a good example of providing a more productive business model. As a start-up, the firm pioneered a new form of Pap-smear testing that is more accurate than its predecessor. If a woman has cervical cancer and the disease is discovered early, she can almost always be cured. Previously, many women received erroneous information about their risk of cervical cancer. Some were told that they did not have cancer when they did, and thus received no treatment.

Others heard that they did have cancer when they didn't and were frightened by an incorrect test result. These patients may have received unneeded treatment if a repeat test report was also faulty. The health, economic and psychological benefits for women having the tests are obvious. The cost of treating early stages of this cancer is also much less expensive than starting later. Early treatment means that insurers and health care providers need to do less in the long run. Those who pay for health insurance will have lower premiums than would otherwise occur. The community benefits by having these women live longer, healthier lives. Those who care about the women benefit from avoiding worry and having to provide less care. Employees, partners, suppliers, shareholders and lenders benefit from Cytyc's success as long as benefits from the company's technology are better than what competitors offer.

Make It More Attractive for Stakeholders to Support Your Company Than Anyone Else's

The best business model impresses each stakeholder that she or he will benefit more by encouraging the success of this company's business model than by supporting any other, or by ignoring the company. When the competitive advantage in providing for each current and potential stakeholder is large, the company's best interests become the individual stakeholder's best self-interests as well. This alignment can reverse the tension that occurs when a company's stakeholders' interests are at odds.

Haemonetics's business model offers an example of clearly unique stakeholder benefits. Haemonetics is a global company engaged in the design, manufacture and marketing of automated blood processing systems. Blood banks and hospitals use these systems. The company's business model vision is making safer and more economical blood components readily available. Many of the company's innovations have followed this vision.

For example, in the late 1980s and early 1990s there was worldwide concern about transmitting viruses such as HIV through blood transfusions. One of the technologies invented by

Haemonetics, intraoperative autotransfusion, addressed this issue. This technology allows for salvaging and washing of the red cells (a critical blood component) that would otherwise be lost by a patient during surgery. As a result, patients having high blood loss surgeries are less likely to need red cells that are not their own.

> The best business models seek to equitably share with all stakeholders the economic benefits they generate.

In recent years, the company has followed its business model vision to address growing shortages of donated blood components. One solution was to offer a new intraoperative salvage device allowing patients to receive their own blood products in a broader range of surgeries. Another solution came from introducing systems that allow blood centers to collect multiple units of needed blood components from a single blood donation without harm to the donor. With the new blood donation technology, costs are reduced, safety can be improved and donors get the satisfaction of helping more people.

Many stakeholders benefit from Haemonetics's business model vision and technology, including the patient, the patient's family and friends, the hospital, blood donors and other patients needing blood. For each of these stakeholders, there is a clear benefit from having more, safer and less expensive blood components available when needed. Satisfying this need is essential to the economic health of Haemonetics's employees, partners, suppliers, shareholders and lenders. Each can also feel great satisfaction from having a role in supplying the many desirable benefits the company produces for other stakeholders.

Fairly Share Benefits with All Stakeholders

The best business models seek to equitably share with all stakeholders the economic benefits they generate. Doing so creates a trust that encourages people with otherwise widely differing interests to protect and support the business model. Being successful in doing so is hard to accomplish. (Methods for achieving successful sharing are described in Chapter 5.)

Timberland is a good example of this sharing approach. The footwear and apparel company sees its role as serving its stakeholders, and advocates that perspective visibly and persuasively. Mr. Jeffrey B. Swartz, the company's third CEO from the founding family, puts it this way. "Doing good and doing well are linked." He sees customers and consumers not as passive recipients of the company's offerings, but as "citizens" with a stake in the company who should be given every opportunity to tell what they want.

Employees are not "hired hands" to be ordered around, but "paid volunteers" who come to work because they believe in what the company is doing. As part of this ethic, the company pays each employee for forty hours a year of volunteer work. Employees initiate and choose the volunteer tasks. For example, employees working in the Dominican Republic established a charter school to improve public education and literacy there for all company employees and their community.

Suppliers have to meet standards of quality on the products and for how they produce them. For example, Timberland wants to be sure that its products are not produced by child labor. Many U.S. companies who buy from other countries are not similarly concerned about suppliers' workers.

Shareholders should get good financial results and the satisfaction of owning a stake in a company of whose values they can be proud.

> The best business model would take a company's competitors many years to duplicate or exceed.

Mr. Swartz also sees his role as bringing the community into the company. As an example, Timberland is a national supporter of City Year, a youth service organization located in thirteen cities around the United States. Many Timberland employees also work on City Year projects.

Company-sponsored volunteerism goes in so many directions that Mr. Swartz doesn't even try to keep track of all the activities Timberland supports.

Timberland makes sure there is no mistake about its intent that the excess resources its fine business model creates are fairly shared.

Be Hard to Overtake

The best business model would take a company's competitors many years to duplicate or exceed. In a world where competitive leads are getting shorter and shorter, being hard to overtake sounds impossible to achieve. But the best business model innovators are skilled at developing this core characteristic.

Invacare is a good example of a company that is succeeding in this regard. It started as a manufacturer of wheelchairs. Invacare improved its business model to become the most efficient and easy

> The Timberland and Invacare examples may seem like a far distance from where you are today. How do you get from where you are to there?

to work with, high-quality provider of almost everything you need when you go home from the hospital. By combining product superiority and diversity with low costs in manufacturing and distribution through home medical equipment (HME) providers, the company's business model could only be displaced by exceeding the firm's performance in each model element simultaneously. The company's success in each area reinforces its advantages in all other areas, making Invacare a formidable company to exceed.

As some say, then, "If you can't beat 'em, join 'em." The company's business model advantages have become so significant that other companies are now hiring Invacare to handle their distribution. Each time that happens, the potential to overtake the Invacare business model is reduced.

To further increase its advantages, Invacare is starting to build a consumer brand image to create additional preference for its offerings.

Since many of its products are reimbursed by health insurance and Medicare, forms handling and interaction with health care providers are significant challenges for patients. Invacare's HME customers perform these services well, which lets Invacare benefit from customers' convenience and location advantages in serving end users. Invacare has established a Web site to direct inquires to these stores to help make them more successful in developing consumer business.

Draw on Your Values and History

The Timberland and Invacare examples may seem like a far distance from where you are today. How do you get from where you are to there? Rogers Corporation provides an interesting answer to this question. The company is a long-established one, based in Connecticut. A strong research tradition has made the company rich in polymer-based materials knowledge. Insights from its knowledge are used to create high-performance electronic components used in the telecommunications and computer markets. Prior to 1997, however, the company was not moving fast or profitably enough to take its expertise from the laboratory to the customer.

When Mr. Walter E. Boomer arrived as president and chief executive officer in 1997, he realized the company needed an improved business model. Mr. Boomer began crafting a vision for any new business model before a single innovation test was conceived. He felt that the company could start innovation development with creating a vision because he found Rogers employees operated based on good values, the beliefs that guide ethical behavior. If Mr. Boomer had not found the company's values to be adequate, instilling the right values would have been his starting point.

To establish this initial vision, he analyzed the successful and unsuccessful experiences the company had already had, treating them like business model development tests. His investigation showed him that Rogers was slowing its internal development efforts to reduce making small mistakes. The effect was to create delays in reaching the market with new materials and products, which was a comparatively much larger mistake. A key principle for the company's business model vision became freeing people to make small, quickly correctable mistakes in order to gain speed and overall effectiveness in reaching and performing in the marketplace. Mr. Boomer's initial goal was to reduce the time and perceptual lags in transferring the company's research labs' knowledge to customers' design engineers. To achieve his goal, Mr. Boomer enabled "wires of authority" rather than a hierarchy of authority.

This core insight helped the company choose what to work on in expanding its business model experimentation. Previously,

175

the research labs and manufacturing function had not been very involved with one another during product development. As a result, when a new product came out, manufacturing yields were often low and costly. Rogers's research and manufacturing people worked on improving this functional hand-off problem by creating a new process and organizational focus.

Mr. Boomer was pleased to discover that Rogers had participated in successful undertakings with other companies. One was a joint venture begun in 1984 to produce polyurethane foam in Japan with Inoac Corporation. Another was a 1988 joint venture with 3M to make electroluminescent lamps used to light cellular handset and pager displays. The company's partners bring integrated technology and manufacturing expertise relevant for high potential products that the company would have difficulty developing, producing and marketing by itself. Surprisingly, one strength Rogers brings is its former experience with hands-off relationships between the company labs and its manufacturing operations during product development. That unfortunate internal circumstance was much like having a joint venture partner manufacture new materials for you, and helped Rogers develop skill in such undertakings.

Based on those successes, Rogers began to add to its joint ventures in Asia. Mr. Boomer noticed that geographical markets for its products were predominately located there. Asian joint ventures provided local partners who could help obtain market acceptance. Distribution times would be shorter and costs lower there, as well.

This approach seems to be off to a good start. The company's latest joint venture with Chang Chun Plastics Company in Taiwan should help its new circuit laminate materials quickly reach a higher market share position. In 1999, Rogers solidified its long-term relationship with Mitsui Chemicals to make materials for Hutchinson Technologies "trace suspension assemblies" for hard disk drives.

Based on successful joint-venture experiences, Mr. Boomer is also experimenting with creating autonomous venture teams (like AES uses for its power plant projects, which are referred to later in this chapter) to establish other new businesses for applying the technology coming jointly from its labs and those of its partners.

Mr. Boomer has also tied compensation closer to overall company performance to encourage teamwork. Little had been done in the past in this area, which encouraged the prior lack of cooperation among different functions. He would like Rogers's employees to own a significant amount of Rogers's total stock and will move closer to achieving that goal by introducing an employee stock purchase plan. Additionally, stock options for employees are being pushed as far down into the organization as the company's current situation will allow.

The principles that Mr. Boomer used illustrate how you can start to hypothesize what your new business models should be. Many of the elements that he considered for establishing the company's new business model vision have been important for other business-model innovators. His approach is likely to be accessible to the widest range of your company's leaders, especially those who are new to the industry. To summarize, Mr. Boomer looked at:

- Whether the company had a solid base in values
- Where taking lots of affordable risks could reduce or eliminate bigger, unaffordable risks
- How the company's past performance could serve as a surrogate for experiments in adding benefits, adjusting prices and reducing costs
- Where he could make fast progress on several fronts at once in adding value for customers and other stakeholders
- What kind of organizational structure would work best for creating and implementing his future experiments in business model innovation
- How he could instill a better spirit of teamwork and cooperation for mutual advantage

If you are wondering about Mr. Boomer's background before he became CEO of Rogers, then-General Boomer headed the Marines in operations Desert Shield and Desert Storm, and later

> Strong agreement to apply good values builds a necessary foundation on which to design and implement new business models.

served as assistant commandant of the Marines before retiring after thirty-four years in 1994. Upon that retirement, he became head of the Babcock and Wilcox Power Generation group at McDermott International.

CREATE YOUR COMPANY'S BUSINESS MODEL INNOVATION VISION

In the remainder of this chapter, you can learn more about how Mr. Boomer's principles can guide your search for a better business model. We have designed a process based on the successful experiences of business model innovating companies to launch your organization onto a solid path of continuing innovation.

Check on Your Organization's Values

Strong agreement to apply good values builds a necessary foundation on which to design and implement new business models. Values encourage taking the right kind of innovative actions in a cooperative and effective manner. Values also shape the direction that business model innovation takes. The best companies find that values help them identify high-performing employees and future leaders. Finally, broadly inclusive values help to stimulate innovation and support from partners, suppliers, customers, end users, distributors and the communities you serve.

As Timberland discovered, the more you talk about your values, the more opportunities you will have to act on them. You will draw positive attention from those who are looking to link with companies that have your values.

If values aren't where they should be in your organization, you need to actively involve all stakeholders in establishing what the values should be. Identifying and fostering desirable values is a necessary first step in creating the right kind of mutual commitments.

How do you know if your organization's values aren't sufficient? A good visceral test is to ask yourself if you feel inspired and proud to do your job because of what your company stands for. If you don't feel that inspiration and pride, what would have to change about the company and its relationships for you to feel that way? Ask others those same two questions in private, and listen carefully to what the respondents tell you.

If you doubt that values are important to company success, consider the case of Enron. At one time, the company was viewed as one of the world's leaders in business model innovation. The firm established many new markets for energy and other commodities. When some of these innovations started to falter, Enron chose to create the appearance of success rather than fix

> **Business model innovators began shifting their risk-taking perspective by identifying their biggest risks.**

the problems. Secret partnerships hid debt, and loans were structured to look like successful energy trades. Innovation in the absence of the right values eventually destroyed the company's

---

Values That Support the Best Business Models

While no one can prescribe values for anyone else, some values seem to be present in almost all of the companies that have the best business models. These values direct you to:

- Pay attention to every stakeholder as an individual.
- Respect each person's views and interests.
- Be honest.
- Keep promises.
- Seek to "do good while doing well."
- Create innovative solutions to important, unmet human needs.
- Look for validation of ideas in customer and end-user acceptance.
- Put the interests of all stakeholders on a par with each other.
- Take pride in your work.
- Serve others in continually improved ways.
- Be reliable in looking out for others.

---

competitive advantages, and Enron collapsed into bankruptcy when its questionable activities were disclosed.

Master Taking Affordable Risks to Reduce or Eliminate the Unaffordable Ones

Almost every successful business model innovator we studied nurtured an environment with great latitude to take small risks on personal initiative, balanced with great care to avoid unnecessary big risks that could hamstring the company. Such cultures can stimulate large amounts of innovation without explicit direction, when people simply follow their curiosity.

Business model innovators began shifting their risk-taking perspective by identifying their biggest risks. Here's how many proceeded.

They mentally doubled or tripled sales while increasing profits more rapidly.

Then they asked themselves what the company would have to do to reach those higher levels of performance. In most cases, new products and services were part of the picture. In many circumstances, achieving higher performance in some important customer benefits was essential. Adding new benefits that built on the company's effectiveness, with little likelihood of detracting from it, was often important.

Next, they asked what risks could cause poor performance in accomplishing those key tasks. They started from the customer's perspective rather than a financial viewpoint.

Some companies found that customers had problems that weren't being addressed. For example, Worcester, Massachusetts-based Allmerica Financial had been a traditional full-line mutual insurance company, offering a wide range of products and services in many markets. When Mr. John F. O'Brien arrived from Fidelity Investments in 1989, he recognized the opportunity to create a distinct set of competitive advantages by refocusing the company's financial services business.

Under Mr. O'Brien, Allmerica was one of the first of several large mutual insurers to convert to shareholder-owned organizations, enhancing the company's ability to perform well in the increasingly competitive industry and establishing a more dynamic, results-oriented culture. As part of this transition, Allmerica exited some lines of business no longer in demand and concentrated on helping aging baby boomers save for retirement. As boomers began to approach retirement, Allmerica broadened its focus, helping boomers create financial plans and prepare to manage their money to ensure that they don't outlive their assets.

Initially, Allmerica lacked the skills needed to succeed in the retirement market. Boomers were accustomed to prompt, high-quality customer service, and Allmerica, like most insurers then, had not made service a priority. Over time, Allmerica turned this liability into an asset, creating state-of-the-art call centers, seminar programs and Internet-based services—establishing a leadership position in the market along the way. For example, with strong financial acumen, but lacking call center experience, Allmerica developed its call center capabilities in part by providing service for the high-volume retailer 1–800–FLOWERS before transitioning its call center to provide service for its sophisticated financial products.

Invariably, the second step in shifting risk-taking perspective (often almost simultaneous with the first) was to examine how to instill more, faster, more focused, and better innovation and decision making in the company. Often, this direction dovetailed nicely with an observed need for more innovation. The primary reason that most big companies grow slowly is too little experimentation with new ideas. Experts, such as Gary Hamel in *Leading the Revolution* (Harvard Business School Press, 2000), argue that every successful innovation begins with a thousand ideas, which are turned into a hundred innovation proposals, that become ten tests, which should yield one implemented success.

By contrast, many companies try to get one successful innovation out of one idea. While there is a chance that approach will work, it's highly unlikely. The best way to get more innovations is to be sure that there are lots of ideas in the pipeline, and that low-risk and low-cost ideas proceed rapidly into experimentation and testing. Top management's job is to enable and encourage more inexpensive experimentation as the foundation for turning a few successful experiments into reality. To encourage more ideas, some leaders have told employees they will be evaluated in part on the ideas they generate, appropriately develop and test. Such measurements have been based on the appropriateness of their activity, rather than on the ultimate business success of their efforts.

A typical final step in changing risk-taking views was locating lower-cost and lower-risk activities to reduce or eliminate the big, unaffordable risks. For example, if part of the company was not profitable enough or losses could snowball, successful innovators considered what their choices looked like for improving that area, short of shutting down or selling the operation. Pursuing this line of inquiry is a task at which turnaround specialists excel.

Analyze Past Performance as Though These Experiences Were New Tests

Finding lessons in a company's past is becoming harder to do. Fearing law suits and wanting to save on storage space and costs, many companies regularly trash all their older records. We all know that success has many parents while failure is an orphan. So discussing corporate history may be of limited use in some cases. What else can a leader do to unearth and reconstruct the past lessons?

The most effective business model innovating leaders performed something that is best described as corporate archeology. Archeologists find what remains of the past. After carefully observing what they can locate (which is usually a tiny fraction of what originally existed), they begin to draw lessons from their observations. If bone tools are present and similar bone pieces appear to have been smashed in the same location, an archeologist may hypothesize that the site was used at one time by a tool maker. Carbon dating can tell how old these bones are to narrow down when the tools were probably made. The archeologist can go on to create modern duplicates of the tools and use them in various ways. From these experiences, hypotheses can be developed about how the tools were constructed and what they were originally used for. The archeologist may go one step further and look for possible clues by observing bone implement use today among people living in less industrialized cultures.

Company leaders we studied seemed to do something very similar. In their searches, business leaders were usually looking for the most extreme forms of success and setbacks. Having found these results, they focused on what was different from the company's usual experiences.

> **Tellabs founder and chief executive, Mr. Michael J. Birck, has noted that you have to keep testing your successes for their future relevance.**

Pioneer discount broker Charles Schwab soon noticed that many of the company's telephone calls were from customers to find out if their orders to purchase or sell securities had occurred yet and, if so, at what price. Realizing that this behavior meant that customers probably always wanted this kind of information, the company began automatically calling customers after every trade to share the details. Many customers complimented Schwab for this timely confirmation service. That success stayed fresh in the organization's memory. When the Internet came along, Schwab quickly grasped that this means of communication made it easier for customers to find out about the current status of their accounts, positions and trades. By creating better solutions to serve these customer needs that built on the company's prior successes, Schwab quickly became the leading online broker despite many other brokers either being better known or having lower commission prices.

Tellabs founder and chief executive, Mr. Michael J. Birck, has noted that you have to keep testing your successes for their future relevance. When the telecommunications equipment provider was starting out, Tellabs had to succeed as a supplier to the regional Bell operating companies for its survival. This necessity meant thinking and acting just like Bell Labs had done in the past, and being conservative in adding equipment to the established network. In the meantime, new telecommunications networks were increasingly provided by more agile companies that wanted to establish new technical models and ways of operating. Tellabs found it needed a variable organizational structure and technology focus to match the different needs of the regional Bell operating companies and newer telecommunications network providers.

Make Fast Progress on Several Fronts at Once in Serving Customers

Most CEOs will tell you that if you can get the right people together and turn them loose on an important problem or opportunity, great results will follow. The same CEOs often complain that it's getting tougher and tougher to find and keep such people, and that the markets for the company's products and services are becoming more sensitive to price than to the benefits customers receive. So the need for the right people has never been greater.

> Almost every business seems to have potential to be more innovative when people think that their business requires continuing innovation.

Many companies have taken this employee recruitment and satisfaction problem seriously. Some go so far as to place their employees' happiness with pursuing innovation opportunities at the center of their business model. When companies execute the talent-encouraging approach well, they may quickly outrace the competition.

Former Southwest Airlines CEO and cofounder, Mr. Herbert D. Kelleher, was famous for his devotion to creating an innovative, customer-caring environment among the airline's employees. "But I think showing respect for people's ideas is very, very important because as soon as you stop doing that, you stop getting ideas." Listening does indeed pay off. "Reading letters from customers is extremely valuable. Customers have given us some tremendous ideas. Employees have given us tremendous ideas as well." Responding promptly is even more important. "So the rule at Southwest is, if somebody has an idea, you read it quickly and respond instantaneously."[1]

Encourage Good Values and Install an Organizational Structure That Stimulates Innovation

Many people associate innovation with high-technology products and services, and certainly those industries create lots of valuable improvements. In light of that perception, our research showed something unexpected. Almost every business seems to have potential to be more innovative when people think that their business requires continuing innovation.

Few industries had a greater reputation for being stodgy than steel making during the 1950s and 1960s. Offshore continuous-casting competitors devastated the integrated steel industry in the United States. Some predicted that steel making would disappear from these shores except for specialty steels needed for defense applications. Today, the industry has been totally reshaped by a technology for using scrap steel as a low-cost raw material. Instead of starting with the raw elements required for steel, existing steel is melted down. That recycling saves a lot of time and reduces facility and energy costs. The challenge is to make higher-quality steel products from this variable raw material. This technology was developed and extensively applied in the United States.

Talk to North American profit leader, Nucor, about this success as a technology story, and you have a surprise coming. Mr. Daniel R. DiMicco, the company's CEO, will tell you that you have it backwards. He credits Nucor's success to the organizational culture, values and system developed by former CEO, Mr. Kenneth Iverson.

Mr. DiMicco sees the foundation for this remarkable success as lying in the company's values:

- Don't overextend yourself.
- Be a risk taker and take on the unknown.
- Focus on long-term rather than short-term, whipsaw thinking.
- Treat customers, employees and other stakeholders the way you would like to be treated.

- Minimize barriers to effective communication.
- Build relationships.
- Hold people accountable to honor the relationship and perform.
- Take your time in evaluating people you hire.
- See continuous improvement as a nonstop journey up a mountain.
- Give people the freedom to do it.
- Help people learn.
- Don't penalize failure because big flops are part of necessary learning.

To implement these principles, Nucor made many organizational innovations to its business model to encourage better performance. It flattened the organization chart. To encourage better communication, the company has only two organizational levels between a division head and floor workers in mills. Responsibility and authority are delegated as much as possible. Education is generously supported for employees, their spouses and children. The company emphasizes promoting from within. In hiring, Nucor looks for people who want to move ahead in life. To encourage them, everyone in the company gets variable compensation based on the firm's profit performance. And production bonus incentives are paid weekly to constantly reinforce the "pay for performance" culture of profit consciousness.

The business model innovation vision that directed this culture and organizational structure was to be a growing company by leapfrogging the competition through commercializing new technology.

If such opportunities can be found in the steel industry, why should your company and industry be any different in terms of developing profitable business model innovations? Work on your values and organizational structure, and you may be surprised at what you can accomplish.

Instill a Spirit of Teamwork and Cooperation for Mutual Advantage

A number of the companies described in this chapter worked effectively on teamwork and cooperation. Certainly, Nucor, Rogers and Southwest Airlines could also serve as examples for this subject.

> **What does your company do to drive customers away?**

Before considering any other examples, let's think about the typical company. Turnover of employees may be from 20 percent to more than 50 percent a year (in some low-paying service businesses). Such turnover means that companies expect the whole work force to turn over on average every few years. The good news about that turnover is that it creates potential for new ideas to come into the company. The bad news is that a lot of talented people leave who initially came energized and filled with good ideas. What happened in between? Clearly, many employees and their companies see their interests as opposed to one another.

Next let's look at the customer base. A similar level of turnover occurs with those people. Many of today's customers will decide they will be better served by a different supplier in the future. Does such turnover suggest that the company is fulfilling its potential? Probably not. Competitors' offerings and prices are frequently similar. The typical reason for switching is because a supplier makes the customer feel abused and disrespected through providing poor service. Honest errors can be forgiven by most customers, as long as a company shows that it is sincerely interested in doing the right thing . . . and doesn't repeat the errors. What does your company do to drive customers away? Taking advantage of customers' ignorance is particularly infuriating. How hard do you think customers try to help improve suppliers that continually annoy them?

Now, consider suppliers. For a typical company, 60 to 70 percent of suppliers will be gone or be receiving dramatically lower orders within five years. If a supplier decides that its company has little chance of being a survivor in serving your business, how hard will it work to find new ways to improve your business model?

As you can see from looking at these sources of friction with stakeholders, the typical company takes actions every day to drive off most of its potentially most committed allies: those who invest their working lives and hard-earned money to serve or be served by the company.

To overcome this harmful cycle of uncaring, fractious relationships, you must establish trust and cooperation through mutually supportive, continuing relationships. Xilinx seems to be a leader in focusing on this opportunity, and has been recognized as one of the best U.S. companies to work for (*Fortune*, December 2000 and 2001). Xilinx is the leading provider of programmable logic devices (microprocessors that you can customize with software). It attributes much of its success in having positive stakeholder relationships to a long-standing practice of creating an innovation-focused workplace. The company looks at everything carefully in this regard, from its marketing activities and how products leave the shipping dock to the way the company keeps the financial community informed. Xilinx employees are urged to take risks and are not punished when they fail. The company's philosophy is that occasional failure is natural and a necessary part of building the "learning organization" that Xilinx wants to be.

The company's business model has always provided for outsourcing product fabrication. This choice frees Xilinx to concentrate its focus on three key competencies: chip and software design, marketing and technical support. With this potential to fascinate and focus employees, Xilinx has succeeded in developing long-term relationships with its employees. The company enjoys an enviable employee turnover of less than 5 percent a year in the job-hopping Silicon Valley environment where 20 percent annual employee attrition has been the norm.

When Mr. Willem (Wim) P. Roelandts arrived as CEO from Hewlett-Packard in 1996, he saw an opportunity to build on the company's sound internal teamwork and cooperation. His goal was to move to even higher levels of cooperation with suppliers and customers. For fabrication suppliers, this approach meant working with two companies instead of five. As a result of being a more important customer to them, Xilinx got faster access to the most advanced fabrication technology from the remaining two suppliers. Xilinx's designers and the fabrication suppliers work together to accelerate the technical development of state-of-the-art semiconductor manufacturing processes used to make Xilinx's programmable chips.

The Xilinx value proposition has always been reducing time to market for its customers. By themselves, Xilinx chips offer the fastest way for customers to create unique logic circuits in silicon. But in other areas of its business, Xilinx also began to take responsibility for speeding customers' products through the supply chain to the end user. Any place where there were delays or inefficiencies, Xilinx directed its attention. It looked at the companies that distribute its products, the semiconductor foundries that make the silicon wafers, and the companies that package the chips and perform final tests on them.

In another area, Xilinx pioneered the use of "intellectual property cores" in its chips. These predefined and pretested cores—from Xilinx or one of its partners—are programming files that make the Xilinx chip perform a specific standard function. Thanks to cores, customers don't have to recreate the function from scratch, and, as a result, they can shave weeks or months from their product design cycles.

As mentioned earlier, Xilinx began more recently to offer turnkey design services. In these cases Xilinx's engineers, not the customer's, create the unique semiconductor logic circuits for a particular piece of digital electronic equipment. This kind of service is especially attractive for customers who are industry entrants and want to reap the time-to-market benefits of programmable logic chips, but don't have the expertise in-house to meet the market's stringent new product development and delivery schedules.

Having created solutions-oriented teamwork among the company and its suppliers and customers, Xilinx will probably continue to extend its connections through stronger and more effective relationships with long-term customers and software partners.

Pile Up the Cash, Rather Than Pile on Debt

Cash in hand creates choices; debt reduces them. In fact, excess debt has been the Achilles heel of many otherwise successful business model innovators. Debt can be most harmful when it encourages you to pursue actions containing underappreciated and hidden risks.

AES, founded in 1981, is the largest global power company. AES provides safe, clean, reliable electricity around the world through its generation and transmission facilities. As of 2000, the company owned or had interests in over 125 generating plants in sixteen countries for an asset value of $21 billion.

At the same time, AES pursued more than 100 business development projects to buy or build more facilities in over forty countries through its independently managed employee teams. These projects were defined and pursued based on the initiative of the teams. Corporate headquarters viewed its role as supporting these teams. Top management's role was to provide the environment in which the development teams could succeed. Mr. Dennis K. Bakke, cofounder and then-CEO, said that the key questions he asked about AES people were:

> "Are they having fun in the work place?"
> "Do they feel like they can use all their gifts and skills to serve the world without being squelched?"

The company had no human resource department and relied on surveys to test the waters for how well it was providing fulfilling work. (This team-initiated development approach is the one that Rogers has considered for its development projects.)

Only two years later, in 2002, the company found itself in a financial quagmire. The stock price had dropped by over 95 percent. Total debt had ballooned to over $23 billion, with much of the increase used to fund acquisitions and build new electrical generating capacity. How were the benefits from the company's admirable management methods blunted?

Rather than reducing risk through size and diversification, AES's investments and ways of funding them had often combined to increase the company's total risk. Using borrowed money, AES made risky investments that it could not otherwise have afforded if limited to its own cash and cash flow. For example, 55 percent of revenues came from South America and the Caribbean, where economic conditions became very weak. In addition, 29 percent of revenues came from merchant power generation where prices fluctuated with demand, rather than being tied to long-term contracts. When volume or prices dropped in weak markets, AES had a problem. Most savvy borrowers know that you shouldn't borrow long-term funds for operations that will have volatile results. As a result, most power providers who borrow money seek as many fixed-price contracts with their customers as possible.

Debt made the business risk problem worse for AES by adding to the cash flow demands for principal and interest payments while cash flow and debt capacity were drying up. With less debt, AES could have more easily ridden out the storm. Instead, it had to drastically cut back on investments and sell poorly performing facilities at low prices.

This otherwise superbly run company could have been much more successful in the long run. AES needed a different business model innovation vision, one that emphasized reducing unnecessary risks and financing growth with an eye to lean times. A lower rate of growth, as a result of less reliance on debt, could have caused the company to be more selective about the operating risks it accepted. If more of the expansion had been funded with sales of company stock, the firm could instead

> **Be practical about risk, rather than follow old finance and strategy theories designed for the unusually stable 1950s that can backfire now.**

have been in a position to use the worldwide economic problems of 2001–2002 to acquire more facilities at bargain-basement prices, rather than having to be a seller in a distressed market.

By contrast, many thoughtful business model innovating technology companies eased the pain from the recession of 2001 with hefty cash balances and no debt. Dell, EMC, Linear Technology, QLogic, Red Hat, Xilinx and Zebra Technologies were among them. As a result, business model innovation for these companies was unaffected by those troubled times in the technology markets.

Finance theory, investment bankers and many security analysts will tell you to pile on the debt, especially when interest rates are low. If your level of business risk is low enough (especially as measured by the steadiness of your cash flow in good times and bad) and you keep lots of cash on hand, this can be good advice. However, as the frequency of competitors' business model innovations and worldwide economic volatility expand, few will be able to afford much debt risk. Instead, be like the thrifty farmer who piles up surpluses in good times to weather the hard ones. Be practical about risk, rather than follow old finance and strategy theories designed for the unusually stable 1950s that can backfire now.

KEY QUESTIONS

- *Do you feel inspired by your company's current business model?* If you are like most people, the answer will be "no." Ask yourself, then, *what's missing to make me feel inspired by our business model?* Ask other people in your company and exchange ideas about what is missing. As you think about potential business models, focus on those with potential to inspire.

- *Does your company's business model provide greater economic and non-monetary benefits for all stakeholders than the alternative of not doing business with your company?* In asking this question, consider each end user, customer, distributor, partner, supplier, employee, shareholder, lender, regulator and community you serve. If your answer is no, ask *what's missing?* The answers should help you see where your business model could be improved so stakeholders see that their self-interest is best furthered by your success.

- *What would have to change for economic and nonmonetary stakeholder benefits to double?* A more successful business model will distribute the surplus rewards it generates from supporting customers efficiently to all those who contribute to enabling the company's success. Answering this question should flesh out whether your challenges are to push innovation in new directions or simply to redirect the way the fruits of that innovation are shared. Most companies will have issues in both dimensions.

- *How long would it take an existing competitor or new entrant to overcome your business model's advantages in providing for stakeholders?* If the answer is less than five years and declining, you definitely have some work to do.

- *What are the biggest risks your company takes now that could set back your progress?* Although it is exciting to "bet the company," the most successful business model innovators avoid doing so except when they can find no alternative. It only takes one large loss when the stakes are high for disaster to occur.

- *How can you turn those big risks into smaller ones?* For example, if each new investment is too big for setbacks to be easily swallowed, can you share the risks and rewards with others? Of, if you lack resources, can you team with organizations that complement your own?

- *If all of your current business model improvement tests were successful, how close would they come to providing an ideal business model?* There will still be significant gaps. How can you fill those gaps? Tests aren't the only way to establish new business models. Sometimes you should look at your history for ideas. In many cases, new business relationships are needed, because it will be too slow and expensive to do everything from scratch. Like Rogers, you can be building those perspectives and relationships while any tests you need are developed and conducted.

- *Would your cash and debt levels allow your company be as active as you would like with business model innovation during bad economic times?* What would your company results look like if a very bad recession hit next year, and then lingered for four years? What business model innovation activities would have to be curtailed? If your innovation would be significantly affected, look at how you could use different expansion plans, financed with more equity and asset sales, to reduce debt and build a substantial cash buffer for future lean times.

CHAPTER 5

SHARE BENEFITS FAIRLY WITH ALL WHO CREATE THEM

You get the satisfaction of being heard, and that is the
whole possible scope of human ambition.
—John Jay Chapman

*Corporate scandals involving executive self-dealing abound now.
These misdeeds have shown that the greed and rapacity of
unchecked corporate leaders have few limits. Nothing more
quickly sinks a company than for key stakeholders to withdraw
their support. Stakeholders always do so when they perceive that
their interests are being harmed or disregarded by corporate leaders. Companies can easily discourage their stakeholders in other
ways, such as by either favoring some and disfavoring others, or by
offering the wrong forms of shared rewards. Companies that
fairly and appropriately share benefits with all who create them
can expect that this important best practice will be even more
valuable than usual in the current business environment.*

Mr. Michael Cogliandro was born in Lawrence, Massachusetts, to
an Italian-speaking mother, but was raised in Italy between the

ages of three and fifteen. English was a second language to him when he returned to Massachusetts as a teenager, but he soon mastered it. He was excited by the opportunities around him. What would he do with his life?

During the Depression, he learned to be a barber. Being ambitious, he purchased his first shop in East Boston for $300 and proudly improved the decor and four barber chairs in it.

Then disaster struck when Pearl Harbor was bombed. Mr. Cogliandro was among the first men drafted into the U.S. Army. Because so many others were being called into military service, he had a hard time finding a buyer for his barber shop. Finally, the seller bought it back for a mere $70, despite the expensive improvements.

Mr. Cogliandro rose to be a corporal in the China–Burma–India theater during World War II. After his discharge, he picked up barbering again, working in the shop he used to own.

In 1949, a friend persuaded him to try a new job at the Harvard Barber Shop in Cambridge, Massachusetts. He liked it there, but decided he wanted his own business again. Mr. Cogliandro set up his next barber shop on Dunster Street in Cambridge, adjacent to Harvard Square. In his new shop, he proudly served the first of several generations of Harvard students, employees and professors. He was honored to do so and wanted to help his customers in any way he could. When he learned that many poor students couldn't afford hair cuts, he would cut their hair for free. Some received this benefit all through college and graduate school. If you could pay, but were a little short that week, Mr. Cogliandro would say, "Pay me when you can." At Christmas, each customer would receive a beautifully wrapped gift, whether or not they paid for their hair cuts.

Mr. Cogliandro also listened carefully to his customers. After he understood how they wanted their hair cut, he would ask them about their families, their backgrounds, their work and their cares. If he didn't understand something, he would keep asking questions until he did. And he never forgot a single thing anyone said. After years of these conversations, he would sometimes realize that he had information that would help his customers. But why would they listen to a humble barber? Mr. Cogliandro became a master of the Socratic method, asking questions to help hearers learn. He would begin, "Excuse me. May I ask you just one question?" By the end of the haircut, that one question would become dozens. Many report that it was like taking a Ph.D. oral on the subject of one's own life. But each customer learned something that he or she (yes, he cut women's hair, too) needed to know. In the process, he created a new business model as a barber, providing helpful advice at no extra charge.

Mr. Cogliandro wanted to encourage good behavior and happy lives. He was surprised to learn that many of his customers were psychiatrists who seemed to have worse problems than their patients. He was shocked to learn that most were divorced or had troubled children. How could they justify charging other people when they made such messes of their own lives? Mr. Cogliandro was blunt with them. They needed to straighten up their own lives and set a good example. He often wondered why the psychiatrists returned, considering how tough he was on them. When asked, one psychiatrist told him, "I come here to listen to you because you're better than a psychiatrist."

Then, disaster struck again. Harvard terminated his lease to build its new administrative offices, Holyoke Center. What would happen to Mr. Cogliandro? He moved to the northern edge of the campus on Massachusetts Avenue, just a little over a block from the northwest corner of Harvard Law School. Almost all of his customers made the hike up there. After all, didn't Mr. Cogliandro make it to work for them every day, regardless of the weather and his own health? Once, he walked all the way from his home in Revere, many miles away, during a terrible blizzard. Harvard rarely closes for bad weather, and Mr. Cogliandro didn't want to disappoint his customers. He became the Cal Ripken, Jr. of barbers by never missing a day of work.

The new barber shop's location turned out to be a blessing in disguise. Many of his new customers were law professors and law students, who used the Socratic method in class. They were expert questioners and respondents. Mr. Cogliandro sharpened his skills.

Word spread about Mr. Cogliandro's great conversational ability, knowledge, caring and common sense. Students told other students. Professors told other professors. Colleagues told colleagues. People would drop in during a reunion visit after hearing about Mr. Cogliandro from a reunion classmate. Over the years, his clientele grew to include many of the most prominent Nobel laureates, deans, politicians, judges, physicians and foundation heads in Massachusetts. Waiting for your turn was great drama as you listened to Mr. Cogliandro question his influential customers.

Mr. Cogliandro was able to share even more information as a result. He could help you identify and get to a top doctor, make a referral to a nationally known lawyer for an unusual legal problem or tell you which academic was the brightest in a given area. Politicians loved his sense of what people were thinking about. They often asked for his blessing before running for office. He had an unerring ability to tell them how they would do. Each customer got the best of what all of the other customers had shared with Mr. Cogliandro, seasoned by his sage questions. He built a new community among his customers in the process. He asked you if you knew so-and-so. If you did, he would tell you about them every time he saw you. If he hadn't seen them lately, he would ask you if you had heard from them. If you didn't know someone and he thought you should know each other, he would arrange an introduction. Becoming a communications facilitator and conduit among his customers so they could help each other was his second business model innovation.

Disaster struck a third time. His partner decided to retire, and the barber shop was sold. Mr. Cogliandro didn't want to retire, but felt he had no choice. Helped by some of his customers, he was able to carry on. Whenever someone was sick, Mr. Cogliandro had always driven to their home or hospital to cut their hair. Why not provide a mobile barber shop? Pretty soon, Mr. Cogliandro was driving to homes, offices and even airports to help busy customers. He carried all of his gear in a neat briefcase, looking very much like a lawyer himself in his conservative sports coat and tie. After arriving and setting up, he would say, "Excuse me. There's just one thing. . . ." You knew you were in for the challenge of your life then. This mobile service was his third business model innovation.

He also found employment in a unisex salon that had replaced his shop. So Mr. Cogliandro had made another change in his business model, his fourth innovation, by allowing women to feel more comfortable coming to him as a customer.

When Mr. Cogliandro retired from the second of two unisex salons that had employed him, his family held a surprise celebration for him at the Harvard Faculty Club and invited many long-time customers. It was probably the most eminent gathering ever held there to celebrate a retirement by someone who never worked for the university. Many deans haven't had such a send-off when they retired. A Nobel laureate rose to speak Mr. Cogliandro's praises. The *Cambridge Chronicle* and *The Harvard Law School Bulletin* covered the gala event.

A number of years later, we were invited to a small reunion gathering of Mr. Cogliandro's family and his customers in a restaurant on Holyoke Street, near the site of his first Cambridge shop. Although one of us had had hair cuts from Mr. Cogliandro since 1965, we were surprised to realize that everyone else in the room had been getting their hair cuts from him since the early 1950s. Each one stood to tell many moving stories about how their lives had been improved by the man each of us first knew as "Mike, the barber."

> **CEOs have often told us their most difficult decision is how to divide economic rewards among stakeholders.**

Mr. Cogliandro has never met a person he didn't want to help. If he heard that a customer had died, he would be among the first to call the family to express his condolences. If a customer's family member or friend needed help, Mr. Cogliandro would work on the problem, just as though it were his own. He would ask every customer what they thought the person in trouble should do, until useful answers emerged. Then he would call the person to share what he had learned. To Mr. Cogliandro, everyone is a stakeholder who deserves help. He has been a second father to all his younger customers. We can all learn from his caring example.

OVERCOME THE PROBLEMS OF FAIRLY SHARING ECONOMIC REWARDS WITH STAKEHOLDERS

CEOs have often told us their most difficult decision is how to divide economic rewards among stakeholders. This challenge is increased by the distrust that stakeholders may feel toward the company and each other. That distrust is often based in bad past experiences. Suppliers sometimes learn that "partnerships" mainly involve giving more to their customer and receiving less and less. Partners can find the delivery on bold promises disappearing as people and priorities shift. Local communities have learned to be wary of hidden corporate agendas. Lenders see what helps shareholders, employees and suppliers as often coming at the lender's expense. Customers aren't sure they are getting all they need and want to be at the top of the pecking order. Shareholders and employees often see themselves in opposition.

> **Most stakeholders have a poor understanding of how serving their needs affects the company's ability to prosper in the future, and what the costs of providing benefits for them are for other stakeholders.**

Regardless of damaged relationships, when a company isn't as successful as it would like to be, the question of how to share the limited, available benefits becomes tougher. What should the CEO do? The improved economic performance that follows implementing a better business model provides the opportunity to realign benefits.

Yet even if these stakeholder interests can somehow be aligned and benefits fairly shared, the form of shared rewards can be unsatisfactory. For example, payments that suggest disrespect make people feel cheapened. Respect and honor without appropriate financial payment eventually cause people to feel used. Standards for respect and reward differ among reasonable people. Providing the wrong benefits sends a fundamental message of not being respected to almost anyone.

> **Most companies look only at the company's financial results, without considering the costs to and rewards for other stakeholders. Look at the potential financial results last, instead of first.**

How can the proper balance be established? In each case, the equity of the decision is important, but the perceived equity of the result is even more so.

Most stakeholders have a poor understanding of how serving their needs affects the company's ability to prosper in the future, and what the costs of providing benefits for them are for other stakeholders. Your improved business model will cause even more confusion, unless you fill in this gap in stakeholder understanding. Before making a business model decision, find out whether your stakeholders are willing to support the alternative model, how they would like to benefit and what adjustments they think are required to make the new business model more exciting and rewarding.

DESIGN, DESCRIBE AND PROPOSE POTENTIAL BUSINESS MODELS FOR STAKEHOLDER EVALUATION AND IMPROVEMENT

Identify business models that maximize the benefits of stakeholder cooperation, while minimizing the potential conflicts. Start by measuring stakeholder benefits and costs. Most companies look only at the company's financial results, without considering the costs to and rewards for other stakeholders. Look at the potential financial results last, instead of first. For instance, many new business models require extraordinary sacrifices in time and effort by partners, suppliers, employees and distributors. A business model that provides sustainable competitive progress without extraordinary sacrifice is a better choice.

Improve stakeholder benefits and lower their costs. For example, your business model choices may show that rewards will grow fastest for company owners. In that case, you should spread ownership to more stakeholder groups. Another business model requires employees to make sacrifices. Can these sacrifices be reduced by relying more on partners and suppliers?

Is there some major new beneficiary of the improved business model who can afford to help implement the new model? Cytyc's new Pap smear test is much more expensive to provide than the old test. Historically, insurers only reimbursed policyholders for a new test at the same or lower rate than the alternative test.

> **Avoid business models that harm more than help any stakeholder.**

Cytyc persuaded insurers to reimburse more for the new method because women would have less pain and suffering, and total medical costs to be paid by insurers would be reduced. The insurers' decisions to pay more for the test allowed physicians and Cytyc to make the test available faster to more women than would otherwise have happened.

Eliminate the appearance of stakeholder conflicts of interest. Many companies now suffer from a perceived split between the interests of executives and the rest of the company's workers. For instance, a firm may have large layoffs and salary cuts, while the top brass receive large salaries, bonuses and stock options. Reductions in employment costs may be necessary. How can unavoidable pain be spread more equitably? One way is to cut everyone's compensation by the same percentage amount, rather than incur layoffs. How can the resulting benefits be fairly shared? After reducing cash compensation, some firms offer gain-sharing bonuses based on company-wide performance to help workers regain what was temporarily lost.

Avoid business models that harm more than help any stakeholder. Mr. Cogliandro did this by putting poor students' needs for haircuts ahead of improving his personal income . . . rather than the reverse approach that is commonly used by many barbers. Some might say he was shortchanging himself as an owner. Mr. Cogliandro knew that every barber has free time, so there's always room in the work schedule to cut more hair. He also enjoyed his relationships with the students, which was worth more than money to him.

After eliminating harm in every way you can think of, your remaining tool will be to shift more benefits toward those who are harmed to redress the balance. If after making all the improvements and shifting all the benefits you can think of and afford, someone will still feel or be victimized by the new business model, you should not even propose it. To do so undermines your moral authority to set an exciting and fair direction for the company. Stakeholder harm can usually be overcome with a little more attention. Sleep on the problem. Then try again with a fresh perspective and address the issues with new people until you find a better solution.

Find and share the most exciting purpose for the new business model. Many people today find that their work fails to provide the meaning they want. As a result, volunteers are often attracted to organizations like the Girl and Boy Scouts, Habitat for Humanity International, literacy groups, the Red Cross and the Salvation Army that serve important humanitarian concerns. One of the best psychological rewards any company can provide for stakeholders is to be part of such a heart-warming humanitarian purpose.

How can an ordinary business attach that kind of significance to what it does? Begin by looking more closely at the positive implications of what you do well. Southwest Airlines offers low fares to passengers as part of its business model. The company's stakeholders have been encouraged to think of this service as a way to bring families closer together and to allow people to see parts of the United States they could not otherwise afford to visit. Rather than seeing a plane full of low-fare passengers, a Southwest flight attendant is likely to be pleased by thinking about helping more people on their way to family reunions, birthdays and weddings. A retailer or a shipping company could think of itself as providing timely delivery of products and parts needed to make life run smoothly and safely for everyone. A publishing company could see a role in advancing knowledge and progress. A television production company providing quality programs could see itself as enriching both the lives of the poor who have few entertainment choices and the perspective of all who watch. How would the products and services of such companies change if employees and other stakeholders were following such inspiring purposes?

After you have considered such implications, reexamine your

business model choices and refine them to better match your most appealing purposes. In making these adjustments, ask stakeholders to tell you what purposes would be most exciting to them.

SHARE THE CONCERNS YOU HEARD AND HOW YOU RECOMMEND ADDRESSING THEM

Have you ever been asked your opinion, and then felt ignored? Your sense of not being heard is often caused by a misunderstanding about why your views were sought.

The best way to avoid this problem is to check with the stakeholders to be sure that their observations have been accurately understood and addressed long before making a decision. Let everyone know you plan several rounds of communication, feedback and adjustment. Then, when you unintentionally goof in dealing with an issue, people will feel like they can still correct the problem rather than becoming frustrated and alienated. Here are some communications ideas for this process.

> Treat all stakeholders as considerately as you would a customer whom you could not afford to lose.

Summarize concerns. Outline possible solutions and ask for better ideas. Like a good town meeting does, keep the process open. When you inform stakeholders about each others' concerns, individuals can see how their needs fit in with the circumstances of all who must perform well.

Ask stakeholders for ways to monitor the resolution of their concerns. You will probably not succeed initially in creating fairness. Working to improve fairness helps, though. Less harm will occur, and you can establish the company's genuine desire to do the right thing. Think about how principle- and process-driven political agreements like the Mayflower Compact and the U.S. Constitution helped establish and maintain the goodwill necessary to create appropriate democratic solutions. When tempers were strained

> Think about providing individualized compensation, tangible and intangible benefits, and recognition for stakeholders as important parts of any superior, new business model.

by tough issues following these agreements, voters, legislators and judges were calmed by realizing that all were pursuing the same purposes in a fair way.

Keep sharing what you learn and looking for solutions until stakeholders are satisfied that the new business model is better for the company, for other stakeholders and for them than what competitors or you offer today. In the process, treat all stakeholders as considerately as you would a customer whom you could not afford to lose. The consideration and care that you show in this process will become part of the fabric of your new business model.

ASK STAKEHOLDERS HOW THEIR PSYCHOLOGICAL AND TANGIBLE BENEFITS SHOULD BE SELECTED AND SHARED

Motivational research has shown that most people feel they should only get psychological benefits in some circumstances (such as a sense of satisfaction from unselfishly helping someone in need), more tangible than intangible benefits in other circumstances (like being asked to accept a company-wide pay cut in exchange for stock options to potentially make up some of the loss and to make one feel more like part of the team), and a balanced mixture of psychological and tangible rewards in other situations (like the pleasure of seeing a new product succeed from one's own thinking and efforts, and receiving a bonus for correctly pursuing that success). The right blend and nature of rewards also varies by person for the same deed. For instance, some people want recognition in public while others may want a handwritten note for the same accomplishment. Think about providing individualized compensation, tangible and intangible benefits, and recognition for stakeholders as important parts of any superior, new business model. Because of their closer contact with stakeholders, many smaller companies can have a big advantage here. Larger companies will have to get many of their employees involved to correctly implement this approach throughout their larger stakeholder base.

Many companies have tried to provide fairer reward sharing by simply helping stakeholders become shareholders. Some only apply this approach to partners and employees. Why not include suppliers, lenders, distributors, customers, end users and the communities you serve? If the entire company's business model will be able to operate more productively, you should be expanding those tangible benefits more broadly. For example, if you offer lenders a chance to advantageously convert their loan principal into company shares, lenders will lower the rate of interest charged. As a result, the company will be able to afford to borrow more money at the same interest cost, allowing stakeholders to benefit more from the business model's expansion. Some communities might be willing to provide more benefits, such as enhanced training for current and potential employees, if they can count on receiving more income and property taxes and owning more valuable shares. You won't know what you can gain from fairer sharing until you explore the alternatives.

As important as it is to explore the alternatives, explaining to stakeholders how to create and exercise the potential benefits is even more important. For example, expanding shareholding potential without adequate explanation usually backfires. One company that didn't describe its stock option grants often found that employees thought that they had received something with no value. Employees treated the options accordingly. Some let "in the money" options expire unexercised. Those companies that explained the economic value of stock options usually convinced employees that they had something valuable, but seldom made much headway in improving performance. The potential for gains seemed out of an employee's control. The best results were achieved by those companies that explained how the option values increase with better economic performance, and showed how an employee can affect that performance by increasing sales, reducing unneeded costs and eliminating unnecessary assets. For example, buying airline tickets sooner sometimes reduces costs while providing the same or a better seat assignment and itinerary for the traveler. Both those who fly and those who book the flights could have an impact here.

Recognition is a little tougher to evaluate because many people are reluctant to ask for what they would like to have. In some cases, potential recipients of recognition have thought so little about it that they don't know how they would be affected until they receive recognition. For instance, a technology company invited all stakeholders who were not shareholders to the company's annual shareholder meeting. The CEO asked each one to stand, described the contributions the person had made during the prior year, and asked for applause. Every single honoree was thrilled to her or his toes. Needless to say, each person thought about what they could do to help the company more in the year ahead, anticipating the pleasure from their praise at the next annual meeting. Since most companies don't do anything like this, most stakeholders would never think of asking for such recognition. It would seem out of place to do so.

> **Interesting work will be the best benefit that many business models provide.**

To be able to offer the right benefits to be shared, plan to supplement the ideas you get from stakeholders for recognition and other intangible rewards with ones that you have read or heard about, as well as your own ideas of what you would like to receive if you were a different type of stakeholder.

IMPROVE THE INTRINSIC SATISFACTIONS OF WORKING WITH THE IMPROVED BUSINESS MODEL

Interesting work will be the best benefit that many business models provide. Yet many companies will focus on how they can do a task at the lowest near-term cost, instead of the most satisfying way to encourage lower costs over both the near and long term and future improvements.

Although people will differ in their preferences, here are some areas to consider:

- Help stakeholders see, hear and feel the positive impact of the new business model. For example, a Haemonetics stakeholder should get a chance to meet people whose lives have been saved by the company's latest technologies.

- Open the way for all stakeholders to work more closely with others to make a greater direct contribution to creating new benefits. Getting different types of stakeholders together to work on important issues is a good way to begin.

- Let stakeholders help individualize your offerings. Begin by imagining what types of individualization are important and follow through to delivering the results.

- Encourage stakeholders to get involved in innovation tasks they love doing. They will be more creative, inspired and satisfied as a result.

HELP STAKEHOLDERS UNDERSTAND HOW UNEXPECTED CIRCUMSTANCES COULD AFFECT THEIR BENEFITS

Since life isn't very predictable, you need to anticipate that the benefits you expect to share may not be available in the quantities and ways that you have planned. Be sure to check how well benefit sharing will work in good times and bad, and with greater and lesser success in initial implementation. Think of this checking as the sort of "torture" pretesting that product manufacturers use to find flaws before placing a new item into customers' hands, such as EMC uses for its storage hardware. Look for ways your new model's benefits and methods for sharing them could crash and burn in the world of imagination, so that stakeholders won't be harmed in reality.

After you turn up potential flaws, locate ways to shift burdens and windfalls more appropriately. Making those adjustments before inaugurating a new business model is easy to do. Adjusting the benefit structure in the same way after it has been operating for a while is more difficult and painful, and can undermine the new direction. However, make needed changes whenever you notice problems occurring, or your inaction will signal a lack of integrity that will be even more harmful. Most companies are better at alleviating painful extremes than protecting against unbalanced windfalls for some. For example, CEOs and executives will usually receive bonuses and stock-option gains occurring solely due to a competitor's independent misfortunes, such as a plant being shut down by regulators. Companies can help ensure against unjustified windfalls by putting caps on how much is received by someone when other stakeholders are not prospering nearly as much. These caps are especially needed when the outsized benefits of some actually reduce the benefits of others, such as where a fixed-size benefit pool is being shared.

KEY QUESTIONS

- *How can you be sure that benefits are being shared in ways that are both fair and perceived that way?* Surveys can help. Also, tell everyone that the company wants and needs to know about inequities, and will address them. What method will work best in your culture to do this? Many leaders describe having frequent hands-on meetings in small groups with stakeholders as one helpful communications device, when the stakeholders understand that their challenges to the status quo are welcome.

- *What can you do to be sure that the benefits that are received are the ones that stakeholders most appreciate?* Ideally, give benefit choices. Think of this approach as being like cafeteria benefit plans. In those plans, employees receive a certain economic value, and each person chooses the benefit combination that works best for them. A young person may select more time off. An older person may want greater payments into a retirement plan. Extended further, stakeholders should be able to swap tangible for intangible rewards and vice versa to best fit their needs at the time.

- *How can your business model serve more purposes that are meaningful to stakeholders?* Berkshire Hathaway has a charitable giving program where shareholders determine to whom the corporation's donations will be given. Timberland lets employees decide where to spend their paid volunteer time. Partners often participate in each other's family and cultural observances as a way to deepen relationships and respect. When Chrysler was in trouble after Mr. Lee Iacocca became CEO, suppliers, dealers, union employees and the government were all willing to make sacrifices and investments to help the company survive because that goal was important to them all. Chrysler emerged stronger for their contributions and with a new willingness to create a better business model built on its new platform of minivans, SUVs and higher quality.

PART THREE

EXPAND BUSINESS MODEL INNOVATION

Opportunities multiply as they are seized.
—Sun-Tzu

Succeeding with a competitively advantaged business model is like running downhill with a tail wind. But as you run with your advantaged business model, strategic treasures also surround you, waiting to be grasped. Each treasure provides additional ways to improve your business and extend your competitive lead. How can you carry and make the best use of these treasures as you run on? It's an exciting prospect!

An uninspiring and potentially threatening circumstance is to have a business model that offers instead no new ways to improve your competitive position. An even worse alternative is to stick with a business model that competitors are overtaking. That's scary!

What's involved in developing the first situation, rather than one of the latter two? Let's return to your role as the parent of two children operating a neighborhood lemonade stand to show how such strategic treasures can be obtained and best employed. As you think about the lemonade stand, look for parallels to your own opportunities to be a business model innovator.

You and your children should prefer to make each of your innovations while you have no competition. Then you'll have more time to make changes, and your sales are less likely to be hurt if you briefly stumble while making the changes. You will also have more access to scarce resources like good locations and workers to support your expanded concept when you add new locations to serve other areas in the city.

Naturally, your children may be tempted to simply copy a neighbor's next-generation business model. That route involves less hard thinking. Unfortunately, the competitive heat they could feel from that competitor would make it harder to succeed, and the success would have to be divided with the competitor. If that innovator kept making successful improvements to a newly advanced business model, your children might always be at a disadvantage. This situation would mean smaller sales and profits from the same effort.

So the lesson is: *Start first and stay focused on adding business model innovations to gain and keep a profitable competitive advantage.* Each successful innovation you make can help you expand your potential to do even more. This subject is explored in Chapter 6 by looking at several case studies of what to do . . . and what not to do. You'll float over the Atlantic with Sir Richard Branson, take a snapshot with a Polaroid camera, remodel your kitchen with American Woodmark, upgrade your cell phone with TriQuint Semiconductor, improve your record keeping with Iron Mountain and start a new career in commercial art with Education Management.

At some point, your children's opportunities to innovate with lemonade stands will require adapting to local customer needs in flexible ways. Part One's introduction mentioned selling used golf balls near golf courses, as one example. In some areas, people may prefer pink lemonade to the yellow kind. Limeade may make a good second offering in other neighborhoods. Near a park filled with young children, play group services might be a good offering.

Next to a beach, selling sun tan lotion and renting sun umbrellas might make sense. And so on.

Coming up with these ideas doesn't have to be hard or expensive. Central planning favored by many companies for all such individual adjustments would quickly add costs while slowing down the rate of experimentation. Obviously, a better solution is to have the people running each lemonade stand look around, think, listen to their customers and ask questions to learn about their customers' unmet needs. Then, use low-cost, low-risk experimentation to validate that stand's new concepts before making any changes permanent.

Sharing best practices among lemonade stands can also increase local innovation and the rate of spreading successful ideas. Hearing about success with pink lemonade might encourage another stand to try selling pink grapefruit juice. By hearing how others' experiments turned out, each stand will get more and better ideas for its own tests. Then, if enough stands can use the same supplies, look to develop product benefit or cost advantages as well.

Create an effective operating organization that focuses on producing business model innovation, as much as it does on excellence in providing current offerings. Chapter 7 describes how business model innovation can become a new core competency in your organization. Examples there show you a variety of methods for adding this key skill. You'll also explore the mindset that leads to more business model innovation.

CHAPTER 6

START BUSINESS MODEL INNOVATION AHEAD OF COMPETITORS AND STAY FOCUSED

Get there first with the most. . . .
—Nathan Bedford Forrest

Some business model innovations allow only the innovator to prosper among all industry suppliers. Even better for the innovator is the business model that permanently closes many potentially attractive paths to competitors. In most other cases, the business model innovator normally gets most of the early benefit, even if followed by copycat competitors.

Mention continuing business model innovation, and British billionaire Sir Richard Branson comes to many minds. In 1966, the dyslexic sixteen-year-old dropped out of school to establish the national English publication, *Student*. At twenty, he founded Virgin Records as a mail-order record retailer by advertising in *Student*. Sir Richard saw this as an opportunity to provide more customer value through discount prices after the law changed so that record producers could no longer dictate retail prices. He picked the name while talking to some friends, noting that "since we're complete virgins at business, let's call it just that: 'Virgin.'" The Virgin brand has since become part of more than 100 businesses that Sir Richard has established and is one of the best recognized in the world. These businesses have included many diverse activities such as an airline, bridal wear, financial services and soft drinks.

Virgin Records went rapidly from exclusively mail order to opening retail stores, the company's first reinvention, in response to a postal union strike. Within two years of its founding, Sir Richard built his own recording studio and produced his first record album, *Tubular Bells*, as the company's second reinvention. It sold over five million copies, yet was produced with inexpensive talent. He later recruited top recording artists as diverse as the Sex Pistols, Boy George, Paula Abdul, Phil Collins and the Rolling Stones, many from other recording companies, in creating his third reinvention. How's that for business model innovation? Most people would have stopped there.

Not satisfied, Sir Richard cofounded Virgin Atlantic Airways in 1984 to redefine long-distance airline travel from being a drudge into being a pleasure. Business-class travelers were transported by limousine, pampered like royalty in a special club on the ground and given superb service in flight. Economy passengers got the latest forms of electronic entertainment for free. It was very easy to earn free flights on the highly rated airline. Severe competition from British Airways almost did him in, however. Due to this pressure, he had to sell Virgin Records to EMI. Later, he won an enormous legal award from British Airways for its excessive tactics used against Virgin Atlantic.

Personally flamboyant and unstoppable, Sir Richard publicized his airline and had fun while setting boat and hot air balloon records (crossing both the Atlantic and a short route across the Pacific aloft). For a fascinating account of his approach to business model innovation, read his entertaining, and often colorful, autobiography, *Losing My Virginity* (Times Books, 1999).

Sir Richard's business model innovations give the impression of being single-mindedly focused on providing something better for customers in a way that most people would prefer. Get that customer benefit part right, and he found that the rest of the business model can usually be worked out. To make the customer benefits affordable to provide has often required numerous rounds of business model innovation by the boundless billionaire. When asked what kind of financial analysis he does before starting a business, he is reported to have indicated that he doesn't do any. As proof, he pointed out that no sane person who had done any financial analysis would start an airline. Airlines are notoriously capital intensive and unprofitable.

By having Virgin stand for such recognizable superiority in products and services, he can expect customers to eagerly try his latest innovations. His unabashed flair for self-promotion helps. For instance, he wore a bridal gown to launch Virgin Bridal. How many male billionaire CEOs would do that?

AVOID THE TECHNOLOGY TRAP

New companies normally focus on providing a better alternative for customers. Often this solution is built around a new technology. Come back to the same company two decades later, and the same "breakthrough" solution may not have been replaced with something better. This company is vulnerable both to start-ups that bring improved ways to serve customers and to established companies that add better solutions.

Think about Polaroid. Founded by the inventive Dr. Edwin Land, the company was the first to provide photographic images straight from the camera within seconds through ingenious chemical, electronic and mechanical interactions. Professional photographers used these images to test the lighting for traditional photographic exposures. Families could be sure a snapshot meant for the family album had the desired image. If not, they could reshoot until an image met their expectations.

> **Focus on providing more superior results for customers than the competitors, regardless of the method used. You can do that with a new business model, a new technology or a combination of the two. If that means pioneering, do it.**

But traditional photography kept rolling on with quality

improvements. Professional quality cameras, lenses and film became affordable for many people, and the skill of amateurs developed. Polaroid photography came to mean fast, but expensive and not very good.

The company's processing speed advantage became less significant, too, when many drug stores began offering one hour prints from ordinary film. Then digital cameras came along, which provided a test image faster and cheaper than Polaroid. Photography fans could also more conveniently store, crop, print and send their images electronically.

> **Notice that business model innovation usually requires more mental agility than resources, so when you focus your thinking on this kind of innovation the playing field is initially either level or slightly tilted in your favor.**

Polaroid sales and profits were ultimately overexposed to the competitor's advances. The company filed for bankruptcy protection in 2001.

Focus on providing more superior results for customers than the competitors, regardless of the method used. You can do that with a new business model, a new technology or a combination of the two. If that means pioneering, do it. Polaroid may have needed to partner with firms that had other kinds of business and technical expertise to fully develop its purpose of providing high-quality, fast images. By focusing innovation on a lagging technology rather than on its business model or a better technology, the firm faltered. Its traditional technology was a filter that kept better solutions unexposed.

START FIRST ON BUSINESS MODEL INNOVATION

Being first with business model innovation sounds impossible for a start-up or a small business. The world is full of long-standing companies that seem to serve virtually every conceivable need.

Can you better serve those needs with a new business model? Probably you can. And if you can, then you may be the first in the industry to compete based on continuing business model innovation. Notice that business model innovation usually requires more mental agility than resources, so when you focus your thinking on this kind of innovation the playing field is initially either level or slightly tilted in your favor.

Examples of Pioneering Innovators

Here are four examples of relatively new businesses that pioneered new business models. Later in the chapter, we show how new advantages were added to their initial business model innovations.

Faster Kitchen Cabinets

American Woodmark was already a high-volume kitchen cabinet manufacturer when it realized that greater profitability required even more volume. The company thought that it could use the rapid geographical expansions of Home Depot and Builders Square stores to become the first cabinetmaker to offer one-week delivery for builders, remodelers and do-it-yourselfers. When time was of the essence, American Woodmark would have the advantage.

In 1980, the company set up a new production schedule and distribution centers to make one-week delivery available. Selling its cabinets faster through Home Depot and Builders Square meant lower distributor markups to the kitchen cabinet purchaser. As a result, when price was of the essence, American Woodmark had another important advantage. When both time and price were issues, American Woodmark had a double-edged advantage.

The new distribution channel provided a further edge. Homeowners, builders and architects could see the cabinets locally to pick out the ones they liked best. Because they could compare samples of countertops and flooring to the cabinet finishes, homeowners could enjoy a better looking kitchen.

Volume soared as these cutting edge advantages took business away from expensive cabinetmakers who took longer to deliver. By 1985, the company (which was started by acquiring a Boise Cascade operation) went public to raise the capital to finance its rapid expansion.

Getting the Message

By 1991, TriQuint Semiconductor had learned how to make high-quality, low-cost gallium arsenide semiconductors, which was an emerging electronics technology. The company's expertise was bolstered in that year by having merged three pioneering firms: Gazelle Microcircuits, Gigabit Logic and TriQuint. But there were few established uses for this new technology.

TriQuint decided to specialize in two applications: high-performance wired optical networks and wireless communications. For optical networks, it looked at how to speed up traffic. For wireless communications, it anticipated that the new higher frequencies that regulators made available would require better electronics to provide clear signals.

This dual focus led TriQuint to become the leader in applying its technology to those applications. Developing knowledge about the end-market issues was critical to TriQuint's success, because these circuits are designed to optimize certain kinds of communications performance. By being the first to focus on many of these problems with its technology, the company was able to make rapid progress in learning and creating products that provided helpful solutions.

Setting the Records Straight

Iron Mountain started as a data and paper records storage service for the New York and New England areas. Auditors usually insisted that companies employ off-site storage for their backup computer files. Iron Mountain's first facility was in a cave, which provided unrivaled security. Since its trucks were carrying data storage from and to customer locations and there was plenty of empty space in the cave, it was logical to bid for the customers' paper storage business as well.

Management next developed a vision to provide all of a customer's records and information storage and management. Served by many tiny companies, the industry was ripe for consolidation and an improved business model to deliver all of these needs.

Bell & Howell had the same idea and started in this direction by purchasing the Bekins records storage business in California and small operators across the country. When Bell & Howell's management decided to take the company private, it sold the records storage business to Iron Mountain. Iron Mountain thus became the only national vendor of these services.

The company could now add value to local storage companies when it acquired them by bringing in national account volume and more professional management of outsourced customer accounts. Soon, business was growing rapidly.

Launching More Successful Careers

Commercial art schools had been teaching for decades when Education Management started out in 1969 by purchasing the Art Institute of Pittsburgh. How could the company develop an advantage?

Education Management expanded its focus from teaching commercial art to also serving employers' needs. The company learned to help its students get and hold commercial art jobs and make better career progress in them. Education Management initially made seven business model changes:

1. Continually define, update and add to the curriculum around employers' current and future needs, by actively involving employers in the curricula development process.
2. Employ faculty who are practicing professionals for career specific subjects.
3. Build the curriculum to concentrate on what students need for job success.
4. Create facilities and technology like the professional career environment.
5. Help graduates get jobs.
6. Make potential students aware of these educational and career choices.
7. Start up or acquire small local schools and convert them to the Education Management business model

through substantial investments, and install detailed planning and information systems to manage those operations.

This new business model meant that Education Management was often the first commercial school in a metropolitan area to offer a diversity of art, design and culinary programs, along with a superior faculty, facilities, technology and job-market outreach. This business model could either shift an acquired school's direction (like the Art Institute of Pittsburgh) or direct a new school to effectively employ the company's improving acumen. In 2002, Education Management had twenty-four art institutes located in twenty-one major metropolitan areas across the United States, with a student population of 32,000 as of the fall 2001.

The Advantages of Starting First

Each of these companies developed close relations with important customers and noncustomer stakeholders through its new business model. American Woodmark optimized cabinet manufacturing and distribution, while making life easier for those who would use and install the cabinets. TriQuint was hearing the cries of the biggest customers for wired optical networks and wireless applications, and helping equipment designers establish improved solutions. Iron Mountain showed customers the benefits of outsourcing data management while providing the biggest, national customers with safer, more reliable storage. Education Management looked to provide a more productive employee to the largest local, regional and national employers, while making it more economically attractive for students to learn.

Once you have such relationships, keep them inaccessible to competitors. To wall off competitors while maintaining the relationships, first learn about the newest and most difficult problems these key stakeholders have. You can also create dialogues with stakeholders to improve on your business model.

You start with a base volume that can make everything new

you do more profitable, allows you to offer more stakeholder benefits, lets you provide more attractive pricing and lowers your costs. American Woodmark operated its factories more intensively with longer volume runs. TriQuint sold higher volumes of its chips than competitors in these same applications, which lowered its development and production costs on a per unit basis. Iron Mountain filled its storage sites faster and collected more revenues per facility than those who did

> In planning your improved business model, locate enhancements where being first will provide the most ongoing competitive advantages.

not have national accounts or data management services. Education Management saw its revenues rise in fully developed schools, with relatively little additional investment.

In the cases of Education Management and Iron Mountain, business model advantages also made it possible for the companies to expand geographically through acquisitions and local start-ups, while enjoying superior economic results compared to competitors. With this enhanced geographic scale came the opportunity to develop even more potential business model advantages.

In planning your improved business model, locate enhancements where being first will provide the most ongoing competitive advantages. The four strategic questions you should be continually asking are:

1. In serving what needs can you be first with the new business model?
2. Where does being first provide the most initial advantage?
3. Where does being first provide the most potential long-term advantage?
4. How large can you become by serving each need?

STAY FOCUSED ON THE FIRST SOLUTIONS WHERE YOU HAVE AN ADVANTAGE AND EXPAND ON THAT STRENGTH

Have you ever watched pent-up, flowing water break through an earthen dam? At first, the water simply washes against the dam's side. Gradually, the water's weight and current begin eroding the weakest sections of the dam's soil. Next, earth along the entire dam begins to fall into the water. But the sections that eroded first continue to succumb more rapidly than the rest. Suddenly, a small trickle of water escapes the dam. The trickle rapidly becomes a stream and then a torrent. Meanwhile, the water cuts an ever-wider channel through the breached sections of the dam. Adjacent sections collapse from the wetness and water pressure. Soon, the water has escaped the dam.

This natural physical process also captures the way that business model innovations work. The innovation attracts open-minded customers with great potential to benefit. Other similar customers will be attracted next. In subsequent business model improvements, the innovator must first concentrate on the advantage that has breached the dam of customer indifference. In this way, the next innovation can gain more rapidly than the last one. When a company shifts attention to serving dissimilar customers or to unrelated benefits, stout indifference to the new offerings will probably hold back the innovation.

Examples Updated

Let's look again at the four innovating companies to see how they built on their initial business model advantages to accelerate growth and profitability.

From Low-Priced Fast Delivery to Just-in-Time Differentiated Products

American Woodmark's fast delivery to home improvement outlets propelled the company forward. The company received a wake-up call when competitors began to match and, in some cases, exceed its performance. An improved business model was needed.

The new vision was to become a fully integrated, just-in-time manufacturer providing a broader choice of brands, styles, better quality and lower costs with fast delivery and low prices. Manufacturing centered around a team-based cell. This new direction required changing the company's culture, learning new ways of working, and replacing almost every procurement and manufacturing process. Building on these new strengths, the company was able to expand its offerings to include bathroom vanities. As a result, more fashion is appearing in America's kitchens and bathrooms.

Despite its success, the firm serves only about 5 percent of the market. Additional business model innovations will undoubtedly be required to capture more of the market and to fend off hard-charging competitors.

From Message Specialist to Component Subspecialties

TriQuint Semiconductor found that more specialized knowledge of customer needs allowed it to create even more and better solutions through designing its analog circuits. Early on, the company hit on the idea of continually splitting its organization into smaller and smaller units to help focus its design talent more closely on specific application opportunities. Currently, the company has a wireless communications division for products such as cellular telephones, a telecom/datacom division for fiber optics, and a division for higher-frequency applications such as satellites and wireless data links that was originally acquired from Texas Instruments.

The wireless communications group could be split further in the future along the lines of the different end-market component needs. For example, since Europe and the United States use different cellular telephone technologies, this group could become two divisions by having each work on handsets for just one of the two technologies. Undoubtedly, that focus would help drive further innovation and product improvements.

The ongoing principle behind these splits is to focus on an ever-narrower set of applications that represents large volumes. In essence, the company is getting the best of two worlds. It is operating the divisions as if it were spinning them off to make them more focused and autonomous. At the same time, the company maintains and builds its combined strength through the ways it manufactures all of the semiconductors.

To succeed with this approach, the company needs to maintain or build its competitive strength in manufacturing. To increase its strength, the company takes on the designs of customers and manufactures them as a foundry. This added volume and diversity of designs injects new challenges and skill-development opportunities.

From Orderly Records to Cutting Records Costs Everywhere

Iron Mountain realized that its national coverage needed to expand to meet all of a customer's storage needs. The company acquired other firms to fill the geographical gaps, often making eighteen to twenty purchases a year. This domestic consolidation was capped in 2000 when Iron Mountain purchased Pierce Leahy, one of the company's largest competitors for paper storage.

Large companies do business globally. Recognizing that, Iron Mountain began acquiring a worldwide capability in 1999. Europe and Latin America were the initial focus. By 2001, the company was clearly the world's leader in records and information management services.

In this business, customers seldom change suppliers. The average account lasts for fifty years. As a result, Iron Mountain is building a long-term relationship with customers that enables the company to add new services. These new services build on its knowledge of how each customer uses storage and information, and increase the profitability of existing accounts and acquisitions.

All Iron Mountain employees are eligible for gain-sharing incentives based on both the performance of their unit and the entire company. This stake in the company's overall success may have encouraged service innovation in support of the company's business model.

Here are examples of new offerings. One service helps ensure that digital records can be read and used when they are retrieved from storage. Iron Mountain will also do confidential shredding and disposal of outdated paper records inside its secure sites. Its consulting services are always adding new ways for customers to reduce records cost while increasing the integrity of those records.

From Teaching Commercial Art to Creatively Improving Education

Commercial art applies artist talent and skill to commerce. Education Management soon learned from employers that they needed commercial artists with broader backgrounds. The company first expanded the variety of educational disciplines at the associate of arts level. The firm later added bachelor degree programs that required an additional eighteen months of learning, but led to a much higher economic return for graduates on their educational investment.

These changes created a win-win-win situation for students, employers and Education Management. Soon, the expanded curriculum was being successfully taught throughout its nationwide system.

When computers became more important to design work, Education Management added significant workplace technology to the classroom to prepare students for multimedia and Internet work.

> **Focus adds to knowledge of what customers need and how to provide better solutions.**

To test the relevance of these changes, Education Management paid attention to the percentage of students who finish the bachelor's program compared to those who start. Currently, 55 percent get their degree. By comparison, the national average completion rate of all bachelor's degree programs is 40 percent. Many factors contribute. Students with a vocational interest are more likely to complete their education when they see the education as relevant. Students enjoy their subjects and the way that

Education Management enables them to learn leading-edge practices. The schools also make it easy for students to find part-time,

> **Adding superior new solutions for a long time increases customer stability.**

summer and full-time employment with interesting companies.

The company now sees the opportunity to provide Internet-based learning for those who don't have the time to study full-time or don't live near its schools. It has three bachelor's degree programs online and has trained more than 200 faculty members as online facilitators. Student and industry reaction to online course work has been very positive. Ultimately, online courses are expected to operate at a higher profit margin than those that are site-based.

> **Make your competitive advantage in customer performance good enough, and you can afford to acquire your most significant competitors through the profits earned by upgrading them to your business model.**

Reflecting its development, Education Management describes its art institutes as "America's leader in creative education." Future company opportunities include applying this business model to other educational disciplines. In December 2001, Education Management acquired Argosy Education Group, which has undergraduate and graduate academic

programs in the behavioral sciences, education, business, law and health sciences with nearly 6,000 students as of the fall 2001.

The Advantages of Staying Focused on Building from Initial Advantages

As you can see from these examples, focus adds to knowledge of what customers need and how to provide better solutions. Without that focus on continuing business model innovation, competitors can gradually catch up to an advantaged business model as happened briefly to American Woodmark.

Adding superior new solutions for a long time increases customer stability. From such longer-term relationships, even more can be learned. At the same time, your reputation can be improved with these customers, making them more willing to try your new products and services.

Most interestingly, adding new benefits onto your business model innovations can expand your competitive advantage. Make your competitive advantage in customer performance good enough, and you can afford to acquire your most significant competitors through the profits earned by upgrading them to your business model. The price premium they demand is easily justified by the value your improved business model brings to their operations. Clearly, Education Management and Iron Mountain understand and apply this lesson.

> Unlike most areas in life where more is less (like eating too much), building these business models, adding onto them and rebuilding them seems more like designing and filling an expandable museum of new wonders. Each new attraction draws your attention, and the mass appeal of them all keeps you coming back.

Can this process of constantly improving business models ever stop? No. TriQuint's approach to constantly seeking to specialize its divisions into smaller and smaller sets of problems is a good model here. Even that fine approach will probably require reworking in the future. For example, at some point the company will probably have to address how to take its customer knowledge and apply it to designing components using other semiconductor technologies. In addition, extreme narrowing of focus may eventually make it organizationally hard to optimize solutions across the customer's total systems needs, unless divisions become very good at teaming up with one another.

Continuing business model innovation is an exciting challenge. Greater opportunities to apply creativity and gain competitive advantage are constantly being opened, like automatic doors responding to your progress along a never-ending hallway of success. Unlike most areas in life where more is less (like eating too much), building these business models, adding onto them and rebuilding them seems more like designing and filling an expandable museum of new wonders. Each new attraction draws your attention, and the mass appeal of them all keeps you coming back.

KEY QUESTIONS

- *Where have you been first to offer an important stakeholder benefit?* For American Woodmark, it was providing fast delivery through home improvement centers. If you are not sure, ask your customers why they initially selected your company. Listen for what you did better or differently than competitors.

- *Are you still the only company to provide this benefit?* If you made your innovation more than ten years ago, someone has probably either duplicated or surpassed you in this area. You need to build a new customer advantage from the base of the old one, especially if its effectiveness is waning or gone.

- *How can you add new competitive advantages to your initial innovation?* Although you already looked at the most common sources of new advantages in chapters 1, 2 and 3, focusing now on where you innovated in the past should stimulate new ideas. Your customers probably have unfilled needs and preferences that favor further innovation in those same areas.

- *If you have not improved your business model at least every five years, what has held you back?* Most companies feel that they could have made their most successful business model innovations many years earlier. The most common reason given for the delay is that business model innovation was assigned a lower priority than expanding the last innovation. That's usually a major mistake because the competitive advantages and growth associated with the next innovation will normally be much greater than is achieved from expanding and optimizing the last innovation. You can see that difference from the examples in this chapter. By moving faster, you cut off the opportunity for someone to get there first.

- *How can you build more often on your first competitive advantage?* More focus is needed on this question. Are you testing all the promising ideas you should be? Can you use recognition and financial incentives to shift attention? What else has worked well for your company in the past to create more attention on useful innovation?

CHAPTER 7

ENHANCE YOUR ORGANIZATION'S ONGOING BUSINESS MODEL INNOVATION CAPABILITY

Sweet and low, sweet and low. . . .
—Alfred, Lord Tennyson

Visit any orchard where customers pick their own fruit, and you will find the lower branches relatively bare. All the branches that require a ladder to reach will be drooping with ripe fruit. Imagine creating orchards that bear more fruit, all of which can be reached from the ground. Creating such accessible bounty is what continuing business model innovation can do.

New business models often produce greater stakeholder harvests. Yet time and competitors will erode the advantages that created the bounty. The most successful companies see each new business model as being like a single tree producing one variety of fruit . . . just one dimension of the potential harvest among many varieties and trees in a large orchard. Nurturing business model design skill will provide more low-hanging fruit. Otherwise, companies will find themselves having to reach for harder to find gains from the existing model, like stretching to reach higher-hanging fruit without a ladder.

Few individuals have been involved in more business model innovations of their own activities than Professor Peter F. Drucker, the well-known pioneer of management studies. Professor Drucker was born in Austria in 1909 at a time when the modern corporation did not yet exist. While many follow Professor Drucker's precepts in managing their companies, few know the process that led to those precepts being developed.[1]

His story contains many lessons about the importance of directing your curiosity in the right way. Some of the basics were taught to him by two of his fourth grade teachers, Miss Elsa and Miss Sophy. He was new to the school, and the teachers had him try a full range of activities. After three weeks, he was asked what he did well and what he did not. They agreed with his self-assessment. He was encouraged to set down his learning goals and to track his progress. It was learning by objectives, very similar to today's management by objectives. Throughout the rest of his formal education and in his self-education thereafter, Professor Drucker applied the same method.

As powerful as the method was, it failed in one area . . . penmanship. His parents had transferred him into the new school primarily to help improve the legibility of his handwriting. In those days before computers (or even electric typewriters), few could appreciate what you wrote unless they could read your inky squiggles.

He discovered that learning by objectives failed to help his penmanship for two reasons. First, he had little manual dexterity and few helpful instincts in this area. Cutting a simple milking stool's three legs to the same length using a miter box and saw was beyond him. Second, he had no interest in penmanship. Consequently, his first innovation was to shift learning by objectives from everything he studied (including subjects where he was doing poorly, such as penmanship), to just the areas where he could excel. Rapid educational and career progress followed.

He soon found himself drawn to journalism. That craft helped him learn how to express his ideas in simple, clear language, which was his second personal innovation. How many academics are known for their clarity? Throughout his long career,

Professor Drucker was able to communicate his ideas to mass and influential audiences through newspaper and magazine articles. *Harper's*, *The Saturday Evening Post*, *The Wall Street Journal* and *Harvard Business Review* counted him among their most frequent and widely read contributors. Considering that English was an acquired language for him, his felicity is all the more remarkable.

After coming to the United States to flee from fascism in Europe, Professor Drucker was well established in an academic career by the beginning of World War II. His first book, *The End of Economic Man: The Origins of Totalitarianism* (Transaction, 1995), drew lots of attention in the economic and political science academic communities. He was recruited by a number of American universities. Instead of choosing the most prestigious, he chose the one where he could have the most freedom to teach whatever he wanted. Bennington College in Vermont was a happy academic home for many years. There he came to his third innovation: He found that he could best learn a subject by teaching it. As you probably know, most academics take the opposite tack. From this experience, he became a superb teacher, partly inspired by the lessons he retained from Miss Elsa and Miss Sophy.

Then his path began to veer in a new direction. He completed *The Future of Industrial Man* (Transaction, 1995) in 1941, and argued that "the business enterprise had become the constitutive institution of industrial society and the institution within which both principles of governance and the individual's status and function had to be realized." This view that seems obvious to us today was so radical at the time that both academics and business people were alarmed. Professor Drucker knew that he could make no further progress in this area until he could study a large industrial enterprise. But none wanted anything to do with him. In those days, companies shunned any outsiders, and an academic would have been the last person sought. Corporate executives with college degrees often hid that distinction. So this path was temporarily stymied by academic alarm and corporate indifference.

World War II experiences brought his fourth innovation. The federal government wanted his help with the war effort. A proffered full-time job turned into part-time consulting. He found that he enjoyed the consulting and could be far more effective in that role rather than as a full-time employee. Thus was born his long and distinguished career as an individual consultant.

In the fall of 1943, General Motors beckoned. The company's vice chairman, Mr. Donaldson Brown, had read *The Future of Industrial Man* and recognized in it many themes of what he and Mr. Alfred Sloan, the chief executive officer, had been working on. Mr. Brown was concerned that the company's pioneering initiatives might be ignored by younger executives if the initiatives were not made more explicit and fully understood. He invited Professor Drucker to help. After interviewing executives who could see no purpose to the assignment, he learned that they would all love to have a book about General Motors. Mr. Brown encouraged him to proceed, and he was given remarkable access. In 1946, *Concept of the Corporation* (new ed., John Day, 1972) was the result. This was Professor Drucker's first management book, and his fifth innovation, as he began to define the basic parameters of what we now know as "management."

He went on to create dozens of innovations in the field of management. In every book about management we read, we find echoes of his earlier thoughts, questions and observations. Certainly, the type of corporate access he successfully pioneered at General Motors was essential to making a book like *The Ultimate Competitive Advantage* possible as well as the many excellent case-study-based business books that are available today.

Let's mention just a few more innovations, though, that pertain to directing future business model innovation. Professor Drucker soon learned that management is a task, and that all organizations require someone to do this task. He expanded his studies to include nonprofit and governmental organizations. Throughout his career, half of his consulting was done at no charge for nonprofit organizations, including the Salvation Army and the Girl Scouts. In this way, he often learned important lessons that he could share with others because nonprofits often innovated first. Those who wish to improve should follow his example and study the most successful innovators.

Professor Drucker also organized a style of life-long learning by employing education by objectives. Each year he reads widely on a subject about which he knows nothing and that seemingly has no connection to his professional work. One year the subject was Japanese art. The Druckers developed many insights into that culture as a result and assembled a wonderful collection of Japanese art. Professor Drucker has often employed this understanding to help Japanese companies and to explain Japanese management methods to non-Japanese executives. This cosmopolitan reading broadens his understanding of management and organizations in ways that specialization normally precludes.

Much of the latter part of his career was focused on teaching experienced executives who traveled to Claremont College in California. From this work, he developed many insights into how teachers and executives need to interact to continually improve the ways they help one another. His experience with mass education expanded through providing many speeches and lectures over live video feeds from a local television station.

> When a company produces a superior business model, the abundance of low-hanging fruit can dazzle the senses . . . to distraction.

As you can see, Professor Drucker's innovation advances were built on disciplining his curiosity about how to help people lead more effective, satisfying and free lives, and make more progress. His innovations and conclusions are great gifts to us all. When we focus our curiosity about our business innovation opportunities into a disciplined, wide-ranging search, great results can frequently follow.

LEARN TO FIND PRODUCTIVE
NEW BUSINESS MODELS

New management practices often work well for a time, and then seem to stop creating advantages. Their appeal may wear off. In time there may be some backsliding. Competitors may catch on and match the improvement. In this chapter we examine how continuing business model innovation can provide increasing benefits by expanding on competitive advantages through enhancing innovation skills.

The Bible advises teaching a man to fish to help him more than by simply giving him a fish. But if everyone then knows how to fish, too many fish are caught and the supply eventually declines. As a result, everyone would be fishing a lot and not catching very much. It's much more beneficial for an organization to learn how to fish and produce other healthy food . . . and to perpetually expand the supply of easily captured fish and healthy food supplies in ways others cannot duplicate. As a result, everyone can be more efficiently fed.

There's a problem, though, with increasing an organization's bounty. When a company produces a superior business model, the abundance of low-hanging fruit can dazzle the senses . . . to distraction. While everyone is grabbing and eating the fruit, little attention is paid to improving the next harvest. Frozen vegetable processors have had this problem.

Processing plants were originally located where the lowest-priced vegetables were grown in the United States. These plants were usually idle because most areas produced only one vegetable crop for one brief period during a year.

Following the concept of processing the lowest-priced vegetables, the Birds Eye division of General Foods moved some of its processing into northern Mexico because agricultural labor for hand-picked crops was less expensive there. For over a decade the company missed another important advantage: These crops could be grown during three seasons a year in Mexico, greatly reducing processing costs and asset intensity. When financial returns were calculated, these Mexican-based products often yielded more than five times the return on investment available in one-crop areas. The company was slow to expand in Mexico, however, due to the difficulties and one-time costs of improving farming practices there to produce the necessary vegetable quality. Also, the company failed to realize that it could more profitably provide vegetables from three-crop areas, even when the vegetable prices were somewhat higher than in one and two-crop areas.

While taking this toehold in Mexico, Birds Eye also introduced frozen products without vegetables in them. Of these, Cool Whip (a frozen nondairy topping resembling whipped cream) created a bonanza due to its large volume and high profit margins. Cool Whip also added a business model advantage. Any frozen vegetable plant that also made and stored Cool Whip saw its costs and asset intensity lessen for all products. Making Cool Whip was like processing a vegetable that could be harvested every day.

With this low-hanging fruit dangling in front of its eyes, Birds Eye immediately focused on adding new high-margin, non-agriculturally based frozen foods and high-priced vegetable mixtures. Almost all of the subsequent new products failed. The annual losses from these unsuccessful efforts were tens of millions of dollars in today's purchasing power. Distracted by

> **Developing successful business models faster requires that each innovation serve as the beginning of an immediate further improvement.**

the Cool Whip success and the subsequent new product disasters, management continued to ignore the enormous Mexican potential.

Following a management change, agriculturally focused executives had more influence, and they increased emphasis on Mexican production. Birds Eye was able to expand there before competitors perceived the opportunity. However, the time and money lost on the unsuccessful frozen novelties and high-priced vegetable mixtures could, unfortunately, not be regained.

How could such misplaced focus on developing the wrong business model have been avoided? How could the correct business model's implementation have been accelerated? Developing successful business models faster requires that each innovation serve as the beginning of an immediate further improvement. For example, Birds Eye's successful Mexican entry should have immediately stimulated questions about where the company's business model should go from there in Mexico and other three-crop locales, even if vegetable prices were initially higher there.

LOOK AT THE ORCHARD
AS WELL AS THE TREE

During recessions, companies focus on reducing costs and debt. During boom times, hiring people, developing new products and increasing marketing draw attention. If companies always worked on both kinds of opportunities, more progress would occur.

How can you achieve and maintain that progress-enhancing balance in pursuing opportunities? A business model innovation focus will help.

Graft a Branch from the Improved Business Model onto Another Tree

Acacia Research took continual innovation seriously in 2000–2001. Founded as a private early-stage venture capitalist, the firm went public in 1996. The company's management looked for start-ups with competitively advantaged business models that would attract public market investors.

Most initial investments were for Internet-related businesses. One of its last investments with the initial public capital was in a start-up company, CombiMatrix, whose technology promised to make low-cost, quickly produced biochips for testing new pharmaceuticals, diagnostics and agricultural products. The same technology could also provide breakthroughs in materials science (in applications like fuel cells with longer battery lives).

Acacia Research saw the potential of CombiMatrix as being greater than all of its other portfolio investments. Acting on this observation, in 2000 Acacia Research began selling and liquidating everything else in order to focus its management attention and financial resources on this technology.

Next, Acacia Research simplified what CombiMatrix had to do. CombiMatrix would work solely on biochips, its most developed product area. An independently managed joint venture of the two companies would apply the technology to other materials. Creating this new organization allowed Acacia Research to extend the technology innovation into another business model while CombiMatrix's original business model was developed. This approach is like grafting a branch from a superior tree onto another one, so that the advantages of the superior tree can be spread more rapidly.

Acacia Research management will advance the technology's development and start other organizations to pursue further business model innovations as they are warranted. Meanwhile, it will seek independent public financing for each new operation to help them along their separate paths. If this technology is broad enough and Acacia Research is nimble enough, the result will be an ever-

> **Your search for a better path should start back at square one every day, building on what you learned yesterday.**

expanding orchard filled with more productive, cross-bred business models. Acacia Research will play the role of the farmer who continually grafts shoots from the best trees onto other, less productive ones so they can bear more low-hanging fruit.

Start Back at Square One Every Day

When asked about his thought process for making these changes in focus, Mr. Paul R. Ryan, chairman and CEO of Acacia Research, observed that: "You first have to think as a shareholder. . . . Ask yourself, 'what would I want my CEO to be doing?'" Often the answer means having to do things you find distasteful, like eliminating businesses and letting people go. This shareholder focus helps Mr. Ryan overcome procrastination.

Then, ask your management people what they want the CEO to be doing.

In addition, he suggests you continually ask yourself if you are acting as a good custodian of investors' capital. As a test of how well prepared you are for improving your business model, assume that everything will go wrong. Are you prepared for those problems? Are you taking action quickly enough in light of the results you are experiencing?

Finally, Mr. Ryan recommends that your search for a better path should start back at square one every day, building on what you learned yesterday.

Mr. Ryan's questions and approach can easily be expanded to include the interests of other stakeholders. Doing so will bring more focus and helpful insights to eliminate procrastination in identifying and dealing with today's critical, business model innovation opportunities and issues.

TO REACH THE NEXT OPPORTUNITY QUICKLY, HAVE A BUSINESS MODEL VISION BASED ON AN ACCURATE CORE INSIGHT

Without a vision of an orchard filled exclusively with many varieties of low-hanging fruit, such an orchard is unlikely to be developed. Likewise, many people will tell you that it is all but impossible for a company to shift focus from one technology to another. How much harder must it be to shift technologies and business models at the same time? Undaunted, business model innovators are successfully doing both. A vision based on an accurate core insight of what's needed can help guide and speed such difficult focus shifts. In biotechnology, such vision is taking one company past technical innovation to the full enhancements that only business model innovation can make possible.

Mr. Tony L. White joined Perkin-Elmer (a so-so scientific instrument maker) in 1995, and quickly shifted the company's focus from a variety of measurements into a single area: DNA sequencing. Deciphering DNA was a difficult process because so much of the genetic code is comprised of apparently meaningless sections. Where does meaningful information begin and end? No one knew until recently. The U.S. government had started a long-term study to answer the question, and the process was expected to take many years.

To emphasize this shift in the company's focus, the corporate name was sold, along with most of the company's operations to EG&G, which now calls itself PerkinElmer.

Mr. White decided that he could profitably speed up DNA sequencing by providing better equipment for the purpose and employing more effective analytical techniques to the data developed by this equipment. By 1999, the remaining company was organized to accomplish this DNA sequencing speed up. The firm was divided into two symbiotic units, which each had public shares. One unit (now called Applied Biosystems) made improved DNA sequencing machines used to decode the human genome. The other unit was Applied Biosystems' biggest customer, Celera Genomics, which employed sophisticated mathematics and information from the sequencing machines to speed decoding. As a result of Celera's success, a worldwide race to decode the human genome ensued. Hoped-for commercial prizes included patents on influential genes needed for improved medicines.

Pushed by Celera's rapid progress in using advanced mathematical analyses similar to those used in breaking enemy codes, other customers of Applied Biosystems bought more sequencing equipment. Applied's sales, profits and value soared. Medical knowledge advanced much faster than anyone had expected as a result of Mr. White's bet.

Celera planned to sell its completed research to other companies as its ongoing source of profits. The company had expected to beat the public effort in this area by many years. Instead, the government effort speeded up and finished the task shortly after Celera did. When the human genome was decoded by the U.S. government, that information became available for free. How could Celera now earn a living? A new business model was needed.

Celera quickly refocused on turning the newly available genetic data into useful information for developing gene-based medicines. Similar to the race to decode the human genome, Celera will be aided by protein-analyzing machines from Applied Biosystems.[2] This business model switch occurred with very little delay, which indicates that advanced thinking must have been focusing on this opportunity for some time. How was the thinking behind this business model switch accomplished?

> The most fascinating parts of this approach involve Applera's ability to earn a greater profit by encouraging more competition, rather than less, and its ability to influence government-sponsored research to speed up.

Applera's (the new name for Applied's and Celera's parent company) underlying vision for each business model is finding faster and cheaper ways to locate what causes and prevents disease. Applera's core insight is to use improved mathematical models in combination with its own developments of new types of measurement equipment to explain poorly understood biological interactions (including genes and proteins, and probably including enzymes at some point) to fulfill the vision. Applera wants to get full benefit from its knowledge development, so it adopts the necessary business models and organizational structures to make that knowledge harvesting more productive. For now, the business model for this harvesting includes selling equipment, licensing data and developing medicines. In the future, new value-adding methods will probably be employed.

> **Company leaders should always have an improved business model ready to go.**

To us, the most fascinating parts of this approach involve Applera's ability to earn a greater profit by encouraging more competition, rather than less, and its ability to influence government-sponsored research to speed up. It's as though a private company had initially fostered the race to the moon between the United States and the USSR by having establishing an early lead with its own space-exploration program. Further development of business models like this one hold great promise for accelerating breakthroughs in basic science, a field normally characterized by irregular progress through individual academic studies sporadically supported by government funding.

WHILE THE HARVEST IS STILL INCREASING, START SEARCHING FOR THE NEXT BUSINESS MODEL

Even seasoned business remodelers may find themselves running up against limitations. Company leaders should always have an improved business model ready to go.

Zebra Technologies Corporation is a leader in portable printers for making bar-coded labels. When the butcher cuts something special for you, the price label probably comes from a Zebra Technologies printer.

Mr. Edward L. Kaplan, CEO and cofounder, says the company started in 1969 with no business model. He was one of two engineers working part time to provide custom electromechanical designs. The company's first continuing success came from paper tape punches and readers for directing machine tools. After initial growth, Zebra realized that market potential was limited.

So the search was on for a new business model. After two years the company had its first bar-code printer. The timing was good. The Universal Product Code (the largest initial use for bar coding) was adopted in 1973 and went into wide-scale use soon after. The company's initial printer was used at meat and produce counters. Zebra later expanded into industrial markets, prospering when an industry or a large company required its suppliers to use bar codes for supply-chain management. For example, if General Motors wants to simplify its accounting for inventory, having bar codes on all supplies can help. Those handling the supplies simply scan the bar codes, and computers tally what's received and on hand, and what has been used. Naturally, if General Motors tells suppliers they must use bar codes, they will. In 1987, Zebra Technologies sold its paper tape business, completing its first business model evolution.

Gradually, competitors began to make inroads with lower-cost bar code printers for end markets where bar codes had not been previously employed. In many cases, Zebra Technologies chose to acquire a company rather than to develop a more competitive offering. From these acquisitions, the company learned a lot about what the printers could be stretched to do.

Recently, new technologies that involve other ways to identify a product, such as radio-frequency-based devices, began to threaten bar code printing. Stores hoped that such devices could be used to replace checkout counters. A customer would pay with a radio-frequency-enabled credit card while exiting the store's door. Although the new technologies have been unattractive to many customers because of their high cost, Zebra was quick to develop these products.

The bar code printer marketplace was maturing in 2001. In response, the company's top management began a business model redesign. In this work, Zebra Technologies focused on developing the rest of its orchard, while continuing to pick the available fruit.

Many different inputs were sought about what the company's

new business model should be, and how to develop it. Each person agreed that the time to create and deploy an improved business model was before it was needed. The search for an improved business model was undertaken with a sense of urgency and importance.

Since the business model development process was completed, the company has been seeking to expand its worldwide distribution in bar-code printers and increase market share in the plastic card printers and readers used for security. The plastic card printer and reader business should have many similarities to what made the company successful with its bar code printers. Zebra Technologies seems to be well on its way to benefiting from its latest business model development efforts. That's nice progress for a company that initially didn't realize the importance of business models. By involving many people in the latest development, Zebra Technologies has increased the likelihood that business model innovation will become a stronger company skill in the future. The company will also be more likely to work on such innovations long before weak business conditions force the focus.

> **Creating a business model innovation advantage is just such an area where pursuing perfection pays off.**

ESTABLISH AND BUILD ON BUSINESS MODELS THAT ACCELERATE STAKEHOLDER PROSPERITY

For information on how new business models can accelerate industry growth, refer to the Linear Technology example in the Prologue.

DEVELOP YOUR BUSINESS MODEL INNOVATION PROCESS

What is "good enough"? Pursuing perfection can be folly. You may only get 1 percent more benefit from adding 20 percent more improvement. Conversely, there are places where a 1 percent improvement can provide 20 percent more benefits. Creating a business model innovation advantage is just such an area where pursuing perfection pays off.

In our studies, we failed to locate companies that had turned business model development and innovation into formal, nonstop processes, like those used in most larger companies for new product development and quality improvement. Instead, sporadic business model developments are mostly driven by some near-term business problem that looks like it will become worse in the future. Some exceptional companies like Acacia Research, Linear Technology and Xilinx are now responding to one-time opportunities instead of only to problems. Such sporadic innovation efforts are similar to those used by companies to build a new manufacturing plant when more capacity is needed.

> In the near future, continually improving business model innovation will become an essential skill in all industries. Otherwise a company won't be able to keep up.

That observation may surprise you, but, actually, it shouldn't. If your competitors are not yet threatening you with new business models, business model innovators can take their time and still be ahead, as Birds Eye found with its Mexican operations. Such companies will have lost opportunities, but those losses don't show up on a profit and loss statement.

Also, we are just on the threshold of the era of continuing business model innovation. How do the management practices that GM used in the 1940s compare to today? Few would be impressed by the old practices, yet those practices were often the best in the world then.

Companies discussed in this book like Acacia Research, Applera, Business Objects, Education Management, Goldcorp, Iron Mountain, Linear Technology, Mandalay Resort Group, Paychex, QLogic, Xilinx and Zebra Technologies are on the cusp of being able to make this transition to a continual innovation process. Perhaps they will. Stay tuned to their progress.

In the near future, continually improving business model innovation will become an essential skill in all industries. Otherwise a company won't be able to keep up. As we saw from Professor Drucker's example, even an individual can make great progress in business model innovation. A company should be able to do even more by drawing on its greater resources and access to other organizations. To shift to continual business model innovation, focus on both establishing and improving an explicit business model innovation process, while enhancing the capabilities of those who work with the process to employ it well. What are some key elements that companies should focus on to create learning by objectives in this crucial activity?

Make the Process You Have Used Explicit

In the average growing company, most employees have been with the organization in their current job for only a few years. To these people, today's reality often seems like all that there is, or ever has been. As a result, people usually want to optimize what they have. But if the company had only done that kind of optimization in the past, it might not have reached its current prosperity. Leaders need to think about how the company got where it is today, and then use those observations to determine what should be done now.

Most companies have used a process (a sequence of work steps) to create the current business model. Make that past business model innovation process explicit, and you can begin to see what elements need to be repeated and by whom. Most larger organizations have internal consultants and training available for process mapping. Other organizations will find this skill residing with reengineering staffs and consultants. Whether or not you know how to do process mapping, you can make helpful progress by answering the following seven questions and thinking about how to improve on what you learn from the answers:

1. How did the business model innovation process begin?
2. How were objectives set?
3. What questions were asked?
4. How were the questions answered?

5. What did the output look like?

6. How was the output used?

7. How was this thinking turned into operating reality?

Note that for smaller companies, you may be describing the inner dialogues that some senior executives had with themselves. You may be mapping a thought process.

Locate Opportunities to Improve Your Past Innovation Process

If you have only seen one example, it may look pretty good. The first telephone was a marvel in its time, but today it would seem hopelessly ineffective. If Mr. Alexander Graham Bell had known what we do today, the original telephone would have looked much different. How can we see beyond the first example of a business model innovation process?

You may have difficulty in seeing how to improve it, but five methods can help you. You should use them all. Each one will teach you something you need to know.[3]

1. *Compare the process you have used to the best one employed by your current and potential competitors.* What elements are present in their processes that would enhance yours? Draw on published articles, presentations you see at conferences and ethically appropriate conversations with former employees of and suppliers to these companies.

2. *Ask those who would use the process what seems most difficult to do.* Ask them to separate their responses into two categories: (a) where the process can be simplified or speeded up and (b) where they lack knowledge, information, experience, tools and other resources to make the work easier and more effective.

3. *Ask your stakeholders how the process could be improved to better serve their needs.* You may find that stakeholders have not been considered or involved enough.

4. *Think of the most effective innovation process you have seen employed by any other organization.* What elements does that process have that yours does not? What elements does yours have that the other one eliminated? Which changes make sense for you?

5. *Imagine perfection in creating new business models.* Perfection might mean developing a business model overnight that immediately increased your competitive lead over competitors, could be instantly implemented and reduced costs from where you are today. What can you do differently to move closer to that image of perfection? For example, you might have a worldwide competition to improve your business model development process along the lines that Goldcorp used for expanding its known gold reserves.

> Enthusiasm sparks the inspiration that leads to the best business model innovations.

Test Your Improvement Options for the Stakeholder Enthusiasm They Generate

Think back to your company's greatest successes. Were they shrouded in gloom or sparkling with excitement? Chances are there was some gloom along the way from temporary setbacks. Yet, potential success probably dispelled some of the gloom to lighten the spirits of those involved. Enthusiasm sparks the inspiration that leads to the best business model innovations.

Creative effectiveness and skill in employing its results are boosted by feeling in control over the creative process. Almost everyone spends more time on activities that he or she likes doing. You can expect the best results by choosing process improvements favored by those who will be working with the process.

Begin Running Nonstop Business Model Development

Do teams get better by practicing all the time, or by only practicing when they lose? Everyone who has played on a winning team knows that regular practice is critical to success. Otherwise running or countering a play (football and basketball processes) is done poorly. Business model innovation is no exception.

Constantly reexamine, improve on and replace your business models. Set goals and provide incentives to accomplish this continual activity. As you do, also be sure to constantly reexamine and improve the process you are using for this innovation. Most organizations find that they need to vary the process to stimulate improved ideas. At a minimum, change the questions you ask.

Measure Your Organization's Effectiveness in Business Model Innovation and Implementation Compared to Key Competitors and Challenges

"How are we doing?" Many companies answer that question based on current profits, but financial performance mostly reflects the business environment and past actions. Answering this question about business innovation compared to competitors is very difficult. It's like answering the question of what will be the most successful new products five years from now. But answering the question is critical to creating the ultimate competitive advantage. After mapping your business model innovation process, you should do the same for competitors. Then track how they are doing in each step, based on reviewing public information. Pay particular attention to improvements they make in the speed or productivity of their business model innovation processes.[4]

In conceptual areas, organizations often lose their way. What is the right direction for one time is often the worst for another time, as Polaroid discovered.

Objective measurements will help steer you in the right direction. Improving the power supply on portable electronic devices will not always be the best use of Linear Technology's attention. For example, enhancing the usefulness of portable electronic devices in all ways might be better. The company should measure the economic value for itself and its stakeholders of improving battery performance compared to potential progress in other important problems. When other customer and end-user problems will become more important than power supply management, Linear Technology would see the need to shift its vision, core concept and business model. By adjusting in this way, companies can create a more bountiful orchard for low-hanging fruit.

KEY QUESTIONS

- *What was the reasoning behind the actions that led to your competitive advantages and disadvantages in serving customers?* A new business model often fits the current and expected business environment well. Permanently changed conditions, however, can make a business model obsolete. A business model innovation process should create models that will work well in a broad range of business environments, and redirect work for establishing better business models when circumstances require.

- *Is that reasoning still the most compelling?* If not, think about when changes took place that required a response. Connect that observation to the next question.

- *If your company did not make timely business model innovations, what were the probable causes of the delay?* Separate out the issues of not noticing the changed circumstances, wishful thinking that the new conditions will go away, not focusing on the business model and not having the skills or resources to create a new business model.

- *How should your business model development process have been improved for you to have a more ideal business model today?* Likely problems are having too few people working on the opportunity, running too few improvement experiments, not doing enough to identify stakeholder issues, insufficient consideration of different business environments and too infrequent business model evaluations. For some companies, the problem can be inexperience with thinking about innovation processes and how to improve them. Feel free to add your own thoughts about weaknesses. This list of likely problems is just to start your thinking.

PART FOUR

PURSUE HIGHER-POTENTIAL BUSINESS MODEL IMPROVEMENT

And thick and fast they came at last,
And more, and more, and more. . . .
—Lewis Carroll (Alice's Adventures in
Wonderland, 1865)

Many companies find that when they first do something new, the results can be pretty modest . . . even disappointing. If they knew that the initial rewards would be so limited, they might not have started. How can you avoid such remorse with business model innovation? Work on a business model that has a hundred times the potential of your current one, and even a weak beginning can turn into a runaway success.

> **Work on a business model that has a hundred times the potential of your current one, and even a weak beginning can turn into a runaway success.**

Let's return to the lemonade stand example and your role as parent to see how you can successfully pursue larger opportunities. Your children have already expanded geographically throughout your community. What else could they do? It may be impractical to add stands in exactly the same way in other cities, but clearly the same business model would apply in those cities.

One possibility is to expand around your family connections. Do your children have clever, hard-working cousins who are interested in having a similar business and live in a different city? Your children could help these cousins learn from what you have done, supply some of the start-up capital and be compensated through a small fee based on future sales. It may be that you could extend your purchasing knowledge and experience to save money in both cities. And certainly, your children will want to hear about successful experiments in other cities.

You have just created the rudiments of an association or possibly a franchised network. After adding a new city with your nieces and nephews, you and your children might next be able to learn how to work with people who are not your relatives to add other stands in that community. After you have mastered that approach, you can experiment with opening new cities by involving families who are not relatives.

Your children should ultimately expand internationally in some appropriate way because you could learn ways to improve

> **See what else can be accomplished by combining your business model with those used by other, seemingly unconnected, organizations in powerful new ways.**

existing stands. For instance, favorite beverage flavors vary a lot around the world. Chances are you would get some excellent product ideas for other markets through all stands testing favorites from the other countries. As a result, lemonade may no longer be your lead beverage! In addition, the rest of the world's population is much larger than in your home country so there's lots of untapped volume potential.

The sooner you properly pursue these options, the less likely you are to have competitors pursuing your new business model, and the more potential benefits you will have gained to share and enjoy.

Ways to find much higher-potential and more attractive business models than your current one are described in Chapter 8.

Now that you've covered the world in pursuing your lemonade stand opportunities, it's a good time to see what else can be accomplished by combining your business model with those used by other, seemingly unconnected, organizations in powerful new ways.

Many people don't get the right nutrition, despite consuming too many calories. Can your beverage and food offerings be improved to make them more healthful? With enough volume, manufacturers may be willing to create special products to meet your specifications.

Time spent working at your lemonade stand might steal away from reading, visiting museums and other worthwhile activities for children. How might you add educational enrichment to the work experience? For example, could you provide classes to learn important skills using examples connected to situations that arise at the lemonade stand? Math studies might build around designing potential new pricing structures. To support your classes, curricula designers might be willing to adapt their texts to include examples from your business.

Most companies have employees do "busy work" when no important work is needed. That seems like the wrong thing to do for your lemonade stand. What about having regular exercise breaks during quiet periods so that youngsters develop their bodies as well as their minds? McDonald's restaurants have play areas for children. Perhaps you should, too. Both customers and employees could benefit. Exercise experts who wanted to help children might be willing to create special programs to fit your working and play environment.

You want your customers to enjoy visiting the stand. What about relandscaping the area around your premises? The children could learn about gardening in the process. Many gardening books come with detailed plans for creating borders and garden areas. Maybe your customers would enjoy looking at shrubs trimmed to resemble animal characters, like those at Disneyland.

Most businesses give money to help charitable organizations. Yet, time and effort are usually worth more to those organizations. Can the lemonade stand help recruit volunteers for walk-a-thons and other healthful fund-raising activities?

And so it goes. We would enjoy hearing about your ideas for the lemonade stand. Feel free to share them with us at mitchell@ mitchellandco.com.

Enhancing your business model by combining what you do with other successful organizations is explored in Chapter 9.

CHAPTER 8

Focus on the Areas
of Highest Potential
Growth and Profitability

Everyone is surrounded by opportunities.
But they only exist once they have been seen.
And they will only be seen if they are looked for.
—Edward de Bono

Many natural processes expand rapidly, until some important resource is exhausted. For water lilies, a pond's surface area ultimately limits their growth. Start them in a larger pond, and more will grow. With the same number of new plants, the growth rate will be initially similar in smaller and larger ponds. But choosing the larger pond's ultimately greater potential to support water lilies reliably provides increased blooms that add more appeal. Similarly, a business plan for developing a larger pond of opportunity can earn greater stakeholder rewards.

Break out of the box. That's the advice that many creativity experts give. Few ever followed that advice quite as literally as pioneering American architect, Mr. Frank Lloyd Wright. The rooms in his custom-designed, Prairie-style homes literally burst out at the edges to extend beyond their foundations and vertical supports by using cantilever construction methods. Rather than having a room closed in by walls meeting in each of four corners, Mr. Wright often had corner windows instead, extending the openness of the room. One of our favorite examples of this home style is the Frederick C. Robie House near the University of Chicago.

But window-cornered homes weren't his sole contribution to architectural innovation. One of our favorite ways that Mr. Wright broke out of the box can be found at his home, Taliesin, in Wisconsin. From the top floor, a delightful walkway is suspended outward into the air like a spring board from a diving tower. As you stroll to the end, the downward sloping grounds fall away beneath you creating the sensation of gently floating upward in the air while you enjoy looking at the beautiful river and meadows around you.

He broke out of the box with designs in many other ways. For example, his landmark Solomon R. Guggenheim Museum on New York City's Fifth Avenue visually spirals upward like a seashell in a way that is as unique today as when it opened many decades ago. Inside, you see the spiral above you converted into a sloping walkway facing galleries arranged to receive natural light from the central atrium. An elevator whisks you to the top so you can easily amble down the walkway. After this artistic tour, your perspective will never be the same. The building redefines the art museum experience.

While many admire Mr. Wright's Prairie style, few realize that he was also breaking out of the box with his business models, constantly looking for a larger pond to fill with his energy and creativity. He wanted to serve more people in more ways.

He began his own business by moonlighting at home to design houses for Oak Park, Illinois, neighbors while working for another firm, something that he wasn't supposed to do. Eventually his employer found out, and Mr. Wright became a full-time self-employed home designer. In those days, few had homes custom designed and even fewer hired young architects with revolutionary ideas. Still fewer hired architects not in a "name" firm. By walking around his home and his neighborhood, potential clients could quickly decide if they liked Mr. Wright's work. His "living cata-logue" of nearby box-breaking homes quickly drew enough clients to make his small firm a success.

Part of the appeal of his homes, especially for wealthy clients who wanted to make a statement about themselves, was that they were distinctive. More fundamentally, these homes were designed to encourage families to spend more time together in pleasant sur-roundings. Entrance foyers and hallways are cramped and have low ceilings that make anyone yearn for more space. That space typically is provided most abundantly in the living room. These rooms are so spacious that a whole family and its friends could stretch out in different areas, without disturbing one another in pre-television times. Wonderful vistas usually beckon the eye looking for relief and contrast to the interior surroundings, while maintaining discreet privacy. Throughout his career, a large per-centage of his income came from designing individualized homes. That was his first business model innovation.

His second innovation was to extend his firm's architectural design work to include furnishings and decor. His homes feature fascinating stained-glass windows, skylights, furniture, sconces, rugs and even musical instruments created specially to comple-ment the building's design and environment.

Understanding the architectural potential to improve family life, he also became interested in encouraging spiritual life. The earliest example of this work was Unity Temple in Oak Park, Illi-nois, built to replace a church that had burned. Working with a site lacking inspiring vistas and limited by a small budget, he built a cubic masterpiece employing low-cost cast-concrete construc-tion and ornamentation. The church seems unimposing from the street. Inside, though, it's a different matter. In a cozy, intimate setting, the congregation finds itself bathed in screened light entering through the roof above . . . and feeling comfortably embraced in God's love. Seated so that they can see the faces of most other people in the congregation, church-goers feel a stronger connection to one another. Also located near his Oak Park home, Unity Temple helped inspire potential clients to favor a more spiritual environment when selecting an architect for their public commissions. Adding spirituality to public places through out-of-the-box designs and modern materials was a continuing third innovation, something seen in both his religious buildings such as the Beth Shalom Synagogue in Elkins Park, Pennsylvania, and in his secular, public ones like the Marin County Civic Center in San Rafael, California.

His subsequent business model innovations were all directly or indirectly influenced by the Depression.

His fourth innovation was to redesign how an architectural firm works. Projects were hard to find, and Mr. Wright needed inexpensive ways to serve what clients he had. Neophytes could provide energy and enthusiasm. Mr. Wright decided he wanted apprentices and associates who shared his values and concepts. He created the Taliesin Fellowship to train young architects in his methods. They would share the physical labor of construction as well as the same working and living space. If you have a chance to visit either Taliesin or Taliesin West in Arizona, you can see architects who began working for Mr. Wright still living and working in these spaces. The architects in Mr. Wright's firm built all of Taliesin West by hand. Today, that experience is continued there by having architectural students build their own shelters on concrete pads in the desert. Mr. Wright got an unexpected benefit from this innovation when one of his apprentices helped him get the commission for Fallingwater, probably his most famous home, from that apprentice's father. We have more to say about Fallingwater a few paragraphs ahead.

Mr. Wright became impatient because his architectural innovations weren't being enjoyed by very many people. His fifth innovation revolved around creating lower-cost building methods and materials that could allow ordinary people to own custom-built homes, by doing much of the construction work themselves. For example, he created unique molds for concrete blocks with appealing designs, constructed from inexpensive ingredients. This was an improvement on his earlier work at Unity Temple. You can see examples of this approach at Taliesin West. During the Depression, he established a new style, the Usonian, that emphasized lower-cost construction. The work of Habitat for Humanity

International, which we discuss in Chapter 9, clearly builds on his vision of inexpensive, self-constructed housing for all.

Not satisfied, Mr. Wright made his sixth innovation. He began working on a new form of urban living that made the city more like the country. He called his project Broadacre City. The eventual design was intended to be replicated throughout the United States so that everyone could live in a more ideal environment. This project occupied his apprentices during many of the most dismal early days of the Depression. Perhaps no architect ever sought to have such an encompassing effect on the lives of those who used his buildings. Although never built, Broadacre City has influenced generations of those who have designed model communities to include more open space, harmonize with the natural habitat and provide variety in neighborhoods and homes.

Naturally, Mr. Wright still wasn't satisfied with his achievements. His seventh innovation, establishing a more organic relationship between buildings and nature, reached its fruition when he designed Fallingwater, located in Mill Run, Pennsylvania. While buildings had historically been sited to take advantage of the natural terrain, the natural surroundings usually took second place to the egos of the building's architects and owners in wishing to subdue nature. Instead, Mr. Wright had always sought to harmonize with nature. For example, Taliesin is located below the peak of a hill like an eyebrow (the home's name means "shining brow" in Welsh) on a human face. To Mr. Wright, placing a home at the top of a hill served to visually obliterate the hill from a distance while little improving the residents' views from the home. At Fallingwater, that harmonizing vision was transformed into having design and construction be subservient to nature. The owners greatly loved a waterfall on their property, and Mr. Wright built the home above and around the waterfall. He got most of his materials from the property, so that the construction would blend with the natural surroundings. Nestled comfortably on a hillside in the woods, the views and pleasant water sounds are wonderful. With this approach, it becomes possible to create even more unique and wonderful homes by letting nature play the leading role.

While reshaping personal living with his business model

innovations, Mr. Wright also sought to reshape life at work. This was his ongoing eighth innovation. He began developing this concept early in his career with his design for the Larkin Company Administration Building in Buffalo, New York. Some commentators have likened that building to a secular cathedral, reflecting his interest in adding spirituality. Light and space radiate out from a central atrium that is now often replicated in modern office buildings. This concept was carried much further in one of his most famous commissions, the S.C. Johnson Administrative Building in Racine, Wisconsin, designed during the Depression. In this building, his workplace innovation reached its fulfillment. There he employed a novel series of freestanding columns to support the ceiling and roof weight, and to create a skylight effect of warmth and airiness across the entire building on even the gloomiest winter day. Mr. Wright wanted to make the working day lighter for people, both literally and figuratively. This vision marked his final business model innovation. Today, architects know that their designs affect how people feel and work. They follow Mr. Wright's lead in making workplaces more pleasant and productive.

With his stunning perception of how life can be improved by creating better surroundings, Mr. Wright has left us with an enduring vision to inspire our business model innovations.[1]

ENVISION BIGGER OPPORTUNITIES WHERE YOU CAN BRING MORE ADVANTAGES

Companies have many ideas to increase sales. Make offerings smaller, less expensive, more rapidly available or tidier, and more people buy. Or so the theory goes. Yet the results usually fall far below the expectations. How can you avoid disappointment with your business model innovations?

Some businesses downplay the importance of an opportunity's potential size, while others focus on big ponds of opportunity. Different size and shape ponds lead to different business models and profit potential.

Supercomputer makers chose a small, obvious pond to cultivate, while overlooking what would become an increasingly larger, more desirable one. Code breaking and weather forecast calculations take too long unless computers are very large and fast. Whoever made the largest, fastest computer could count on selling it for these applications. But this view of the opportunity was flawed for creating the best business model. Here's why. First, a supercomputer's capabilities become available on smaller, cheaper computers in a few years. That trickle-down aftermarket for supercomputing capabilities at modest prices is enormous. Second, you can link millions of ordinary computers to perform any conceivable calculation by accessing unused processing time and

> Rather than extrapolating trends into the future, you need to understand the trends' causes to find the best opportunities ahead of competitors.

capacity. The SETI (Search for Extraterrestrial Intelligence) project pioneered this approach using personal computers. The supercomputer business inevitably began to shrink as a percentage of all computing as more applications could be performed on less expensive machines.

Mr. Michael S. Dell has always focused on serving the most people in the best way. From the beginning, Dell Computer customized machines for customers to improve their usefulness while reducing unnecessary costs. Dell's methods for delivering on this key concept have been refined and improved through many business model innovations, but its competitive advantages have been based on the same business model vision of what must be done. As a result of its focus on a better pond and its innovations, Dell's *profits* often exceed the *revenues* of all supercomputer makers.

LOOK FOR THE BIGGEST FUTURE POND

Rather than extrapolating trends into the future, you need to understand the trends' causes to find the best opportunities ahead of competitors.[2] Finding untapped ponds of future demand is more than just looking globally. Supercomputer makers looked globally. They failed to consider what most potential customers would ultimately need.

Finding the best opportunities ahead of competitors sometimes means developing alternative products and services to meet different needs . . . ones that don't connect to today's offerings. Let's head to the mall to meet a wig importer who looked ahead and decided to move his resources from a shrinking pond into a larger, growing one.

Mr. Rowland Schaefer reached the top of U.S. wig importing while women's wigs were a big business. To increase sales and profit margins from wigs, he changed his business model to include retail distribution by buying The Harry Camp Co., a department-store chain of leased millinery and accessory counters. This distributor also operated Claire's Boutiques, a few freestanding millinery and accessory shops located in enclosed malls.

When fashion preferences changed and the wig business shrank, Mr. Schaefer sold The Harry Camp Co. That sale allowed him to escape the shrinking pond for wigs while retaining a sound capital base.

But he kept Claire's Boutiques because they always made money. As fashions shifted, Claire's changed from carrying wigs and hats to featuring costume jewelry and hair accessories. This retail concept was refined into Claire's Accessories, small mall shops now offering inexpensive fashion accessories and costume jewelry attractive to preteen and young teenage girls, a totally new and larger pond for Mr. Schaefer. Chances are that many of the young women and girls you see sporting earrings had their ears pierced for free at Claire's. The stores appeal to girls who are just starting to select their own accessories, a market most retailers ignore. Claire's provides a welcoming, inexpensive, safe place to start learning about fashion.

How was that shift accomplished? Ms. Marla Schaefer, vice-chairman, reports that Mr. Schaefer is always looking for the next big thing. In our way of thinking, he's looking for larger future ponds. The company's culture encourages new ideas because Mr. Schaefer listens and acts quickly on promising ideas. That quest has led Claire's to expand storekeeping units and store design based on measurements of how tested changes enhance effectiveness. When there were enough stores, Claire's directly imported

Asian-made goods to cut costs and ensure more timely supplies. The well-developed Claire's concept then bought similar retail operations outside the United States and converted them into Claire's-type boutiques. Each outlet has some items that are special for that country, but 75 percent are common to U.S. operations. This mix works because American entertainment is influential in creating global fashion tastes.

> **Ask yourself where your current successes can allow you to serve a larger, more attractive market with substantial competitive advantages.**

Following an unsuccessful experiment with acquiring a young men's fashion retailer, Mr. Rags, Claire's continues to search for retail concepts that fit with its business model's core insight of providing inexpensive fashion to the youngest consumers. The parent company will acquire such concepts, apply Claire's management processes, and then expand such retailers globally through new store openings and complementary acquisitions. Eventually, Claire's search for ever-larger future ponds could help the company cover the worldwide lily pond of young people looking for value and comfortable shopping experiences in their first fashion choices. That's quite a distance from its beginnings in finding and importing the least expensive hairpieces for fashion-conscious, well-to-do women, essentially a purchasing-focused vision.

What can you learn from this experience? Ask yourself where your current successes can allow you to serve a larger, more attractive market with substantial competitive advantages. Be especially attentive to opportunities to add new competitive advantages, as Claire's did in learning how to become an effective retailer for a different kind of customer. If you don't keep searching for larger, more attractive, future markets, you will stay stuck in the mud in your old pond. If the pond shrinks or dries up, the effects can be quite harsh. Instead, with a focus on finding paths to larger, more attractive future opportunities with more competitive advantages, you can accomplish, share and enjoy much more!

ADD MORE CUSTOMER VALUE DIMENSIONS TO SPEED YOUR WAY TO THE BIGGEST FUTURE POND

Refer to the Huffy example in the Prologue to consider the many ways that a new business model can open up larger, more exciting opportunities.

Go to the Best Place in the Biggest Future Pond to Plant Your First Water Lilies

Where do you plant your water lilies in the biggest future pond? Put them all together in one almost land-locked corner, and they will expand more slowly than if you plant them in several sheltered places about midway between the center and the shore from where they can spread unhindered in all directions. The fewer water lilies you have to start with, the more important it is to put them in the right places.

Mr. Bernard Liautaud worked for Oracle in Paris when he saw an exciting software prototype. With the software, you could organize information from an Oracle database around common terms understood by business people. Oracle wasn't interested, but he was.

From watching Oracle, he knew that software companies have to operate worldwide and function on any software platform. How should his new French company, Business Objects, organize itself to operate universally? He decided the company should be transnationally based from the beginning. His objective was to combine the best people and knowledge from different countries.

For example, he sought capital for the company like a Silicon Valley start-up would. To access business resources beyond Paris, he obtained venture capital from American and Dutch firms in addition to French ones. He wanted Business Objects to access advice and contacts from these firms, not just money. This approach was a sharp break from what new French firms usually did. The typical goal was for the founder to keep 100 percent ownership. Business Objects became the first start-up French company to offer stock options to employees. This capital sharing enabled Business Objects to attract top people globally who had worked at many leading technology companies. To reinforce this transnational perspective, the top management team now combines American, French and U.K. natives.

The firm had a strong technical base in Paris, but the biggest potential markets were elsewhere. Mr. Liautaud soon opened major subsidiaries in the United States and the United Kingdom, as well as offices across Europe and in the company's Asia-Pacific region. He moved to the United States to become closer to that market, but continued to nurture his top French software development team.

From this strong well-located base, Business Objects improved its initial business model, which allowed better access to Oracle databases, so that its software also worked with other database software platforms. The company's software architecture operates independently of all databases, so that it can be quickly installed and used—kind of a "Switzerland" for its open and heterogeneous technical strategy. The second improvement added query tools to allow users to answer more of their own questions without involving programming professionals. The third improvement expanded the software's application footprint. Initially, all company databases could be queried. That capability was then expanded to allow a company to permit customers, suppliers, partners and other stakeholders to query any databases within the company as well as their own. Business Objects has been building the information connections that allow companies to better apply this book's communications concepts for business model innovation. Undoubtedly, future improvements will help people access, interpret and employ even more valuable and timely information.

HELP WELL-SITUATED WATER LILIES GROW FASTER

By improving a pond's balance of nutrients, access to sun, filtration and water flow, well-situated water lilies grow faster and more abundantly. The most successful business models do the same for stakeholders by improving their environment.

Dr. Henry Yuen scanned for technology opportunities in developed countries and was intrigued by television. More people have televisions than computers, and televisions can be found throughout homes. Most people spend more time at home watching television than with telephones and computers combined.

What was missing to increase television watching? Because VCRs were hard to program, viewers had to choose between competing shows and spending time on other activities. Working with colleagues from Cal Tech, Dr. Yuen developed VCR Plus+ that makes recording a show easier.

Cable and satellite systems provide so many programs now that viewers can't easily know what their choices are. Dr. Yuen created a patented electronic program guide for his company, Gemstar. To enhance that opportunity, Gemstar purchased the venerable publication, *TV Guide*, so that advertisers could reach viewers in more ways. Gemstar began a multiprong strategy to make its electronic program guides available on every television. Dr. Yuen worked with television set makers to add components necessary to receive the guide. Outside the United States, he found cable operators willing to add the guide to their cable boxes in exchange for a split of the advertising revenues. In the United States, cable operators were reluctant to work with the renamed Gemstar-TV Guide. Because of this resistance, Gemstar-TV Guide also arranged for the company's program guide to be sent and received over local broadcast and paging channels, should a local cable operator try to strip the guide out of local television station programming.

Dr. Yuen noticed that electronic commerce can potentially be more accessible for consumers by using a television set rather than a computer. Following that concept, he began developing the programming guide's potential as a portal to find product information and special offers. Advertisers may prefer this approach to the Internet because television provides better video and audio quality for their messages.

Other information can be more conveniently accessed via television. The company offers electronic books that can be quickly downloaded from your television set onto convenient, portable readers. We can probably expect that television guides of this sort will be created as well.

As a result of its efforts to expand television's usefulness prior to 2002, Gemstar-TV Guide improved the environment for its offerings so that its stakeholders could hope for greater harvests from the company's competitive advantages.

Then in 2002, the company lost two legal cases involving patents for its electronic program guides. These setbacks to its patent strengths and questions about

> **Always look to expand your opportunities to locate and follow unimpeded pathways to progress.**

its accounting practices caused the stock's value to plunge. The setbacks need to become spurs for the company to once again improve its business environment, business model and competitive advantages. Because Dr. Yuen is no longer CEO, we will watch with interest to see if the company will continue to implement his business model innovation vision of continually improving the television environment for stakeholders.

LET YOUR GROWTH BE UNFORCED

When companies grow too rapidly, the results are catastrophic. Rapid growth can be like a forced march over difficult, uphill terrain carrying a heavy pack. At first you move rapidly. But gradually fatigue slows you down. Without rest and refreshment, you eventually drop . . . exhausted. Rapid corporate growth is usually unnatural and unsustainable. Too many companies operate this way, and naturally drop behind the competition.

In contrast, water lilies in an optimum pond environment grow unabated until the pond is covered. Expand the pond's circumference, and more growth will occur. A business model innovation that enlarges and improves your competitive environment, your pond of opportunity, while adding competitive advantages can expand your unencumbered potential. Then your growth can continue rapidly to a much larger size. Always look to expand your opportunities to locate and follow unimpeded pathways to progress by simplifying your tasks and inexpensively testing more competitively advantaged ways to improve the stakeholder environment.

KEY QUESTIONS

- *How does your business model harmfully complicate your operations?* Companies usually perform too many functions for themselves. Time and talent are spent on executing the existing business model, which could be better employed developing and implementing improved business models. In many cases, outside suppliers can do today's business model tasks better than you can. Even if they can't, your talented people can be free to work on higher-value activities. Huffy's simplification increased its effectiveness, even with many fewer employees. Downsizing, by contrast, is like a speed-up on a production line. It usually harms the existing business model's effectiveness while reducing the time available to improve business models because people are being asked to do more with the same business model in less time and with fewer resources.

- *How can a new business model free you to pursue larger future opportunities?* Are you nearer to the top or the bottom of the opportunity barrel? Up to half of all business areas have, by definition, below-average potential. What are some high-potential areas that connect well to your business model strengths? Are there other ways to add business model strengths? For example, could you partner with more talented companies?

- *How can a new business model focus you on the highest potential areas?* Business Objects can provide you with insights. If you could make already valuable products and services even more valuable, how successful could you be? Huffy's selection of Nike as a partial role model can be a guide. If all you did was market products or services that you designed, how much more effective could your organization be? Gemstar-TV Guide can also be a partial role model. If all you did was develop intellectual property that could be licensed and sold to others, how much more effective could your organization be? Think about other companies that have successfully emphasized just a few activities related to high-potential needs.

- *How can a new business model expand your potential to prosper?* In each of this chapter's cases, the company innovations encouraged more customers and essential stakeholders to be receptive. How can your company more effectively encourage new customers and stakeholders?

CHAPTER 9

EXPAND THE BENEFITS
YOU PROVIDE AND SHARE

Be not deceived; God is not mocked:
for whatsoever a man soweth, that shall he also reap.
—Galacians 6:7

*When you stock and feed fish in a previously empty pond, you cre-
ate reliable harvests from fallow resources. Feed minds with better
questions, thoughts and information, and you create other reliable
harvests. Seed the future with better innovations today from those
minds, and you will create plenty wherever resources are idle.*

In the late 1960s, Mr. Millard and Ms. Linda Fuller felt that their
marriage was failing. Mr. Fuller's success in helping found a marketing firm had led to material riches and increasing spiritual
poverty. They decided to sell their business and possessions, give
the money to the poor and seek a life of contribution. As Mr.
Fuller said, "I see life as both a gift and a responsibility. My responsibility is to use what God has given me to help His people in
need."[1]

Working with Mr. Clarence Jordan at Koinonia Farm in

Georgia, they developed the concept of a partnership with poor people to build homes in 1968. Forty-two homes were built there on half-acre plots. This experiment was the seed of Habitat for Humanity International, a nonprofit ecumenical Christian ministry that builds decent housing and helps eliminate poverty. Donors provide land and capital, volunteers and the families who are buying the homes help with the building, and the houses are sold at cost with no-interest mortgages to deserving families. That home-building partnership experiment was the first innovation. Since that time, more than 125,000 homes have been built through this program in over eighty countries.

Mr. Fuller realized that people outside the United States needed this help, too, especially in developing countries. In 1973, the Fullers decided to test the partnership concept in the Democratic Republic of Congo, formerly known as Zaire, to build housing for 2,000 people. Using different plans and building methods than at Koinonia Farm and working with much poorer people, the second experiment was also a success. Taking the concept to an underdeveloped country was the second innovation.

Returning to the United States in 1976, Mr. Fuller established an ongoing organization to implement the home-building partnership concept, the third innovation. By turning that concept into an organization, others could share the vision behind the first experiments more easily, learning could proceed in a more organized fashion and partners could be more easily attracted.

Mr. Fuller's marketing skills soon led him to develop a number of ways to interest others. Some of the early activities involved writing books about the experiences, sponsoring fund-raising and volunteer-attracting walks, speaking at churches and operating events like special building days when more building occurred than usual. Developing this marketing expertise was the fourth innovation. Skill in this area continues to grow.

Soon after founding the organization, the concept of the local affiliate was established. Each affiliate would operate along the Habitat model, but would be responsible for finding its own resources, volunteers and families to build and purchase the housing. The affiliate-based organizational structure was a brilliant fifth innovation because it allowed local initiative to drive the program forward. By 1978 the affiliate program was well on its way, when the first affiliate outside of Georgia was established in San Antonio, Texas.

Affiliates were encouraged to donate one-tenth of their funds to support home-building in other countries. Encouraging that sharing was an inspired sixth innovation because it meant that the program could be extensively expanded into poor countries where the needs were greatest. In those countries, volunteer labor was easy to access. Both land and materials were cheap. But financial donors were scarce. In 2001, $9 million was contributed by U.S. affiliates for this program. That money goes a long way. While the average U.S. home built under the program costs almost $50,000 now, some homes in poor countries are built for as little as $800. Today, most homes in the program are built outside of the United States.

As a seventh innovation, the organization began to encourage people to establish their own initiatives to support Habitat. One of the most significant new initiatives was when former U.S. president Jimmy Carter and his wife, Rosalynn, began sponsoring an annual event to build houses in 1984. Their example helps attract volunteers and donations. In the 1999 event, 293 homes were built in the Philippines. Other special initiatives include Women Build, which Ms. Fuller heads, to encourage more women to become involved, campus-based programs and home-building vacations abroad.

As an eighth innovation, Habitat for Humanity International began to loosen its controls over national affiliates so that these groups could adapt the overall organizational vision more completely to their own countries. The result was faster and more successful growth.

The organization made other significant innovations in designing lower-cost housing, developing techniques for training inexperienced builders and organizing the building process so that more rapid progress could be made. As part of a special event in 1999, a New Zealand affiliate built a house in less than four hours.

As the organization has grown, the types and quality of the

benefits for all stakeholders have improved as well. The sense of satisfaction is greater now for volunteers and donors, communities benefit from having these new homes, the families are stronger from having decent homes and more financial security, and many unexpected benefits arose for stakeholders. Volunteers developed new skills and self-confidence. Donor churches became stronger spiritually. New friends were met. We know a couple who eventually married after meeting through their Habitat volunteer work. That's not unusual. As the Fullers titled one of their books, *The Excitement Is Building* (Word Publishing, 1990).

> **If you seek many ways for multiple stakeholders to gain as a result of an inspiring purpose, you will ignite even more innovation.**

Notice that Habitat for Humanity International has a fine track record in continuing business model innovation, although it is not a for-profit business. That success suggests that economic incentives for all stakeholders are not essential to business model innovation. We certainly have to take seriously any organization's success that creates thousands of new homes each year. In the United States, Habitat is one of the fifteen largest home builders.

A unique element of the Habitat innovation experience is that enthusiasm for the organization's purpose, rather than an organizational process, helped drive many of the innovations. Keep that point in mind when you consider what your organization's purpose is, whether you are a for-profit or a not-for-profit. With enough enthusiasm, you will soon see much more innovation . . . in ways you could not have anticipated. If you seek many ways for multiple stakeholders to gain as a result of an inspiring purpose, you will ignite even more innovation as Habitat for Humanity International did.

Habitat's progress was greatly aided by its ability to attract volunteers and resources from existing organizations. Home building requires lots of specialized knowledge, and people with that knowledge have to lead the actual building. In many cases, such volunteers are union workers who could earn a great deal of money for themselves with the same effort. Unions, home builders, home building suppliers and architects have generously supported Habitat from its beginning. Keep the importance of accessing key knowledge from other organizations in mind when you look for your innovations.[2]

MULTIPLE HARVESTS
BRING GREATER PROSPERITY

When a paved road becomes a muddy track appearing to lead nowhere, you should realize you may have taken a wrong turn. If you turn around immediately, you are less likely to get stuck. You also save time, gas and aggravation while traveling to your destination. Rather than reversing directions after discovering a mistaken turn, plan your trip so that each paved road connects smoothly to another one so you arrive in the fastest time with the least effort.

Everyone has seen a business model's effectiveness dwindle. Most have also seen new business models flop. You can be in trouble if you don't change, and can have other troubles when you do. With companies becoming more adept at business model innovation, standing pat is less and less viable. What should you do?

Successful business model innovators pursue many potential ways to gain. Think of business model innovation as being like stocking and feeding fish in a flourishing lily pond. Let's look at some examples of creating multiple benefits for different stakeholders from the same activity.

In Hawaii, some lovely resort lily ponds provide similar, multiple benefits. Beautiful fish dart below the blooming lilies while diners watch from adjacent lanais. The wait staff feeds the fish with the diners' leftover bread. Youngsters sometimes load stale bread onto barbless hooks to catch and release the fish. Grown fish undoubtedly find their way onto someone's plate. Those who have enjoyed any of the ponds' attractions are more likely to return, adding yet another harvest.

The lily-pond-as-entertainment approach has also been used to develop knowledge. Dolphins learn quickly, and people love dolphins. Imaginative Hawaiian dolphin researchers designed experiments where gesturing volunteers taught dolphins language.

Through the Earthwatch Institute, a nonprofit organization designed to encourage worldwide scientific research through donations and volunteering, volunteers worked with dolphins, covered their own expenses and paid a pro rata share of all the experiments' costs too![3] Knowledge advanced, and volunteers had fun, meaningful vacations while also boosting Honolulu tourism.

Other multiple-benefit ways of cooperating directly help people. The Grameen Bank in Bangladesh provides unsecured microcredit to poor people. A typical loan is less than $100, far too small to be affordable in terms of most banks' overhead costs. How can such small sums be profitably provided?

The bank is owned 90 percent by saver/borrowers and 10 percent by Bangladesh. Committees of local savers volunteer their services to select the loans to grant and oversee repayment. Loans are used to improve farms and homes and establish local businesses. These investments help borrowers, and their suppliers and employees. Borrowers are anxious to repay due to social pressure and a desire to be able to borrow again. Default rates have been low enough to be affordable by the bank.

The Grameen Bank also educates savers and borrowers about better economic and health practices. The bank teaches planting more vegetables and selling any surplus, obtaining clean water, using sanitary facilities, repairing and building stouter homes, helping one another when troubles arise, avoiding principal-draining dowries and keeping family size and expenses down. The bank emphasizes children's education, creating the seeds of greater future harvests.

In the remainder of this chapter, we look at companies who have replaced yesterday's business models with better ones. In each case, we conjecture how to provide greater and more kinds of harvests from the new business model by involving new stakeholders. Our purpose is to stimulate *your* thinking about *your* business, and not to make judgments about the companies or their managements. Some of these conjectures are undoubtedly inappropriate in ways we don't understand. So, we request that you not ask the companies to take on these challenges!

Here's a brief example of a potential improvement. Earthwatch's scientific tourism could be combined with Grameen-style banks to also develop infrastructure in underdeveloped countries, as Habitat for Humanity International does with its working vacation programs. Tourists would work on interesting scientific experiments, share their practical knowledge with local people, consider investing in local Grameen-style banks and projects, and help create new markets for local suppliers and services after they leave. Tourists would enjoy a safe Peace Corps-type assignment, an Earthwatch experiment and a stimulating diversion for the time and expense of a "normal" vacation. All could feel richer from their contributions. The resulting harvests would multiply in many continuing ways. Such a concept could be quickly tested through a venture combining Earthwatch and the Grameen Bank.

HARVEST MORE PONDS
BY EXTENDING YOUR RESOURCES

Most innovation occurs when two seemingly unconnected ideas are brought together for the first time. Interactions between seemingly unconnected ideas are more likely to be fruitful when you involve new stakeholders. The lesson is to keep an open mind about possibilities and potential.

Mr. P. A. Ridder, chairman of Knight Ridder, sees electronically communicated information as a natural extension of the company's newspapers. Based in San Jose, California, the company is quick to sense the potential of Silicon Valley's new technologies.

When the Internet showed its potential, Knight Ridder established online versions of each newspaper, and encouraged focus on these versions by operating them independently of the newspaper publishers and in separate facilities. This organizational approach allowed the new offerings to move faster and more nimbly than newspapers usually do. As a result, the company soon learned and acted on the knowledge that newspaper information has to be reformatted to be effective in electronic communications.

To make a more attractive package for national advertisers, Knight Ridder joined with other newspapers to establish the Real

Cities online network, reaching fifty-five U.S. markets by 2001. Knight Ridder also used its news strength to acquire and develop Web sites (sometimes with other publishers) built around local advertiser categories including CareerBuilders (for jobs) and Cars.com (for vehicles). Finally, Knight Ridder supplies its information on non-Internet platforms and is the local source for Palm Pilots.

Knight Ridder uses its local news knowledge to build advantages in all forms of information distribution, which is like being able to fish in many ponds simultaneously from one central location.

How else might Knight Ridder expand its attractive business model to involve people who wouldn't normally become stakeholders? Here are a few of our conjectures.

First, local news sources could be expanded by encouraging readers to call and e-mail with more news leads and stories. For the best results, these contributors would need some education and require careful checking, but the gains might be worth the effort. Many people would work for little or no pay because they like to see their names published. Journalists might be assuaged by realizing such a model requires more editors, while eliminating no fully paid reporters. If journalists balked, the readers who provide news could be given access to different publications, which deliver only reader-produced content.

Second, the company might manage similar foreign online operations for other newspapers. As one potential opportunity beyond that, Knight Ridder could then develop new electronic services to help poor foreign workers prepare for and get jobs in other countries as a way to add online viewers and attract foreign advertisers. The employment services could be provided at no cost to local libraries with computers so that poor workers could access the information.

Third, Knight Ridder could add online services to help companies establish foreign-based outsourcing relationships with small firms. Advertising potential from outsourcers and outsourcing companies could be substantial. Other new services could help investors get information to make venture capital and small company stock investments in less developed countries. Financial advertisers could be attracted by such content.

Notice that by expanding its reach, Knight Ridder would also be able to make more money from acquiring and operating newspapers. This expanded business model would add many more harvests by involving new stakeholders that a less electronically adept publisher cannot serve.

LOCATE POTENTIAL NEW HARVESTS FROM EXISTING PONDS FOR NEW STAKEHOLDERS

We have been impressed by how often newly diversified companies retrench from their new areas after an old "slow growth" business unexpectedly turns out to be the company's fastest growing area. Act as though you are missing good opportunities to develop what you are doing today, and you will probably be right.

While Knight Ridder harvested online crops, toy-and-game-maker Hasbro was driven to distraction by the Internet. After fast growth and steady, but low, profit margins in 1997 and 1998 from its interactive operations, Hasbro lost a ton in these areas in 1999 and 2000. Seeing continuing problems, Hasbro sold its stake. And the company pulled in its horns in other ways. Manufacturing was consolidated into three factories. An unsuccessful matrix-style organization was simplified.

Mr. Alan G. Hassenfeld, CEO and grandson of the company's founder, offered this humble, but profound, advice he learned from his wife for guiding the company, "God gave me ears, not to talk with, but to listen." By listening to assessments of Hasbro's mistakes, he learned that you "have to take measured risks" with new business models and organizational structures. The company's new direction reflects that thoughtful caution in moving ahead.

To improve its business model, Hasbro looked at its old fishing holes in new ways. With some development and marketing, much growth could come from adding new versions of existing, well-known brands such as Tinker Toys and Lincoln Logs. Earlier, the board game of Monopoly had yielded substantial growth. The average home went from having the original Monopoly to owning and playing with several versions, as Hasbro increased the game's relevance and fun for the players.

Hasbro expanded its profitable offerings of artificial-intelligence toys. The company was a pioneer with Furby, and recently added Poo-Chi, an interactive electronic puppy.

The company reexamined its online experiences and realized that there will be many new ways to electronically distribute play experiences. The company's goal should be to quickly adapt its offerings to new electronic forms with minimal risk.

What else could Hasbro do to involve new stakeholders and serve existing ones in more beneficial ways? See what you come up with before reading any of the following conjectures.

First, since youngsters love its brands, Hasbro could partner with educators to create learning modules that employ these brands. People learn best when they are playing. Dungeons and Dragons might be adapted for creative writing. Monopoly-based problems could be part of the math curriculum. Interactive toys like Furby could be adjusted to help children master specific lessons in preschools and at home. Since educators often create such materials on a contingent royalty basis, the company's investment could be small. By teaming with an educational publisher, Hasbro could rapidly expand the distribution of these offerings in new ways.

Second, the company could sponsor international competitions for children to design new versions of the Hasbro games and toys that they like. The most promising ideas would be turned into products. This competition could be a modern variation of Roald Dahl's *Charlie and the Chocolate Factory* (Alfred A. Knopf, 2001) to encourage more interest in toy making and play experiences.[4]

Third, toys that spur a child's development can attract new customers, including school systems and government authorities, for whom such toys could be cost-effective learning supplements. Hasbro could provide limited free access to its technical staff for academic researchers interested in toy-assisted learning. Free samples could open the door to experimental sites to validate the applications.

About 40 percent of students have trouble learning to read using standard methods. Perhaps a version of Furby could help a child identify an effective learning style for reading, and then help the child begin to master the basics in that way. Teachers could follow up the Furby-based clues to select educational activities that best fit each struggling youngster's needs.

Fourth, the lessons that the Grameen Bank shares with savers and borrowers could be encapsulated into Furby-type toys and provided to poor youngsters by economic development organizations. Such learning aids could be provided to parent volunteers when they are much less expensive than employing a paid local staff. Toys are no substitute for trained teachers, but could facilitate learning where such teachers are unavailable or seldom available.

Hasbro's new harvests would also improve its knowledge and skill in producing traditional toys and games. Hasbro could create a better way of doing good while doing well.

MOVING ON TO UNDEVELOPED PONDS

If there isn't going to be enough pond water to support lilies and fish, the future is bleak. You'd better pack up some lilies, fish eggs and your fishing gear and head to a better pond, even if it means learning to plant lilies and to stock and catch fish in new ways.

PMC-Sierra's predecessor company was the third largest supplier of personal computer modems in 1994. Newer high-speed technologies would require DSL and cable modems, reducing future demand for the company's products. The company was very excited, however, about the Internet.

By 1997, the company exited modems and never looked back. Mr. Robert L. Bailey, PMC-Sierra's CEO says the decision was "not as hard as it looked." They were guided by a thought from Mr. Don Valentine of Sequoia Capital, "Great markets make great companies." A company's innovation, growth, market share and profitability are potentially enhanced by a great market's rapid growth and dynamism. Becoming number one in providing Internet-enabling chips was such an opportunity.

PMC-Sierra looks at development projects for new products like a venture capitalist would. A market-creating new product costs $30–50 million. When you do one project, then top talent and money are not available for another project. Even with the company's success, it could only afford to fund a few projects when the technology recession of 2001–2002 hit.

As you can imagine, eliminating old activities helps focus attention on new ones. Military commanders, such as Alexander the Great, have sometimes burned boats and bridges behind them so that their army's survival depended on winning the battles ahead. Acacia Research's concentration of all resources on one technology was a similar decision, as was Claire's decision to sell The Harry Camp Co.

What else could PMC-Sierra have done to work with other organizations to provide more harvests for more stakeholders?

Remembering the Hawaiian resort ponds, its technology evolution could have provided more types of customer advantages, such as making wireless and wired networks work better together for data communications. Such combined networks are very important in less developed countries, where land-line telephones are limited. Business Objects might have been a good partner for finding better ways to access data. PMC-Sierra could probably have sold enough high-priced stock during Wall Street's Internet craze to pay for this expanded focus.

In addition, adoption risk could have been reduced by working with customers who wanted the new technologies for expanding their business models to serve more types of stakeholders. The foreign online business services we suggested for Knight Ridder could be ideal for helping PMC-Sierra pursue this purpose. Such customers would help build application knowledge, and add financial resources and access to their customers.

Finally, talent is a key ingredient for new-product-driven business models. By picking more emotionally rewarding new applications, better thinkers and ideas could be attracted. Recruiting key people would certainly be easier. With a nucleus of great developers, even more top people would want to join the company.

IMPROVE THE POND'S ENVIRONMENT, AND THE GENETICS OF THE LILIES AND FISH

Altering the physical structure of life is both an opportunity and a threat. Adjusting genes can create superior health solutions. But a new solution's development cost can be over $200 million and require many years of effort. And more new solutions will fail to repay their costs than will. How can any small company possibly succeed?

The bad news is that the problem is about to get worse. Dr. Frank Baldino, Jr., CEO of the biotechnology company, Cephalon, points out that altering genes isn't enough to cure many genetically influenced diseases. Genes also affect health through proteins. Enzymes are needed to assist in key bodily chemical processes. The best health solutions will probably require changing all three areas and be even more enormously expensive and take longer to achieve than gene-adjusting therapies alone. As the costs of solutions mount, developers need to more accurately predict benefits before development begins.

What business model can work best for biotechnology solution developers? Financial choices are bleak until a company creates a successful product. Otherwise, contributed capital just bleeds away and the company eventually has to fold. Cephalon succeeded in 1999 with its first product, PROVIGIL, which neurologists prescribe to reduce excessive daytime sleepiness from narcolepsy. That product doesn't have the same profit potential as developing the next antibiotic that almost every child will use to cure ear infections, but smaller companies have a better chance to succeed when they target smaller opportunities that the pharmaceutical giants ignore.

After the first product success, Dr. Baldino argues that large, long-term financing needs require you to balance profit performance today with developing new products for tomorrow. Otherwise, you cannot access enough development cash to allow tomorrow to happen. Attracting enough capital means rewarding shareholders, regardless of your new product development progress or lack thereof. As a result, Cephalon has looked for new

PROVIGIL applications, such as encouraging day-time wakefulness (a lower cost and risk direction, with near-term profit potential), while working on high-sales-potential drugs for various cancers, Parkinson's disease and Alzheimer's, projects which have high development costs and risks.

How can a biotechnology company compete with powerful, established drug companies? Pharmaceutical giants can afford many simultaneous biotechnology investments. As Cephalon did with PROVIGIL, you can locate projects that more capable, richer companies are unlikely to pursue, such as solutions for rarer diseases. Unfortunately, these drugs offer less profit because of more limited sales potential, while incurring development costs similar to any other new drug. This apparent problem can be a blessing in disguise. These giants may be willing to license limited potential, partially completed projects to biotechnology firms. This cooperation opens new doors to opportunity and funding. As pharmaceutical companies merge, the technology licensing opportunities improve. So a biotechnology company may be able to cooperate with pharmaceutical companies to access better opportunities, while tapping into new knowledge and funding sources.

How else can Cephalon cooperate with large pharmaceutical companies? Cephalon handles sales and marketing to neurologists for another company's migraine opiate. Cephalon already called on neurologists to sell PROVIGIL, and the other firm did not. Both companies get major cost and effectiveness benefits. Another opportunity is recruiting top talent whose jobs are eliminated in pharmaceutical mergers.

Looking forward, Cephalon sees itself moving toward continuing profitability, but needing better risk-reward opportunities, continued access to lots of low-cost capital and the ability to weather unexpected development delays. These challenges will increase when Cephalon becomes a provider of more complex therapies, as future technologies will require. Dr. Baldino realizes Cephalon should always be open to selling the company when that action provides full value for shareholders, advances product progress for human benefits and creates a strategic fit for the future.

What else could Cephalon do to improve its business model by serving other stakeholders?

First, the company could license other profitable products from foreign companies lacking the interest or resources to obtain FDA approval. Products needing neurologist prescriptions would be best. Project-based financing is usually available for such developments.

Second, Cephalon could joint venture with other companies with similar issues and complementary expertise to obtain a more attractive development portfolio. Most biotechnology companies have limited funding, and many pharmaceutical companies lack enough promising, high-potential projects. More pharmaceutical company funding would probably be attracted.

Third, Cephalon could also partner with less developed countries wanting to establish a native biotechnology industry to cure their diseases that are rarely seen in developed countries. By focusing attention on the country's more unique health issues, Cephalon could increase its expertise advantages. In providing the technology and training as its contributions, Cephalon might be able to expand its projects without spending much more money. International development organizations like the World Bank might be attracted to fund such projects for these countries.

Cephalon needs to focus first on being sure that its scientific acumen is unmatched. Then, it must find low-cost ways to reduce unnecessary risks in selecting development projects. Finally, it must make itself uniquely attractive as a partner to attract the funding to fulfill its scientific potential in alleviating many health problems.

PASS IT ON TO BUILD IT UP

Refer to the example of Mandalay Resort Group in the Prologue for ways that business model innovation can become part of your company's ongoing focus through succeeding management generations.

KEY QUESTIONS

- *Where has your business model provided new resources through involving new stakeholders?* Resources can include unduplicated customer knowledge, inexpensive capital, top talent or insights for making better choices.

- *Where has your business model created resource disadvantages by serving or involving new stakeholders?* Sources of disadvantage can be circumstances such as too few people compared to the opportunities, costly processes lacking corresponding benefits and dispersed communications that harm operations.

- *What were the original reasons for pursuing new stakeholders that led to these new-stakeholder-based resource advantages and disadvantages?* You may find connections to a prior or the current business model. Use these connections to locate potentially destructive and constructive seeds for business model innovation.

- *If you had used the ideal business model to involve and serve new stakeholders when your current business model was set, what would you have done differently?* The idea here is to locate any resource gaps in your business model that should have been filled in the past.

- *How could your past business model development process have been improved to create better resources for involving and serving new stakeholders?* The most common problem is not thinking about how to expand the availability and usefulness of resources. This chapter's examples may not fit your situation very well either. Spend time identifying examples that people in your organization find pertinent, instructive and encouraging.

- *What potential stakeholders are you ignoring now? How could they become a source of added resources and strength?* What do you have to do differently to involve and serve them? Be sure to include potential stakeholders who cannot afford your offerings and are not in contact with your company now.

EPILOGUE

GREATER AND LONGER LASTING BENEFITS

Love our principle,
order our foundation,
progress our goal.
—Auguste Comte

It's twilight following a perfect summer day in suburban Darien, Connecticut, nestled on Long Island Sound astride Interstate 95, a few miles from Westchester County, New York. A happy group of parents and teens are enjoying Chinese food on a picnic table near the train station. All is calm and peaceful.

Clang! Clang! An alarm suddenly shatters the tranquillity. There's an emergency call from Darien High School. Four slight, but well-trained, teens and an adult visitor leave the table and scramble aboard one of Post 53's three enormous ambulances, while one adult EMT (emergency medical technician) prepares to follow in a chase car. A fourteen-year-old young woman on the crew helps the inexperienced visitor find a seat and buckle up just seconds before the ambulance pulls out of the garage.

The siren blares and lights flash as the eighteen-year-old EMT driver heads for the high school. A second EMT, a sixteen-year-old, is also aboard. Arriving at the school, the teens (two young women and two young men) find a man suffering from a painful sports injury in the gym. While the police, the adult EMT who drove the chase car and the visitor look on respectfully, the two teenage EMTs diagnose the probable injury, communicate with the emergency room at a nearby hospital, apply first aid and work with the other two teens to assist the patient into the ambulance. The patient focused all of his attention on the teenagers; he didn't notice the adults.

After a short ride, the man is being seen by an emergency room (ER) physician at the hospital. Meanwhile, the teens fill out their paperwork so the patient's medical records will be complete, and offer the visitor a tour of the ER. Physicians and nurses chat amiably with the teens, as they would with peers.

The teens pack up their stretcher and gear, reload the visitor and head back to Darien Emergency Medical Services, the other name for Post 53. The visitor feels as though an episode from the *ER* television series has come to life.

Once there, the teens notice the ambulance could use a fill-up. Before leaving, they ask if anyone wants them to bring back ice cream. As the orders are taken, it's the first time since the alarm sounded that the visitor saw them act like teens rather than adults.

What is this? Darien gets free emergency medical services from Post 53, sometimes supplemented by the Darien police and fire departments and paramedics from Stamford, an adjacent town. The adults start IVs and provide advanced resuscitation. The teens do everything else . . . twenty-four hours a day, seven days a week.

Sixty teens, ages fourteen through eighteen (fifteen from each high school graduating class) and twenty-five adults operate Post 53, and respond to 1,100 emergency calls a year. Some of these are potentially life threatening, such as heart attacks and strokes . . . and horrific accidents on I-95. The adults carry the day load during the school year, and the teens make up for that the rest of the time. At night, teens who live far from the Post sleep there, when they're not answering a call or doing their homework. That's just part of the dedication that the teens and adults show to their responsibilities. The chase car EMT had children who volunteered at the Post many years earlier. But he stayed involved because the Post needed someone who could break away from a local job to cover emergencies during the day. His business allows him to do that. The group's adult leader, Mr. Richard E. Koch, carries three communications devices on his belt to keep track of Post emergencies and his normal work as an officer at a local company. He is one of several advanced EMTs at Post 53, and is certified to train EMTs. He's been volunteering at the Post since 1981, long before his own children were born. Mr. Koch has never lived in Darien, and serves out of a humanitarian desire to help.

Before they leave the Post, the teens will complete more than 200 hours of training and will become certified EMTs. They will have provided hundreds of hours of volunteer work. They are proud to be part of this service, having been selected by other Post teens from among many applicants. Of the Post's teens, 88 percent are on the honor roll, compared to the 55 percent of the general student body at Darien High School who are. While many colleges run similar programs involving their students, this is one of a very few programs employing high school students as the primary staff. President George Bush honored Post 53 in 1992 by selecting it as one of the "1,000 points of light."

The service is free to patients. Funds are generated first by volunteers working to earn money for the Post, before asking others to help. The Post holds an annual food fair and an art show. The balance of its budget comes from an annual fund-raising letter to town residents. Post 53 members volunteer more than 105,000 service hours a year. Comparable services provided in other towns would cost over $1 million a year.

But saving money isn't the point. Saving lives and encouraging young people are the purposes. Many of the teens will decide to pursue medical careers because they find the work suits them. Others simply develop self-confidence and coolness under pressure.

All the Posties (as the teens call themselves) feel a powerful sense of satisfaction from having made a difference in their community. Ultimately, they earn the respect of top-notch adults and patients, entering the adult world as a peer years before they normally would. It's not easy. After the emergency call described here, each teen shared her or his feelings about the experience with the visitor. Their adrenaline was definitely pumping, and their emotions were jumping . . . even though their exteriors were coolly professional throughout.

Families gain, too. Teens learn to budget their time, and observe firsthand the dangers of drugs and alcohol from seeing patients. The teens have a safe place to hang out and associate with other outstanding teens. It's like a clubhouse for life training.

Leaving Post 53 that night, the visitor's head shook in wonder. Imagine if adults always assumed that teens can function as contributing adults, rather than requiring careful watching for incipient delinquent behavior. There's a tremendous talent pool and energy that can be harnessed by committed adults for their communities. Here's an enormous stakeholder group that families and communities must learn to take more seriously.

Whom else are we overlooking? Are we asking too little from our seniors? What about those with disabilities? Perhaps parts of the growing inmate population would like to contribute more, as well. Question your assumptions about who can do what!

Important actions must begin as thoughts. The most useful thoughts are triggered by questions. Recall some moments when you first imagined something important that you later created. In this epilogue, we look at how shaping thoughts can create the ultimate competitive advantage through continual business model innovations.

Chance is a powerful force causing much of the worst for companies. Mental preparation is a company's foundation for doing better.

Overly circumscribed business model visions are the main limits on human and corporate progress. Expand those mental horizons, shape the focus in the right direction and soon your experience will reflect the greater vision. When a pioneer successfully expands what a company can be, others will copy that thought process. With a better model, success is repeated in unexpected arenas. What a wonderful opportunity for greater mental stimulation and practical accomplishment!

What is the right mental foundation for your business? If vision, core concepts and business model innovation thinking are like a building's physical foundation, the challenges are clear. No building can be stronger than its foundation. Once a foundation is established, it can be strengthened, but it is much easier, faster and cheaper to begin with the right foundation. How can you know if your foundation is large and strong enough? Effective companies often acquire options on extra land and design buildings for potential expansion. Inflexible commitments can limit future choices and potential. Recent movements toward outsourcing and virtual operations are freeing some companies to have more flexibility. Fortunately, a company's mental foundation can be shifted more than a building's . . . like making changes to an architect's computer-designed plan.

Business people often focus on a successful company's minimum requirements. Have customers. Earn a profit. Have enough cash flow to pay bills and make necessary investments. Be able to weather business storms. Improve what you are doing. Outmaneuver competitors when threatened. While those are all essential things to focus on and important activities to do, these tasks are not nearly enough to build the right mental foundation.

Instead, businesses should think about the most that they can accomplish. This focus is also critical for individuals, families and governments. Many important tasks can be done best by companies. Individuals can only do so much, and governments often work best when they do the least to ensure the common good. Nonprofit organizations often lack access to significant capital. Where combined efforts, sustained activity and significant resources are required to fill a critical need, companies can be highly effective. Much progress will either be enabled or retarded by our ability to broaden and strengthen our concepts of what our businesses can do. When you establish a greater mental foundation, a more fruitful and happy future for all life on Earth can follow.

What are the foundation concepts that need to be added to the essential tasks of every company? Here are five principles to guide you.

1. *Serve more people with what they will perceive as improved performance, more rapidly and in more ways with fewer resources.* The potential always exists to do this regardless of what has just been accomplished. Progress will lag well behind potential, unless this purpose is always uppermost. Companies err when they fragment this charge into its component parts, or only focus on it occasionally. The solution is to encourage, measure and reward such overall performance at least as much as any other corporate purpose.

2. *Make each thought and activity apply to people and their pur-*

poses who are not now being served. Optimal results come from balancing interests. Companies miss opportunities to make good decisions whenever they stop thinking about whom and what else should be considered. For example, employee benefits are often evaluated in terms of basic fairness, what the company can afford, and the ability to attract and retain high caliber people. If you also consider the employees' interest in their families having happier, healthier and more successful lives, ideal solutions change even if resources don't. Benefits may shift to providing more flexibility in working hours and locations. Indirect gains may accrue to the company, like having employees be more effective, because their families are better off. Each time you consider more people and purposes, better solutions will arise. By continually expanding your focus, you can fulfill a fuller range and percentage of your company's potential.

3. *Involve more people when considering each thought and activity.* Together, people can be more capable thinkers than individually. But nothing would get done if people collaborated about everything on each occasion. That would be like having each person do their own fishing. Based on interest, perspective and expertise, different people can be involved from time-to-time so that better experiments are identified, more optimum choices are validated and better decisions made. Like Goldcorp, you should find ways to involve all of the world's best thinkers when the opportunity is greatest.

4. *Start each morning with the thought that you are beginning a new company.* Abandon the assumptions that led you where you are today, but use any resources or advantages your current position provides. Think about obtaining resources you lack, what you need to learn and who else can help you.

5. *Strengthen your stakeholders' commitment to these principles.* A stakeholder community that applies these five principles will be more successful than a few individuals in a company operating based on them. Expand the commitment by sharing your own successes, provide encouragement to try these principles, applaud and reward those who follow through, and speak continuously in favor of the principles.

Think back to the *Mayflower*. In a storm-tossed cabin, a community came together to accept and bind itself to some new principles of cooperation. From those beginning principles came many seeds of today's human freedom and progress.

With these five principles, we can intelligently and thoughtfully expand the scope and effectiveness of our companies. In doing so, you should follow the paths that individuals and organizations like Acacia Research, Allmerica, American Woodmark, Applera, Beckman Coulter, Sir Richard Branson, Business Objects, Central Parking, Cephalon, Claire's, Clear Channel Communications, Mr. Michael Cogliandro, Cytyc, Dell Computer, Disneyland, Dr. Peter Drucker, Earthwatch Institute, Ecolab, Education Management, EMC, Gemstar-TV Guide, Gilat Satellite Networks, Goldcorp, Grameen Bank, Habitat for Humanity International, Haemonetics, Hasbro, Huffy, Mr. Ray Hughes, Invacare, Iron Mountain, Jordan's Furniture, Knight Ridder, Linear Technology, Mandalay Resort Group, Martin Marietta Materials, Nucor, Paychex, PMC-Sierra, Post 53, QLogic, Red Hat, Rogers, Mr. Marc Rosenthal, Mr. Douglas Ross, Charles Schwab, Southwest Airlines, Mr. Richard Sumberg, Sybron Dental Specialties, Tellabs, Timberland, TriQuint Semiconductor, Wall Drug, Mr. Frank Lloyd Wright, Xilinx and Zebra Technologies have staked out.

Together, we can establish a better foundation for progress. With this perspective in mind, you will uncover new insights when you return to this book. As you live these principles, you will also develop successful experiences you can share with your company's stakeholders as examples of what must be done. As you help others learn these principles, you will soon benefit by receiving better ideas from them, and having greater resources to employ. As you involve and serve others you do not consider today, you will find new paths for human progress. As you reflect on what these principles have meant for your life, you will be glad that you chose to be a business person. After you are gone from the Earth, you will be remembered as someone whose work supported humane values and contributed to the human family.

Notes

PREFACE

1. If you would like to learn more about how to overcome this stalled progress, visit our Web site, www.fastforward400.com.

2. Free articles are available at www.mitchellandco.com to help you improve.

3. If you would like to read these articles, visit www.mitchellandco.com and click on the "leading" file folder second from the left side of the home page to pull up the article menu. Our first article on business model innovation was in May 2001.

4. Most companies at this time were infamous for not responding to e-mails sent through their corporate Web sites. We wanted to find companies that *did* respond—companies that were effective in reaching out to current and potential stakeholders.

5. Free excerpts and ordering choices are available at www.2000percentsolution.com.

6. Free excerpts and ordering choices are available at www.irresistibleforces.com.

INTRODUCTION

1. An excellent article on EMC and the industry during these years can be found in *Forbes* (October 2, 2000), "Boom!" by Daniel Lyons, pp. 146–153.

2. An update on EMC's latest business model innovations is contained in *Business Week* (September 2, 2002), "Everybody Wants to Eat EMC's Lunch," by Faith Keenan, Spencer Ante and Cliff Edwards, pp. 76–77.

PROLOGUE

1. Have you ever seen the 1971 James Bond movie, *Diamonds Are Forever*? In that film, actress Jill St. John (playing Tiffany Case) wins a stuffed animal filled with diamonds in the upstairs midway of a circus-themed casino. That casino was the original version of Circus Circus. During the scenes in the casino, you can see the location of the gaming tables, circus acts, the net, many of the midway attractions and children looking over the gaming area from the midway.

CHAPTER 2

1. We make several references to Activity-Based Costing (ABC) in the book. Based on analyzing the cost of activities across offerings, ABC is a useful approach that helps you notice strategic opportunities to lower costs and avoid cost increases. It is done in addition to standard accounting. Many business model innovators employ both standard accounting for profit and loss statement and balance sheet reporting purposes and ABC for strategic and tactical decision making. You can learn more about ABC by speaking with your external auditors or by reading *Cost & Effect* (Harvard Business School Press, 1997) by Robert S. Kaplan and Robin Cooper.

CHAPTER 3

1. You can learn more about this process in the fine book, *e-Business Intelligence: Turning Information Into Knowledge Into Profit* (McGraw-Hill Professional, 2000) by Bernard Liautaud with Mark Hammond.

2. For information on how to develop and apply this capability, visit www.mitchellandco.com and click on the "gaining" file folder on the far right side of the home page.

CHAPTER 4

1. *Fortune*, May 28, 2001, p. 70.

CHAPTER 7

1. How he became the honored management sage is partially recounted in his book of autobiographical minibiographies, *Adventures of a Bystander* (2nd ed., Wiley, 1997).

2. *Forbes*, July 23, 2001, "Gene Jockeys," by Robert Langreth, pp. 52–53.

3. For further ideas on how to pursue these improvements and to find business model innovation process improvements, you may find it helpful to read Part Two of our book, *The 2,000 Percent Solution* (AMACOM, 1999).

4. Readers who are interested in improving their strategic measurements compared to competitors should read *The Balanced Scorecard* (Harvard Business School Press, 1996) by Robert S. Kaplan and David P. Norton.

CHAPTER 8

1. If you are not familiar with Mr. Wright's work, we recommend *Frank Lloyd Wright: The Masterworks* (Rizzoli, 1993), edited by David Larkin and Bruce Brooks Pfeiffer with text by Bruce Brooks Pfeiffer. Except for Taliesin and Taliesin West, this book abounds with large color plates of the buildings and interiors we reference accompanied by a compact, but insightful, text.

2. For more information about trends and their causes, see Part Two of *The Irresistible Growth Enterprise* (Stylus, 2000).

CHAPTER 9

1. See www.habitat.org.

2. For more information about Habitat for Humanity International, including how to become involved, visit www.habitat.org.

3. For more information about the Earthwatch Institute, including how to become involved, visit www.earthwatch.org.

4. In that children's classic, young Charlie Bucket wins a much-coveted tour of Willie Wonka's secret chocolate factory and its amazing new product developments and manufacturing methods.

ACKNOWLEDGMENTS

The Ultimate Competitive Advantage was improved by the assistance of well over a thousand people, and space does not permit us to thank each of you individually here. We hope you know we appreciate and care about you, and are indebted to you for what you did to make this book possible. Thank you!

We acknowledge the following people for their special contributions:

Mitchell and Company's clients since our founding in 1977 deserve first mention and thanks because they provided the opportunity to develop the insights in this book. We thank them for providing for our firm's success, as well, so that we had the time and resources to devote to this project. Some of the examples in this book also profile our clients. Although we have not indicated so in the manuscript, they know who they are. We especially appreciate having had the opportunity to serve as consultants in creating some of the business model innovations described here. We appreciate our clients' willingness to let us disclose their stories. Many dozens of client executives also took time to provide helpful comments that were used to revise the manuscript.

The tracking research on which this book is based would not have occurred without the encouragement and support of *Chief Executive Magazine*. We especially want to thank former long-time editor, J. P. Donlon, for his assistance in improving our questions and analyses from year to year. His curiosity helped us first notice that frequent business model innovation was occurring among our study group. Several other editors and writers at *Chief Executive Magazine* assisted us in other useful ways. The magazine's fine reputation helped open many doors that might otherwise have remained closed to us in the study's early days.

We want to specially thank the hundreds of CEOs, their staffs and their companies who assisted us since 1992 to understand the causes of their successes in achieving outstanding business performance. We particularly appreciate those who participated in our surveys, and let us perform in-depth interviews and conduct on-site visits to operations. Some of the top-performing companies opened their doors especially wide, and we appreciate the remarkable ongoing access provided to us by Mike Birck at Tellabs, Tom Golisano at Paychex and Mike Ruettgers at EMC. If you would like to know more about the companies we have investigated, go to www.mitchellandco.com and click on the "leading" file folder second from the left. That will bring up a menu of our past lists of successful CEOs and their companies, as well as our articles in *Chief Executive Magazine*.

Some of the most interesting material in this book came from on-site visits to the companies discussed while accompanied by our clients. We are especially grateful to Alcoa-Fujikura, Cadence Design Systems, Dell Computer, Disney, Electronic Data Systems, General Foods, General Motors, Hewlett-Packard, IBM, Kroger, Motorola, Ritz-Carlton and Tellabs for hosting visits that provided pivotal insights.

Almost every example in the book is based on in-depth interviews with the person, company or organization described. We appreciate having had access to dozens of individuals and companies for developing the book's examples. Many interviewees conducted their own research to develop better answers to our questions and provided detailed company materials for us to study. In all cases where we had access to significant nonpublic information, we asked the individuals and companies involved to review the manuscript for accuracy and for understandability, and almost all assisted us in these ways. We appreciate these corrections and improvements. Any errors in the book are the sole responsibility of the authors.

We are especially grateful to Tom Golisano of Paychex and Bob Knutson of Education Management for providing their thoughts in forewords to this book about who should read *The Ultimate Competitive Advantage* and what readers can expect to gain. Each man is an outstanding leader in more ways than this book addresses, and their companies are benchmarks in their industries of business model innovation. Pay attention to what they say and do.

Some companies helped us with interviews, visits and background material, but did not make it into the book. In most cases, this omission was because the example did not work well with the manuscript's structure. We apologize for leaving these companies out. We have kept our notes and believe that the material may be helpful in future books and articles.

Our quantitative studies of top-performing companies and their CEOs were ably assisted over the years by Zacks Data Services and *Value Line*.

Many executives assisted in the book's conceptual development. We would especially like to thank the members of Loren Carlson's CEO Roundtable for helping us understand what small business

CEOs needed from this book. Roger Fridholm was tireless and effective in his help with the book's fundamental messages. We acknowledge and appreciate the special contributions of Tim Althof, Mike Birck, Neil Bruckner, Dick Koch, Laura Saxby Lynch, Gil Press, Mike Riley, Michael Sharp and Barry Spielman.

During the drafting of the book, many executives, authors and academics took the time to consider our questions and words. The comments and ideas we received from the following people proved to be essential to the final version of the book: Norman R. Augustine, chairman of the executive committee, Lockheed Martin; Robert L. Bailey, chairman and CEO of PMC-Sierra; Dennis W. Bakke, former president and CEO of AES; Dr. Frank Baldino, Jr., president and CEO of Cephalon; Michael J. Birck, chairman and CEO of Tellabs; John C. Bogle, founder and former CEO of The Vanguard Group; Walter E. Boomer, chairman and CEO of Rogers; Monroe J. Carell, Jr., former chairman and CEO of Central Parking; J. Harold Chandler, chairman and CEO of UnumProvident; H.K. Desai, chairman and CEO of QLogic; Daniel R. DiMicco, president and CEO of Nucor; Dr. Peter F. Drucker, professor at Claremont College; David T. Farina, principal and head of technology research at William Blair & Co.; Yoel Gat, chairman and CEO of Gilat Satellite Networks; B. Thomas Golisano, chairman and CEO of Paychex; James J. Gosa, president and CEO of American Woodmark; Don R. Graber, chairman and CEO of Huffy; Alan G. Hassenfeld, chairman and CEO of Hasbro; Roger E. Herman, CEO of The Herman Group; Bill Jensen, president of The Jensen Group, Dr. Rosabeth Moss Kanter, professor at Harvard Business School; Edward L. Kaplan, chairman and CEO of Zebra Technologies; Dr. Robert S. Kaplan, professor at Harvard Business School; Larry G. Kirk, CEO of Hancock Fabrics; Robert B. Knutson, chairman and CEO of Education Management; Richard E. Koch, adult leader of Post 53; Philip Lader, chairman of WPP Group; Bernard Liautaud, chairman and CEO of Business Objects; William F. Mahoney, executive editor of *Shareholder Value Magazine*; Dr. John C. Maxwell, founder of The INJOY Group; Ronald A. McDougall, chairman and CEO of Brinker International; Robert R. McEwen, chairman and CEO of Goldcorp; Harold M. Messmer, Jr., chairman and CEO of Robert Half International; A. Malachi Mixon, III, chairman and CEO of Invacare; Dr. David P. Norton, president of Balanced Scorecard Collaborative; John F. O'Brien, chairman and CEO of Allmerica; James L. Peterson, president and CEO of Haemonetics; Floyd Pickrell, president and CEO of Sybron Dental Specialties; C. Richard Reese, chairman and CEO of Iron Mountain; P.A. Ridder, chairman and

CEO of Knight Ridder; Willem P. Roelandts, president and CEO of Xilinx; Emanuel Rosen, author of *The Anatomy of Buzz*; Michael C. Ruettgers, executive chairman of EMC; Paul R. Ryan, chairman and CEO of Acacia Research; Ronald L. Sargent, president and CEO of Staples; Marla Schaefer, vice chairman of Claire's Stores; Glenn Schaeffer, president of Mandalay Resort Group; Alan L. Schuman, chairman and CEO of Ecolab; Stephen M. Shapiro, founder of The 24/7 Innovation Group; Irwin D. Simon, chairman and CEO of The Hain Celestial Group; Patrick J. Sullivan, president and CEO of Cytyc; Robert H. Swanson, Jr., chairman and CEO of Linear Technology; Jeffrey B. Swartz, president and CEO of Timberland; Roger von Oech, author of *A Whack on the Side of the Head* and *Expect the Unexpected or You Won't Find It*; Deborah Wadsworth, president of Public Agenda; John P. Wareham, chairman and CEO of Beckman Coulter; Richard C. Whiteley of the Whiteley Group; Robert Young, cofounder and former CEO of Red Hat; Dr. Henry C. Yuen, former chairman and CEO of Gemstar-TV Guide; Stephen P. Zelnak, Jr., chairman and CEO of Martin Marietta Materials; and George Zimmer, CEO of Men's Wearhouse.

At Mitchell and Company, we would like to thank all of the staff members who worked on this investigation since 1992. We do not list you by name for fear of mistakenly omitting someone. We know you remember those all-nighters to meet our publishing deadlines. Thank you for making this new knowledge possible.

We have an extraordinary editor and publisher in Steve Piersanti at Berrett-Koehler. The book's original concept was similar to the material contained in Chapter 3. Steve's exceptional leadership and questions helped us to perform a continual innovation on this subject and manuscript, from which this final result emerged over more than two years of intense collaboration. We didn't know we had all of this knowledge in us until Steve helped us to find it. We feel like he deserves credit as a coauthor. He is not only brilliant, he is wonderful to work with. We also wish to thank him for being willing to invest in the book in many ways that most publishers do not. We encourage all business authors to take their books to Berrett-Koehler, and we encourage all business book readers to read this company's many fine books. We also appreciate the unstinting support that Berrett-Koehler's managing editor, Jeevan Sivasubramaniam, has given us as our advocate.

One of Berrett-Koehler's gifts to us was an introduction to five very talented professional readers, who helped us spot our weaknesses and suggested design solutions. These readers are Bob Coleman,

Acknowledgments

Kathleen Epperson, Andrea Markowitz, Ann Sonz Matranga and Cynthia W. Wright. We made dozens of improvements based on the comments of each. We would especially like to recognize the remarkable assistance of Ann Sonz Matranga who reviewed two consecutive drafts, proposed many beneficial structural changes, thoughtfully rewrote sentence after sentence and generally gave us the kind of support that an outstanding business book editor provides. This book strongly bears her influence.

Bernice Pettinato of Beehive Production Services assisted us in many valuable ways. She helped us craft our original book proposal. She also worked with us to create a new beginning for the book so we could pursue a number of Steve Piersanti's suggestions, and she did the final copy editing. Throughout, she was her usual fountain of knowledge and helpful suggestions for improvements. She, too, is a joy to work with. Bernice has helped us make all three of our books much better. We especially wish to thank Bernice for her endless patience with our desire to improve the manuscript as much as possible during the copy editing process.

Our families deserve our special thanks for their willingness to help bear the heavy time and financial burdens we incurred during the eleven years of work that were required for this book. We can never thank you enough for your loving support.

We greatly appreciate all those who read this book. You have made a substantial commitment of your time and thought. Thank you! Without you, these remarkable efforts by so many talented people would be of less benefit.

Finally, as coauthors and colleagues, we would like to gratefully acknowledge and thank one another for the wonderful support and contributions provided to each other, both in writing this book and in managing Mitchell and Company and Leading Executive Organizations 100, Inc. We could not have had this wonderful adventure or accomplished these results without the both of us.

That having been said, we want to reemphasize that the responsibility for any errors or missed opportunities to improve the book is ours alone.

INDEX

Index

Index

Index

Index

About the Authors

DONALD W. MITCHELL is chairman and chief executive officer of Mitchell and Company, a management consulting firm established in 1977 to specialize in business strategy. He is also cofounder of Leading Executive Organizations 100, Inc., which facilitates advanced executive learning by CEOs, CFOs, division presidents, corporate planners and investor relations executives. Prior to cofounding Mitchell and Company, Mr. Mitchell served as director, strategic planning for Heublein, Inc., where he was also responsible for acquisitions and divestitures. After graduate school, he worked as a project manager at The Boston Consulting Group, Inc. in Boston under the direction of well-known strategist, Mr. Bruce D. Henderson.

Mr. Mitchell has contributed to many business process innovations that have been used successfully by companies to create improved business models. These process innovations address improved ways to profitably gain market share, adjust prices, reduce costs, add new customer benefits, develop a more profitable customer and product mix, lower the cost of capital, expand the stock-price multiple, develop a more compatible shareholder base and anticipate stock-market reaction to corporate decisions and performance.

He has led strategic consulting assignments for several hundred major companies during four decades. He often speaks before groups of CEOs and CFOs.

Mr. Mitchell has coauthored *The 2,000 Percent Solution*, helping companies make faster progress by creating outstanding solutions for their most significant problems, and *The Irresistible Growth Enterprise*, helping companies learn how to benefit from unpredictable changes in business, economic and social trends. He has been widely quoted in major business publications concerning business strategy and investments and has published more than twenty-five articles on related subjects. He is listed in a number of biographical references including *Who's Who in the World.*

He graduated *magna cum laude* with an A.B. in modern European history from Harvard College and holds a J.D. degree from Harvard Law School. He attended Harvard Business School and studied marketing there while a second year student at Harvard Law School, receiving a Distinction on his second-year marketing project for *New York Magazine.* He is a member of the bar in Massachusetts.

Mr. Mitchell served on the board of Literacy Volunteers of Massachusetts from 1993 until 2001. He has been treasurer of the Harvard Law School Association and a member of the boards of the Harvard Alumni Association and the Harvard Cooperative Society.

He was born and raised in San Bernardino, California, and now resides in the Boston area with his family.

CAROL BRUCKNER COLES is cofounder, president and chief operating officer of Mitchell and Company. She has spent over twenty-six years designing management processes to help companies develop the strategic potential of their businesses and improve their market value. Prior to 1977, Ms. Coles served as manager of strategic planning for Heublein, Inc., where she was responsible for developing and instituting the strategy audit process and involved in acquisition and merger activities.

She is coauthor of *The 2,000 Percent Solution* and *The Irresistible Growth Enterprise.* She has frequently been quoted in the business press about the future direction of major corporations and the stock market. Ms. Coles has been a guest speaker at annual conferences for *Business Week's* CFO Forum, *Institutional Investor,* the National Investor Relations Institute and YPO. She has been listed in *Who's Who of American Women* and served as a director of Boston chapter of The Planning Forum.

Ms. Coles has a B.A. degree from New York University and an M.A. in economics and education from Columbia University.

She was born and raised in New York City and now lives in the Boston area with her family.

Donald W. Mitchell and Carol Bruckner Coles may be reached at mitchell@mitchellandco.com.

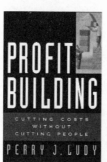

Corporate Creativity
How Innovation and Improvement Actually Happen

Alan G. Robinson and Sam Stern

Alan Robinson and Sam Stern have investigated hundreds of creative acts that have occurred in organizations around the world to find the truth about how innovation and improvement really happen. Rich with detailed examples, *Corporate Creativity* identifies six essential elements that companies can use to turn their creativity from a hit-or-miss proposition into something consistent that they can count on.

Paperback, 300 pages • ISBN 1-57675-049-3 • Item #50493-415 $17.95

Hardcover • ISBN 1-57675-009-4 • Item #50094-415 $29.95

Audiotape, 2 cassettes/3 hrs. • ISBN 1-56511-264-4
Item #12644-415 $16.95

Love 'Em or Lose 'Em
Getting Good People to Stay, Second Edition

Beverly Kaye and Sharon Jordan-Evans

Regardless of economic swings or unemployment statistics,you need your stars to stay. And you need them not just to stay, but to be engaged, motivated and producing at their peak. In this revised and updated edition of the bestselling classic, Beverly Kaye and Sharon Jordan-Evans explore the truth behind the dissatisfactions of many of today's workers and offer 26 strategies—from A to Z—that managers can use to address their concerns and keep them on the team.

Paperback original, 300 pages • ISBN 1-57675-140-6
Item #51406-415 $18.95

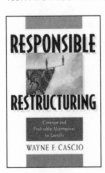

Responsible Restructuring
Creative and Profitable Alternatives to Layoffs

Wayne F. Cascio

Responsible Restructuring draws on the results of an eighteen-year study of S&P 500 firms to prove that it makes good business sense to restructure responsibly—to avoid downsizing and instead regard employees as assets to be developed rather than costs to be cut. Cascio offers specific, step-by-step advice on developing and implementing a restructuring strategy that, unlike layoffs, leaves the organization stronger and better able to face the challenges ahead.

Hardcover, 144 pages• ISBN 1-57675-129-5 • Item # 51295-415 $27.95

Berrett-Koehler Publishers
PO Box 565, Williston, VT 05495-9900
Call toll-free! **800-929-2929** 7 am-9 pm Eastern Standard Time
Or fax your order to 802-864-7627
For fastest service order online: **www.bkconnection.com**

Berrett-Koehler books and audios are available at quantity discounts for orders of 10 or more copies.

The Ultimate Competitive Advantage
Secrets of Continually Developing a More Profitable Business Model

Donald Mitchell and Carol Coles

Hardcover, 300 pages
ISBN 1-57675-167-8
Item #51678-415 $36.95

To find out about discounts on orders of 10 or more copies for individuals, corporations, institutions, and organizations, please call us toll-free at (800) 929-2929.

To find out about our discount programs for resellers, please contact our Special Sales department at (415) 288-0260; Fax: (415) 362-2512. Or email us at bkpub@bkpub.com.

Berrett-Koehler Publishers
PO Box 565, Williston, VT 05495-9900
Call toll-free! **800-929-2929** 7 am-9 pm Eastern Standard Time
Or fax your order to 802-864-7627
For fastest service order online: **www.bkconnection.com**